**Free Video**  **Free Video**

Essential Test Tips Video from Trivium Test Prep

Dear Customer,

Thank you for purchasing from Trivium Test Prep! We're honored to help you prepare for your exam.

To show our appreciation, we're offering a **FREE** *Essential Test Tips* **Video by Trivium Test Prep.*** Our video includes 35 test preparation strategies that will make you successful on your big exam. All we ask is that you email us your feedback and describe your experience with our product. Amazing, awful, or just so-so: we want to hear what you have to say!

To receive your **FREE** *Essential Test Tips* **Video**, please email us at 5star@triviumtestprep.com. Include "Free 5 Star" in the subject line and the following information in your email:

1. The title of the product you purchased.
2. Your rating from 1 – 5 (with 5 being the best).
3. Your feedback about the product, including how our materials helped you meet your goals and ways in which we can improve our products.
4. Your full name and shipping address so we can send your **FREE** *Essential Test Tips* **Video**.

If you have any questions or concerns please feel free to contact us directly at 5star@triviumtestprep.com.

Thank you!

– Trivium Test Prep Team

*To get access to the free video please email us at 5star@triviumtestprep.com, and please follow the instructions above.

CARDIAC VASCULAR NURSING CERTIFICATION STUDY GUIDE:

CVRN Exam Prep Review
and Resource Manual with
2 Full-Length Practice Tests [4th Edition]

E. M. Falgout

TABLE OF CONTENTS

ONLINE RESOURCES

Ascencia Test Prep includes online resources with the purchase of this study guide to help you fully prepare for your Cardiac Vascular Nursing Certification exam.

Practice Test

In addition to the practice test included in this book, we also offer an online exam. Since many exams today are computer based, practicing your test-taking skills on the computer is a great way to prepare.

Flash Cards

Ascencia Test Prep's flash cards allow you to review important terms easily on your computer or smartphone.

From Stress to Success

Watch "From Stress to Success," a brief but insightful YouTube video that offers the tips, tricks, and secrets experts use to score higher on the exam.

Reviews

Leave a review, send us helpful feedback, or sign up for Ascencia Test Prep promotions—including free books!

Access these materials at: **https://www.ascenciatestprep.com/cvrn-online-resources**

INTRODUCTION

Congratulations on choosing to get your cardiac vascular nursing certification! This certification is an important step forward in your nursing career, and we're here to help you feel prepared on exam day.

The ANCC Cardiac Vascular Nursing Certification

THE ANCC CERTIFICATION PROCESS

The **Cardiac Vascular Nursing Exam** is developed by the **American Nurses Credentialing Center (ANCC)** as part of its certification program for cardiac vascular nurses. The cardiac vascular exam measures the nursing skills necessary to excel as a nurse providing cardiac vascular care. To qualify for the exam, you must meet the following criteria:

- have a current registered nurse license in the United States or its territories (or foreign equivalent)
- have practiced for two full years (or equivalent) as a registered nurse
- have at least 2,000 hours of practice as a cardiac vascular nurse in the last three years
- have at least 30 hours of continuing education in cardiac vascular nursing in the last three years

Once you have met the qualifications and passed the exam, you will have the credential Registered Nurse–Board Certified (RN-BC), and you may use the credential as long as your certification is valid. You will need to renew your certification every five years by completing professional development requirements that may include a combination of continuing education hours, academic credits, research, or practice hours.

ANCC EXAM QUESTIONS AND TIMING

The cardiac vascular certification exam consists of **150 questions**. Only 125 of these questions are scored; 25 are unscored, or *pretest* questions. These questions are included by the ANCC to test their suitability for inclusion in future tests. You'll have no way of knowing which questions are unscored, so treat every question like it counts.

The questions on the exam are multiple-choice with four answer choices. Some questions will include exhibits such as ECG reading strips or laboratory results. The exam has **no-guess penalty**. That is, if you answer a question incorrectly, no points are deducted from your score; you simply do not get credit for that question. Therefore, you should always guess if you do not know the answer to a question. The computer testing system will allow you to go back to questions during the exam before submitting your final answers.

You will have **three hours** to complete the test.

The ANCC develops its exams based on feedback from cardiac vascular nursing professionals about the nursing concepts and skills that are most important to their work. This feedback has been used to develop an exam framework broken down into the four sections shown in the table below.

ANCC Cardiac Vascular Nurse Exam Content Outline			
Content Domain	**Knowledge**	**Skills**	**Percentage of Exam**
Assessment and Diagnosis	1. Anatomy and physiology 2. Pathophysiology	1. Patient interview (e.g., history, chief complaint, allergies) 2. Cardiac vascular assessment techniques and tools (e.g., Doppler, stroke scale) 3. Data collection and interpretation (e.g., diagnostic tests, laboratory results) 4. Nursing diagnosis identification and prioritization	25
Planning and Implementation	1. Evidence-based practice guidelines (e.g., ACC/AHA guidelines, quality measures) 2. Scope and standards of practice (i.e., cardiac vascular nursing, vascular nursing) 3. Legal and ethical considerations (e.g., informed consent, advance directives) 4. Procedures (e.g., angiogram) 5. Surgeries (e.g., coronary artery bypass, carotid endarterectomy) 6. Pharmacologic therapies 7. Non-pharmacologic and complementary therapies 8. Risk-reduction measures (e.g., venous thromboembolism prophylaxis)	1. Care coordination (e.g., interdisciplinary teams, discharge planning) 2. Interventions (e.g., therapeutic hypothermia)	35
Evaluation and Modification	1. Expected outcomes 2. Drug interactions (e.g., drug-drug, drug-food)	1. Adverse reactions and events (e.g., heparin-induced thrombocytopenia, hypotension) recognition and treatment 2. Urgent condition (e.g., pseudoaneurysm) recognition and treatment 3. Emergent condition (e.g., STEMI) recognition and treatment	22

Content Domain	Knowledge	Skills	Percentage of Exam
Patient and Community Education	1. Cardiac vascular risk factors (e.g., ethnicity, smoking) 2. Chronic disease management 3. Cardiac vascular education topics (e.g., procedures, medications) 4. Self-management strategies (e.g., daily weights, blood pressure logs) 5. Community resources (e.g., cardiac rehabilitation, anticoagulation clinic)	1. Individualized education planning and implementation (e.g., addressing barriers) 2. Home monitoring (e.g., remote telemetry, point-of-care testing) 3. Health promotion (e.g., wellness counseling, health fairs)	18

ANCC EXAM ADMINISTRATION

The ANCC Cardiac Vascular Nursing Exam is administered at **Prometric** testing centers. To register for the exam, you must first apply through the ANCC website (https://www.nursingworld.org/our-certifications/cardiac-vascular-nurse/). After your application is accepted, you will receive an Authorization to Test. You can then register for the exam at www.prometric.com/ANCC. You will have 90 days from the date you receive your Authorization to Test to take the exam.

On test day, plan to arrive at the testing site 30 minutes early. You will need to bring an appropriate government-issued ID (driver's license, state ID card, military ID, or passport). If you do not have any of these IDs, you may bring two IDs, one with a signature and one with a photograph.

You will not be allowed to bring any personal items into the testing room, such as calculators or phones. You may not bring pens, pencils, or scratch paper, but the testing center will provide a personal whiteboard for note-taking. Most testing centers provide lockers for valuables.

After you check in, you will receive instructions for your exam. You will then be allotted time to practice with the computer testing program before beginning the exam.

ANCC EXAM RESULTS

Once you have completed your test, the staff at the Prometric testing center will give you a score report. The score report will include your raw score (the number of questions you answered correctly) and a scaled score. A scaled score of 350 is required to pass the exam. The number of correct answers needed for a scaled score of 350 will vary depending on the questions in your version of the test (if you took a version of the test with harder questions, the passing raw score will be lower).

If you fail the exam, you will receive scoring information for each separate content area. You may reapply and retake the test after 60 days. You have three chances to pass the exam within a twelve-month period.

The ABCM Cardiovascular Nursing Certification

The **American Board of Cardiovascular Medicine (ABCM)** offers the **Cardiovascular Nursing Level I Board Certification (CVRN-BC) examination** as part of its certification process. The only necessary qualification for the exam is a current registered nurse license. However, the ABCM recommends that nurses have at least a year of cardiac nursing experience before attempting the exam.

You can apply for the exam through the ABCM website (https://www.abcmcertification.com/exam-application). Once your application has been approved, you will receive an email with instructions for exam registration. The exam can be taken on a home computer or at an approved testing facility.

During the exam you will have **three hours** to answer **150 questions**. Questions cover nursing concepts from the following content areas:

1. Bedside Assessment (14.5% of exam)

2. Basic ECG Concepts (18% of exam)

3. Coronary Artery Disease & ACS (9.5% of exam)

4. Hypertension (9.5% of exam)

5. Heart Failure (9.5% of exam)

6. Cardiomyopathy (6.5% of exam)

7. Cardiovascular Pharmacology (11.5% of exam)

8. Pacemakers/ICDs (6.0% of exam)

9. Noninvasive and Interventional Cardiology (15% of exam)

After the exam, you will receive an email with your score and a pass/fail designation. You will need to answer 105 questions (70%) correctly to pass the exam. If you fail the exam, you can pay a fee to retake it. There is no limit to the number of times you may take the exam.

Using This Book

This book is divided into two sections. In the content area review, you will find a review of the knowledge and skills necessary to pass the exam. Throughout the chapter you'll also see Quick Review Questions that will help reinforce important concepts and terms.

The book also includes two full-length practice tests (one in the book and one online) with answer rationales. You can use these tests to gauge your readiness for the test and determine which content areas you may need to review more thoroughly.

Ascencia Test Prep

With health care fields such as nursing, pharmacy, emergency care, and physical therapy becoming the fastest-growing industries in the United States, individuals looking to enter the health care industry or rise in their field need high-quality, reliable resources. Ascencia Test Prep's study guides and test preparation materials are developed by credentialed industry professionals with years of experience in their respective fields. Ascencia recognizes that health care professionals nurture bodies and spirits, and save lives. Ascencia Test Prep's mission is to help health care workers grow.

ONE: ANATOMY and PHYSIOLOGY of the CARDIOVASCULAR SYSTEM

The Heart

- The heart has four chambers: the left atrium, right atrium, left ventricle, and right ventricle.
    - The **right atrium** collects blood from the body.
    - The **right ventricle** pumps blood to the lungs.
    - The **left atrium** collects blood from the lungs.

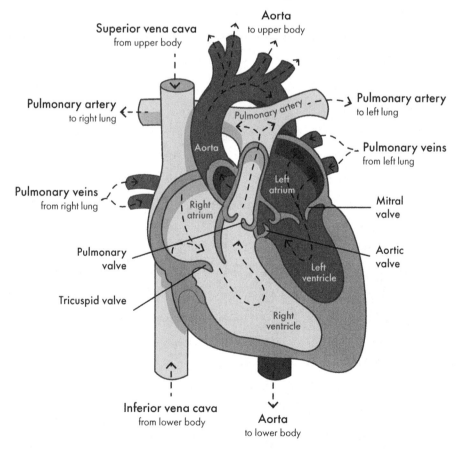

Figure 1.1. Anatomy of the Heart

- The **left ventricle** pumps blood to the body.
- The atria are separated by the **atrial septum**, and the ventricles by the **ventricular septum**.

- The **atrioventricular valves** are located between the atria and ventricles and cause the first heart sounds (S1) when they close.
  - The **tricuspid valve** separates the right atrium and right ventricle.
  - The **mitral valve** separates the left atrium and left ventricle.

- The two **semilunar valves** are located between the ventricles and great vessels and cause the second heart sound (S2) when they close.
  - The **pulmonic valve** separates the right ventricle and pulmonary artery.
  - The **aortic valve** separates the left ventricle and aorta.

- Blood flows through the cardiac valves in the following order: tricuspid → pulmonic → mitral → aortic. (Use the mnemonic **T**issue **P**aper **M**y **A**ssets.)

- The heart is formed by layers of tissue:
  - **pericardium**: the outermost protective layer of the heart, which contains a lubricative liquid
  - **epicardium**: the deepest layer of the pericardium, which envelops the heart muscle
  - **myocardium**: the heart muscle
  - **endocardium**: the innermost, smooth layer of the heart walls
  - The pericardium is divided into two layers: the **fibrous pericardium** and the **serous pericardium**.

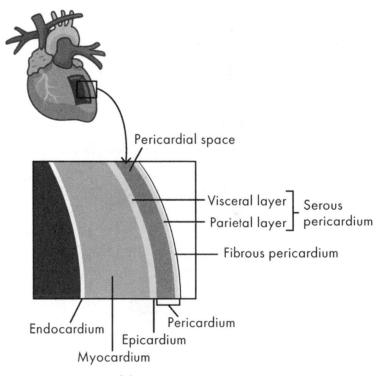

Figure 1.2. Layers of the Heart

○ The serous pericardium is further divided into the **visceral** and **parietal** layers. The space between these two layers is the **pericardial space**, which contains pericardial fluid.

- Blood is supplied to the heart by coronary arteries: the **right coronary artery (RCA)**, **left anterior descending (LAD) artery**, and **left circumflex artery**.

- The heart's pumping action is regulated by the **cardiac conduction system**, which produces and conducts electrical signals in the heart.

  ○ The **sinoatrial (SA) node** sets the heart's pace by sending out electrical signals that cause the atria to contract. It is located in the anterior wall of the right atrium.

  ○ The **atrioventricular (AV) node** relays the electrical impulse of the sinoatrial node to the ventricles. The impulse is delayed to allow the atria to fully contract and fill the ventricles. The node is located at the base of the right atrial wall.

  ○ The **bundle of His** carries the electrical signal from the AV node to the **right** and **left bundle branches**.

  ○ The endpoint of the conduction system are **Purkinje fibers** in the endocardial layer that depolarize muscle cells, causing contraction of the ventricles.

Figure 1.3. Coronary Arteries

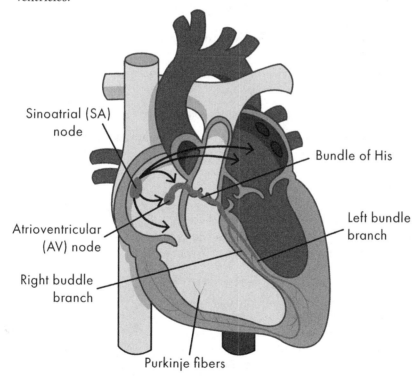

Figure 1.4. The Cardiac Conduction System

- The circulatory system is a closed double loop.

  ○ In the **pulmonary loop**, deoxygenated blood leaves the heart and travels to the lungs, where it loses carbon dioxide and becomes rich in oxygen. The oxygenated blood then returns to the heart.

○ The heart then pumps blood through the **systemic loop**, which delivers oxygenated blood to the rest of the body and returns deoxygenated blood to the heart.

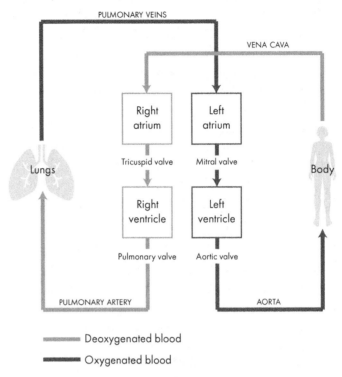

Figure 1.5. The Pulmonary and Systemic Loops

- During the **cardiac cycle**, the heart alternates between **diastole** (relaxation) and **systole** (contraction) to move blood.
  ○ When both chambers are in diastole, the atria passively fill the ventricles.
  ○ During atrial systole, the atria force blood into the ventricles.
  ○ During ventricular systole, the ventricles force blood into the arteries.

QUICK REVIEW QUESTION

1. Left-sided heart failure can cause pulmonary edema, while right-sided heart failure is more likely to cause edema in the abdomen and extremities. How does the anatomy of the heart produce this difference?

Blood Vessels

- The cardiovascular system circulates blood, which carries nutrients, waste products, hormones, and other important substances dissolved or suspended in liquid **plasma**.
  ○ **Red blood cells** (RBCs) transport oxygen throughout the body. RBCs contain **hemoglobin**, a large molecule with iron atoms that bind to oxygen.

- ○ **White blood cells** (WBCs) fight infection.
- Blood leaves the heart and travels throughout the body in **blood vessels**, which decrease in diameter as they move away from the heart and toward the tissues and organs.
- Blood exits the heart through **arteries**.

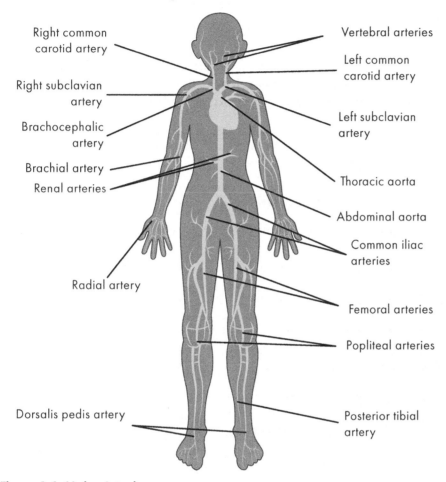

Right common carotid artery

Right subclavian artery

Brachiocephalic artery

Brachial artery

Renal arteries

Radial artery

Dorsalis pedis artery

Vertebral arteries

Left common carotid artery

Left subclavian artery

Thoracic aorta

Abdominal aorta

Common iliac arteries

Femoral arteries

Popliteal arteries

Posterior tibial artery

Figure 1.6. Major Arteries

- The arteries branch into **arterioles** and then **capillaries**, where gas exchange between blood and tissue takes place.
- Deoxygenated blood travels back to the heart through **veins**.
- Some veins have **valves** that prevent deoxygenated blood from flowing back to the extremities.
- Blood vessels have three layers:
  - ○ the **tunica adventitia**, the outer layer, composed of connective tissue
  - ○ the **tunica media**, the middle layer, composed of smooth muscle
  - ○ the **tunica intima**, the thin inner layer
- The **lumen** is the interior space of the blood vessel, through which blood flows.

HELPFUL HINT

Carotid intima-media thickness is a measure of the width of the tunica intima and tunica media in the carotid artery. It is used to evaluate atherosclerosis and cardiovascular risk.

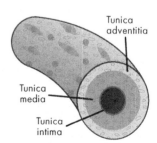

Tunica adventitia

Tunica media

Tunica intima

Figure 1.7. Structure of Blood Vessels

QUICK REVIEW QUESTION

2. A patient presents with weak popliteal and pedal pulses and intermittent claudication in the left calf muscle. The nurse should suspect an occlusion in which artery?

The Coagulation Process

- **Hemostasis** is the process of stopping blood loss from a damaged blood vessel.

- Blood loss is stopped through **coagulation**, the process of turning liquid blood into a semisolid **clot** composed of platelets and red blood cells held together by the protein **fibrin**.

- The process of coagulation is a complex cascade of reactions involving proteins called **clotting factors**.

  ○ Platelet aggregation is initiated by the exposure to **von Willebrand factor (vW)** and **tissue factor (TF)**.

  ○ During coagulation, the protein **fibrinogen** (factor I) is converted to fibrin by the enzyme **thrombin** (factor IIa).

  ○ **Prothrombin** (factor II) is a precursor to thrombin.

HELPFUL HINT

Most clotting factors are designated by roman numerals. These numerals give the order in which factors were discovered, not the order in which they are activated.

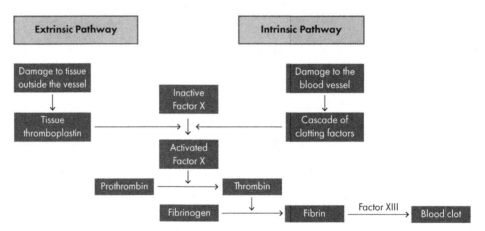

Figure 1.8. The Coagulation Cascade

- Coagulation can follow 2 possible pathways:

  ○ The intrinsic pathway is activated via damage within a blood vessel.

    · This pathway is monitored by measuring the activated partial thromboplastin time (aPTT).

    · Heparin disrupts the intrinsic pathway.

  ○ The extrinsic pathway is activated by damage outside the vasculature.

    · This pathway is monitored by measuring the prothrombin time (PT).

    · Warfarin disrupts the extrinsic pathway.

  ○ Both pathways activate clotting factor X and produce a fibrin clot.

- **Fibrinolysis** is the disintegration of the blood clot.

HELPFUL HINT

The liver is highly involved in the synthesis and removal of clotting components. Chronic liver disease often leads to coagulation disorders caused by the decreased synthesis of clotting factors and the poor clearance of activated factors.

3. Congenital hypofibrinogenemia is an inherited condition characterized by low circulating levels of fibrinogen (< 150 mg/dL). What abnormal laboratory values should a nurse expect in a patient with severe hypofibrinogenemia?

1. Blood from the lungs is returned to the left side of the heart. When the left side cannot pump this blood back out to the body, fluid builds up in the lungs, resulting in pulmonary edema. Blood from the body is returned to the right side of the heart, so right-sided failure causes fluid to build up in the abdomen and extremities.

2. The nurse should suspect an occlusion in the femoral artery, which is located proximal to the weak pulses and the site of claudication.

3. Fibrinogen (clotting factor I) is a substrate necessary for coagulation. Patients with very low fibrinogen levels are at risk for severe bleeding and will have prolonged PTs, INRs, PTTs, and aPTTs.

TWO: CARDIAC and VASCULAR ASSESSMENT

Taking a Focused Cardiovascular History

- A cardiovascular history covers:
    - signs and symptoms
    - current medications (including over-the-counter medications, recreational drugs, herbal remedies, and topical treatments)
    - allergies (food and medications)
    - lifestyle habits (nutrition, exercise, tobacco use, alcohol use)
    - medical history
    - surgical history
    - family history
- Common cardiac and vascular symptoms to look for:
    - chest, jaw, or arm pain
    - upper abdominal or lower back pain (more common in adults > 65, people with diabetes, and women)
    - nausea or vomiting
    - diaphoresis
    - light-headedness, dizziness, or syncope
    - weakness or fatigue
    - dyspnea
    - palpitations
    - numbness or tingling
- Ask about preceding events that could have triggered the onset of symptoms (e.g., extreme temperatures, stress, intercourse, smoking, eating).
- Use the acronym **PQRST** when assessing patient's pain.
    - **Provoking**: What was happening when the pain started? What makes the pain better or worse?

- Quality: What does the pain feel like (sharp, stabbing, dull, aching, burning, etc.)?
- Region: Where is the pain located? Does the pain radiate or move to another area of the body?
- Severity: On a scale of 0 – 10 (10 being the worst pain imaginable), how bad is the pain?
- Timing: How long have you been experiencing this pain? When did it start? How long does it typically last?

- Assess the patient's psychosocial status. Factors that affect the patient's psychosocial status include:
  - psychiatric history
  - current/past work history
  - financial situation
  - educational history
  - spiritual/cultural preferences
  - violence assessment
  - coping skills

QUICK REVIEW QUESTION

1. An 80-year-old female patient with a history of angina states during her interview that she has been experiencing constipation, headaches, and severe lower back pain for the last twenty-four hours. Why would these symptoms require immediate follow-up from the nurse?

Physical Examination

INITIAL SURVEY

- The initial survey is a rapid assessment to identify any life-threatening conditions.

- Assess the general appearance of patient.
  - obvious wounds
  - level of consciousness (LOC)
  - signs of distress
  - skin color (e.g., rubor, pallor, jaundice, cyanosis)
  - race and gender

- Evaluate **ABCs** (airway, breathing, and circulation).
  - **Airway:** Ensure the patient has a patent airway.
  - **Breathing:** Assess the patient's breathing status and the need for any interventions.
  - **Circulation:** Assess for signs of cyanosis or decreased blood flow.

○ If patient is unresponsive or not breathing, look, listen, and feel for 10 seconds or less, and then start CPR/ACLS protocols.

QUICK REVIEW QUESTION

2. Upon entering a patient's room for assessment, the nurse notices that the patient appears newly diaphoretic and out of breath. What should the nurse's priority be, and what actions need to be taken?

VITAL SIGNS

- **Pulse:** A normal pulse should be 60 – 100 bpm and regular.
    - ○ The **apex (or apical) pulse** is heard using a stethoscope at the fifth intercostal space midclavicular.
    - ○ **Peripheral pulses** are taken by palpating arteries in the extremities (see Figure 2.1).

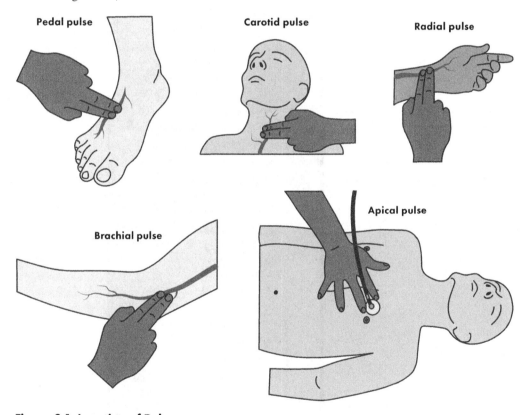

Figure 2.1. Location of Pulses

- **Respirations:** Normal respirations are 12 – 20 breaths per minute.
- **Blood pressure (BP)** is the pressure exerted by blood on the inside of blood vessels.
    - ○ **Systolic blood pressure (SBP)** is the pressure that occurs while the heart is contracting.
    - ○ **Diastolic blood pressure (DBP)** occurs while the heart is relaxed.

- The **pulse pressure** is the difference between the systolic and diastolic blood pressure (e.g., BP 120/80 = pulse pressure of 40).

- **Orthostatic blood pressure** is taken when the patient stands after having been lying down. A drop of 20 mm Hg in systolic blood pressure or 10 mm Hg after the patient has stood up from a lying position is considered abnormal.

- A **pulse deficit** is the difference between the patient's pulse rate and heart rate.

- The **ankle-brachial index (ABI)** is a ratio of the BP taken at the ankle and the BP taken at the brachial artery (upper arm).

  - $ABI = \dfrac{\text{systolic ankle BP}}{\text{systolic arm BP}}$

  - Normal ABI is 0.9 – 1.3. Lower values indicate occluded arteries caused by peripheral vascular disease (PVD). Higher values are caused by abnormally hardened blood vessels.

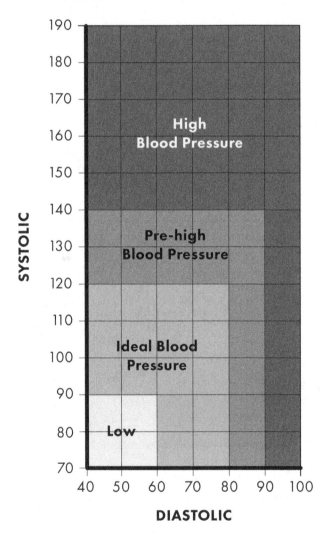

Figure 2.2. Classifying Blood Pressure

- **Oxygen saturation** (blood oxygen) is a measurement of the ratio of oxygen-saturated hemoglobin (red blood cells carrying oxygen) to unsaturated hemoglobin. Normal blood oxygen level is 94 – 100 percent.

NEUROLOGICAL ASSESSMENT

- Assess the patient's mental status, including LOC, alertness, orientation, and speech.

- The Glasgow Coma Scale (GCS) is the most commonly used, systematic, objective scoring tool for judging a patient's LOC.

Table 2.1. Scoring on the Glasgow Coma Scale

Eye Opening (E)	Verbal Response (V)	Motor Response (M)
4 = spontaneous 3 = to sound 2 = to pressure 1 = none NT = not testable	5 = orientated 4 = confused 3 = to words 2 = to sounds 1 = none NT = not testable	6 = obeys command 5 = localizes 4 = normal flexion 3 = abnormal flexion 2 = extension 1 = none NT = not testable

- Assess the patient's motor function. Special attention should be paid to nonsymmetrical findings.
  - muscle tone and coordination (bilateral hand squeeze and foot press, moving fingers and toes)
  - facial symmetry (patient's ability to lift eyebrows and smile)
  - **PERRLA** (pupils equal, round, and reactive to light and accommodation)

- Assess patient's response to stimulus (light touch on an area).

- Assess cranial nerve function. (See Table 2.2.)

Table 2.2. Cranial Nerve Function and Assessment

Cranial Nerve	Assessment
I. Olfactory: sense of smell	Have patient identify a smell with eyes closed, using each nostril individually.
II. Optic: central and peripheral vision	Have patient read something; assess peripheral vision.
III. Oculomotor: constriction of pupils and extraocular movement	Test pupil response with penlight; have patient follow with their eyes a finger making a large "H."
IV. Trochlear: downward eye movement	Have patient follow your finger moving toward their nose.
V. Trigeminal: face	Check sensation on forehead, cheeks, and jaw; test jaw strength; have patient clench teeth.

Table 2.2. Cranial Nerve Function and Assessment (continued)

Cranial Nerve	Assessment
VI. Abducens: sideways eye movement	Have patient look toward each ear and complete the 6 cardinal fields of gaze.
VII. Facial: movement and expression	Assess facial symmetry; have patient puff cheeks, pucker, raise eyebrows, and smile.
VIII. Vestibulocochlear: hearing and equilibrium	Assess gait; hold a ticking watch by patient's ear, have them close their eyes, and ask them what they hear.
IX. Glossopharyngeal: tongue, throat, and uvula	Assess ability to taste sweet and sour on back of tongue; assess gag reflex.
X. Vagus: sensory and motor	Have patient swallow while speaking; have patient say "ah."
XI. Accessory: head and shoulder movement	Have patient shrug shoulders and turn head against resistance.
XII. Hypoglossal: tongue position	Have patient stick tongue out midline and then side to side.

QUICK REVIEW QUESTION

4. A patient is being prepared for cardiac ablation to treat atrial fibrillation (A-fib). During assessment, the nurse notes that the patient has slurred speech and a left-sided facial droop. What priority intervention should the nurse anticipate?

RESPIRATORY AND CHEST ASSESSMENT

- Perform respiratory inspection. Look for abnormalities in the shape of the chest, and assess the rate, depth, and effort of breathing.
    - **tachypnea:** rapid breathing
    - **bradypnea:** slow breathing
    - **dyspnea:** difficulty breathing
    - **hyperventilation:** increase in rate or volume of breaths; increase causes excessive elimination of CO_2
    - **Kussmaul breathing:** type of hyperventilation characterized by deep, labored breathing that is associated with metabolic acidosis
    - **Cheyne-Stokes breathing:** deep breathing alternating with apnea or a faster rate of breathing; associated with left heart failure or sleep apnea
- Perform lung percussion. Tone indicates where lungs are solid or filled with air or fluid.
    - Normal air-filled structures have a **resonant** note (tympanic or drumlike sound).

- ○ Fluid or tissue-filled cavities (e.g., pneumonia) have a **dull** sound.
- ○ Air-filled tissues (e.g., emphysema, pneumothorax) have a **hyperresonant** sound (more pronounced drumlike noise).
- Perform lung auscultation. **Vesicular breath sounds** are heard over the lungs; **bronchial breath sounds** are heard over the trachea and bronchi.

Table 2.3. Lung Sounds

Sound	Description	Etiology
wheezes	continuous musical-like sound; can occur on inspiration or expiration	air being forced through narrowed passages in the airway (e.g., asthma, COPD)
rhonchi	low-pitched, coarse rattling lung sounds	secretions in the airway (e.g., pneumonia, cystic fibrosis)
stridor	high-pitched wheezing sound	air moving through narrowed or obstructed passages in the upper airway (e.g., aspiration, laryngospasm)
rales (crackles)	crackling, rattling sound that can be coarse or fine	fluid in the small airways of the lung (e.g., pulmonary edema, pneumonia)
pleural friction rub	a grating, creaking sound	inflamed pleural tissue (e.g., pleuritis, pulmonary embolism)
diminished or absent breath sounds	decreased intensity of breath sounds due to lack of air in lung tissues	air or fluid around the lungs (e.g., pleural effusion, pneumothorax) or blocked airway
egophony	an "e" sound heard as "a" due to increased resonance of sound traveling across fluid	fluid in the lungs (e.g., pleural effusion, pneumonia)
bronchophony	increased volume of spoken voice over areas of lung consolidation	
whispered pectoriloquy	increased volume of whispered voice over areas of lung consolidation	

QUICK REVIEW QUESTION

5. A patient is admitted to the cardiac care unit with pleural effusion secondary to right-sided heart failure. What sound should the nurse expect to hear when auscultating over the area of effusion?

CARDIOVASCULAR ASSESSMENT

- Inspect and palpate **carotid arteries** with patient positioned at a 45-degree angle with their head turned away.

HELPFUL HINT

Palpate one carotid artery at a time; do not occlude both arteries at the same time.

- Inspect and palpate the **jugular veins**.
  - ○ Have the patient relax the sternomastoid muscle so that pulsations in the interior jugular vein can be observed.
  - ○ **Jugular venous distention (JVD)** can be used to estimate central venous pressure (CVP): JVD indicates an elevated CVP.

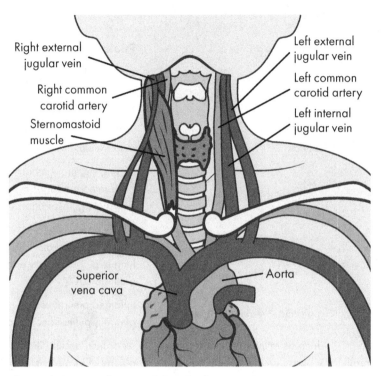

Figure 2.3. Vasculature of the Neck

- Observe the temperature, size, and color of extremities; palpate peripheral pulses simultaneously. Special attention should be paid to asymmetrical findings.

- To perform cardiac percussion, the nurse taps on the patient's chest to identify cardiac margins and underlying structures. (Although percussion is useful to identify cardiac margins and underlying structures, this outdated process has been replaced by X-ray.)

- Perform cardiac auscultation from the apex of the heart to the base of the heart using a stethoscope.
  - ○ **mitral valve:** found at the fifth left intercostal space at the midclavicular line
  - ○ **tricuspid valve:** found at the fifth left intercostal space at the left sternal border
  - ○ **Erb's point:** found at the third left intercostal space at the left sternal border
  - ○ **pulmonic valve:** found at the second left intercostal space at the left sternal border
  - ○ **aortic valve:** found at the second right intercostal space at the right sternal border

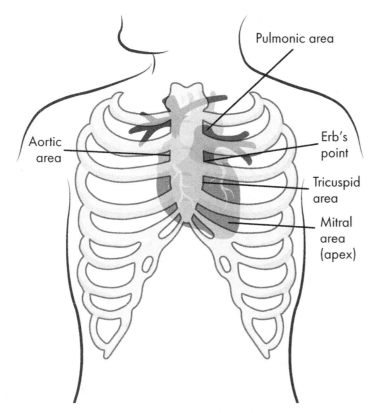

Figure 2.4. Locations for Cardiac Auscultation

- **Heart sounds** are produced as blood moves through the heart.
  - **S1:** caused by the closure of the AV valves; indicates the end of diastole and the beginning of systole
  - **S2:** caused by the closure of the semilunar valves; indicates the end of systole and the beginning of diastole
  - **S3 (ventricular gallop):** an extra heart sound heard after S2; caused by a rush of blood into a ventricle, S3 is a normal finding in children and young adults
  - **S4 (atrial gallop):** an extra heart sound heard before S1; caused by the atrial contraction of blood into a noncompliant ventricle; can be a normal finding in older adults
- **Murmurs** are the sounds made by turbulent blood flow in and around the heart.
  - Murmurs can be systolic (occurring during ventricular contraction) or diastolic (occurring during ventricular filling).
  - Murmurs caused by increased blood flow across a normal valve are soft and systolic; they are commonly caused by anemia, pregnancy, hyperthyroidism, fever, or exercise.
  - Abnormal murmurs can be caused by septal defects, infections, or structural damage (e.g., stenosis or endocarditis).
- **Pericardial friction rub** is a high-pitched, leathery sound heard characteristically in pericarditis.

HELPFUL HINT

S3 heart sound is associated with ventricular dysfunction or volume overload in the ventricles (e.g., MI, systolic HF, dilated cardiomyopathy, or mitral valve regurgitation).

S4 heart sound is associated with decreased ventricular compliance (e.g., hypertrophic cardiomyopathy, hypertension, or aortic stenosis).

- heard loudest at the fourth and fifth intercostal spaces, with patient leaning forward
- will continue even if patient is holding breath
- **Carotid bruits** are abnormal sounds heard over the carotid artery caused by turbulent blood flow. They can be heard with a Doppler or stethoscope and may indicate carotid artery disease.

QUICK REVIEW QUESTION

6. Which abnormal heart sound might a nurse expect to hear in a patient with heart failure?

ABDOMINAL AND GASTROINTESTINAL ASSESSMENT

- Perform bowel auscultation.
  - High-pitched gurgling sounds are normal. Normal bowel sounds can be documented as normal, hypoactive, or hyperactive.
  - **Borborygmi:** loud, rumbling sounds caused by shifting of fluids or gas within the intestines; a normal finding
  - **High-pitched bowel sounds:** often described as tinkling or rushing sounds; may indicate an early bowel obstruction

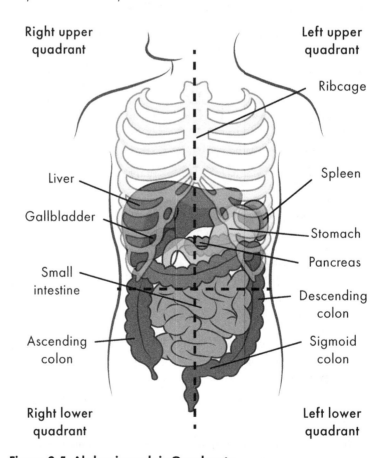

Figure 2.5. Abdominopelvic Quadrants

- ○ **Absent bowel sounds:** an indication of an ileus where no peristalsis is occurring; bowel sounds may be temporarily absent in certain cases (e.g., after surgery), but their absence, combined with abdominal pain, indicates a serious condition

- Palpate abdomen; ask the patient where they are having pain, and palpate this area last.

- Perform abdominal percussion.
  - ○ Start at the umbilicus and move downward.
  - ○ **Tympanic sounds** indicate air-filled intestines.
  - ○ **Dull sounds** indicate organomegaly, masses, or fluid.

QUICK REVIEW QUESTION

7. A patient has been admitted to the cardiac care unit with right-sided heart failure. What is the most likely reason a nurse would note dullness when percussing the abdomen?

HELPFUL HINT

In patients with *ascites* (collection of fluid in the peritoneal cavity), the location of the dull sound will shift as the fluid shifts when the patient changes position between supine or lying on their side.

SKIN AND NAIL ASSESSMENT

- Inspect skin for abnormalities.

- Assess the extent of **skin edema** by pressing firmly into the skin and grading the indentation.

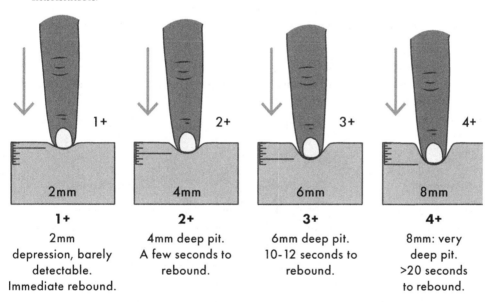

1+	2+	3+	4+
2mm depression, barely detectable. Immediate rebound.	4mm deep pit. A few seconds to rebound.	6mm deep pit. 10-12 seconds to rebound.	8mm: very deep pit. >20 seconds to rebound.

Figure 2.6. Grading Skin Edema

- Observe color and temperature of skin.
  - ○ **cyanosis:** a blue or purplish skin color caused by hypoxia
  - ○ **pallor:** paleness associated with anemia, shock, and other disorders
  - ○ **rubor:** redness of the skin; often caused by inflammation

- hemosiderin staining: brown skin color caused by iron deposits within cells; associated with chronic venous insufficiency and iron overload

- shiny skin in the extremities: a potential sign of peripheral vascular disease

- Observe skins for signs of bleeding (hematoma, ecchymosis, petechiae, or purpura).

- Inspect nails for abnormalities.

  - clubbing: an enlargement of the tissue at the distal phalange; occurs over a long period and is associated with many chronic cardiovascular and respiratory disorders

  - capillary refill time (CRT): how long it takes for blood to return to the skin under the nail after pressure is applied. Normal time is 3 seconds or less.

> ### QUICK REVIEW QUESTION
>
> **8.** A patient presents to the clinic with complaints of left calf tenderness. During assessment, the nurse notes cyanosis of the left foot with no palpable pulse. What diagnosis do these findings support?

Hemodynamics

- **Stroke volume (SV)** is the volume of blood pumped from the left ventricle during one contraction. Stroke volume is determined by:

  - preload: how much the ventricles stretch at the end of diastole (a measure of ventricular end-diastolic volume)

  - afterload: resistance the heart must overcome during systole to pump blood into circulation (a measure of aortic pressure and systemic vascular resistance [SVR])

  - contractility: the force of the heart independent of preload and afterload

Table 2.4. Hemodynamic Parameters

Parameter	Description	Normal Range
Blood pressure (BP)	vascular BP given as systolic pressure (SBP, top number) and diastolic pressure (DBP, bottom number)	90/60 – 120/80 mm Hg
Central venous pressure (CVP), or right atrial pressure (RAP)	pressure in the vena cava; used to estimate preload	2 – 6 mm Hg
Pulmonary artery pressure (PAP)	pressure in the pulmonary artery	8 – 20 mm Hg
Stroke volume (SV)	volume of blood forced from the left ventricle with each contraction	60 – 100 mL/beat

Parameter	Description	Normal Range
Cardiac output (CO)	volume of blood pumped in a unit of time (usually per minute) $CO = SV \times HR$	4 – 8 mL/min
Cardiac index (CI)	CO relative to patient size $CI = CO/BSA$	2.5 – 4 L/min/m^2
Mean arterial pressure (MAP)	average BP during a complete cardiac cycle $MAP = SBP + (2 \times DBP)/3$	70 – 100 mm Hg
Systemic vascular resistance (SVR)	total peripheral vascular system resistance to blood flow $SVR = 80 \times (MAP - CVP)/CO$	700 – 1200 dyne $\cdot$ sec/cm^5
Pulmonary artery occlusion pressure (PAOP), or pulmonary capillary wedge pressure (PCWP)	indirect measurement of left atrial pressure; uses Swan-Ganz catheter to "wedge" inflated balloon into a branch of the pulmonary artery	6 – 12 mm Hg
Pulmonary vascular resistance (PVR)	vascular resistance to blood flow in the lungs $PVR = 80 \times (MPAP - PAOP)/CI$	255 – 285 dyne $\cdot$ sec/cm^5
Left ventricular end-diastolic pressure (LVEDP)	pressure in the left ventricle before systole	5 – 12 mm Hg
Arterial oxygen saturation (SaO$_2$)	fraction of oxygen-saturated hemoglobin in arteries	95 – 100%
Mixed venous saturation (SvO$_2$)	fraction of oxygen-saturated hemoglobin in veins (taken from PAC)	60 – 80%
Central venous oxygen saturation (ScvO$_2$)	fraction of oxygen-saturated hemoglobin in veins; surrogate for SvO$_2$ (taken from central venous catheter)	>70%
Arterial oxygen content (CaO$_2$)	volume of oxygen delivered to tissue per unit of blood	16 – 22 mL/dL
Oxygen delivery (DO$_2$)	volume of blood oxygen being transported to tissues per unit of time	arterial = 1000 mL/min venous = 775 mL/min
Oxygen consumption (VO$_2$)	volume of oxygen used by the body per unit of time	200 – 250 mL/min

QUICK REVIEW QUESTION

9. The nurse is reassessing a patient with severe sepsis after a fluid bolus and the administration of vasopressors. What hemodynamic value would indicate an improvement?

Laboratory Tests

Table 2.5. Common Laboratory Tests

Test	Description	Normal Range
Cardiac Biomarkers		
Troponin I (cTnI) and troponin T (cTnT)	proteins released when the heart muscle is damaged; high levels can indicate an MI but may also be due to other conditions that stress the heart (e.g., renal failure, HF, PE); levels peak 24 hours post-MI and can remain elevated for up to 2 weeks	cTnI: < 0.04 ng/mL cTnT: < 0.01 ng/mL
Creatine kinase (CK)	responsible for muscle cell function; an increase indicates cardiac or skeletal muscle damage	22 – 198 U/L
Creatine kinase–muscle/brain (CK-MB)	cardiac marker for damaged heart muscle; often used to diagnose a second MI or ongoing cardiovascular conditions; a high ratio of CK-MB to CK (high CK-MB/CK) indicates damage to heart muscle (as opposed to skeletal muscle)	normal CK-MB: 5 – 25 IU/L CK-MB/CK suggesting possible MI: 2.5 – 3
Complete Blood Count (CBC)		
White blood cells (WBCs)	a high WBC count can indicate inflammation or infection	4,500 – 10,000 cells/μL
Red blood cells (RBCs)	cells that carry oxygen throughout the body and filter carbon dioxide	men: 5 – 6 million cells/μL women: 4 – 5 million cells/μL
Hemoglobin (HgB)	protein that binds oxygen in the blood	men: 13.8 – 17.2 g/dL women: 12.1 – 15.1 g/dL
Hematocrit (Hct)	percentage of the blood composed of red blood cells	men: 41% – 50% women: 36% – 44%
mean corpuscular volume (MCV)	average size of RBCs	MCV: 80 – 95 fL
mean corpuscular hemoglobin (MCH)	average amount of HgB in RBCs	27.5 – 33.2 pg
mean corpuscular hemoglobin concentration (MCHC)	average concentration of HgB in RBCs	334 – 355 g/L
Platelets	blood components that play a role in clotting	150,000 – 450,000 platelets/μL

Test	Description	Normal Range
WBC Differential		
Neutrophils	first responders that quickly migrate to the site of infections to destroy bacterial invaders	2,000 – 7,000/μL (40 – 60%)
Band neutrophils	immature neutrophils (also called bands)	< 700/μL (< 5%)
Lymphocytes	B cells, T cells, and natural killer cells; all 3 types develop from common lymphoid progenitors	1,000 – 3,000/μL (20 – 40%)
Monocytes	foreign substance cells that engulf and destroy microbes, and cancer cells	200 – 1,000/μL (2 – 8%)
Eosinophils	cells that attack parasites and regulate inflammation	20 – 500/μL (1 – 4%)
Basophils	cells responsible for inflammatory reactions, including allergies	20 – 100/μL (0 – 2%)
Coagulation Studies and Clotting Factors		
Prothrombin time (PT)	how long it takes blood to clot	10 – 13 seconds
International normalized ratio (INR)	standardized PT for patients taking Warfarin	healthy adults: < 1.1 patients receiving anticoagulants: 2.0 – 3.0
Partial thromboplastin time (PTT)	the body's ability to form blood clots	60 – 70 seconds
Activated partial thromboplastin time (aPTT)	the body's ability to form blood clots using an activator to speed up the clotting process	20 – 35 seconds
D-dimer	protein fragment produced during fibrinolysis	negative
Fibrin split products (FSP) or fibrin degradation products (FDP)	components produced during fibrinolysis	< 10 mg/L
Fibrinogen	amount of fibrinogen (clotting factor I)	200 – 400 mg/dL
Plasminogen	substrate involved in fibrinolysis	10 – 16 mg/dL
Kidney Function Tests		
BUN	by-product of ammonia metabolism; filtered by the kidneys; high levels can indicate insufficient kidney function	7 – 20 mg/dL

Table 2.5. Common Laboratory Tests (continued)

Test	Description	Normal Range
Kidney Function Tests (continued)		
Creatinine	product of muscle metabolism; filtered by the kidneys; high levels can indicate insufficient kidney function	0.6 – 1.2 mg/dL
BUN-to-creatinine ratio	increased ratio indicates dehydration, AKI, or GI bleeding; decreased ratio indicates renal damage	10:1 – 20:1
GFR	volume of fluid filtered by the renal glomerular capillaries per unit of time; decreased GFR indicates decreased renal function	men: 100 – 130 mL/min/1.73 m^2 women: 90 – 120 mL/min/1.73 m^2 GFR < 60 mL/min/1.73 m^2 is common in adults > 70 years
Potassium (K$^+$)	helps with muscle contraction and regulates water and acid-base balance	3.5 – 5.2 mEq/L
Sodium (Na$^+$)	maintains fluid balance and plays a major role in muscle and nerve function	135 – 145 mEq/L
Calcium (Ca^{2+})	plays an important role in skeletal function and structure, nerve function, muscle contraction, and cell communication	8.5 – 10.3 mg/dL
Chloride (Cl$^-$)	plays a major role in muscle and nerve function	98 – 107 mEq/L
Magnesium (Mg^{2+})	regulates muscle, nerve, and cardiac function	1.8 – 2.5 mg/dL
Liver Function Tests		
Albumin	protein made in the liver; low levels may indicate liver damage	3.5 – 5.0 g/dL
Alkaline phosphatase (ALP)	enzyme found in the liver and bones; increased levels indicate liver damage	45 – 147 U/L
Alanine transaminase (ALT)	enzyme in the liver; helps metabolize protein; increased levels indicate liver damage	7 – 55 U/L

Test	Description	Normal Range
Liver Function Tests (continued)		
Aspartate transaminase (AST)	enzyme in the liver; helps metabolize alanine; increased levels indicate liver or muscle damage	8 – 48 U/L
Total protein	low levels may indicate liver damage	6.3 – 7.9 g/dL
Total bilirubin	produced during the breakdown of heme; increased levels indicate liver damage or anemia	0.1 – 1.2 mg/dL
Gamma-glutamyl-transferase (GGT)	enzyme that plays a role in antioxidant metabolism; increased levels indicate liver damage	9 – 48 U/L
L-lactate dehydrogenase (LD or LDH)	enzyme found in most cells in the body; increased levels may indicate liver damage, cancer, or tissue breakdown	adults: 122 – 222 U/L
Urinalysis		
Leukocytes	presence of WBCs in urine indicates infection	negative
Nitrate	presence in urine indicates infection by gram-negative bacteria	negative
Protein	presence in urine may indicate diabetic neuropathy, nephritis, or eclampsia	negative
pH	decreased (acidic) pH may indicate systemic acidosis or diabetes mellitus; increased (alkali) pH may indicate systemic alkalosis or UTI	4.5 – 8
Blood	presence in urine may indicate infection, renal calculi, a neoplasm, or coagulation disorders	negative
Specific gravity	concentration of urine; decreased concentration may indicate diabetes insipidus or pyelonephritis; increased concentration may indicate dehydration or SIADH	1.010 – 1.025
Urine osmolality	concentration of urine; more accurate than specific gravity	300 – 900 mOsm/kg
Ketones	produced during fat metabolism; presence in urine may indicate diabetes, hyperglycemia, starvation, alcoholism, or eclampsia	negative

QUICK REVIEW QUESTION

10. A female patient is admitted with an RBC count of 2.8 million. What signs and symptoms should the nurse expect her to present with?

Other Diagnostic Tools

- A **chest X-ray** is used to diagnose abnormalities in the lungs, heart, and bones.

- A **CT (computed tomography)** scan is a type of X-ray that produces a 3-D picture of organs, bones, and tissues. IV or oral contrast can be used for this test, and kidney function needs to be checked before the procedure.

- **MRI (magnetic resonance imaging)** uses large magnets and radiofrequencies to produce detailed pictures of the body. **MRA (magnetic resonance angiography)** uses large magnets and radiofrequency to view and identify abnormalities in blood vessels.

- A **PET (positron emission tomography)** scan uses a radioactive dye that helps identify areas of high chemical activity that could represent disease. Check for iodine allergies before testing.

- A **TEE (transesophageal echocardiogram)** uses a specialized probe that passes through the patients' esophagus to view the heart structure and record images. Check for gag reflex after the procedure; patient must remain NPO for at least 60 minutes after the procedure (or until numbness subsides) to prevent choking.

- A **TTE (transthoracic echocardiogram)** is a noninvasive test that uses ultrasound to view the heart. The ultrasound probe is placed on the chest or stomach to obtain the necessary images.

- During **electrophysiology studies (EPS)**, a small catheter is guided through the femoral vein to the heart to test the electrical system of the heart and identify dysrhythmias.

- During a **diagnostic cardiac catheterization**, a small catheter is threaded through the radial, brachial, or femoral artery and guided to the heart. Dye is then injected through the catheter, and X-ray pictures are taken of the heart.

- **Stress testing** is used to assess the cardiovascular system's response to strenuous work. They can be physical (via treadmill) or chemical.

- The **Borg scale** is used to assess a patient's perception of exertion during physical activity. The rating goes from 6 (no exertion) to 20 (maximum exertion).

- The **six-minute walk test** assesses how far a patient can walk in six minutes. The procedure is done on a hard, flat service, and the patient is able to set the pace.

HELPFUL HINT

Some PET scans require patients to be on a no sugar, low-carb diet for twenty-four hours before scan.

QUICK REVIEW QUESTION

11. A patient has returned to the cardiac vascular unit after undergoing a diagnostic cardiac catheterization. A priority concern for this patient is a risk of bleeding. Why is this a concern, and what should be done if bleeding occurs?

Electrocardiography and Telemetry
ECG BASICS

- A 12-lead **electrocardiogram (ECG)** is a noninvasive diagnostic tool that records the heart's electrical activity. This diagnostic test can help determine a patient's cardiac rhythm and rate.

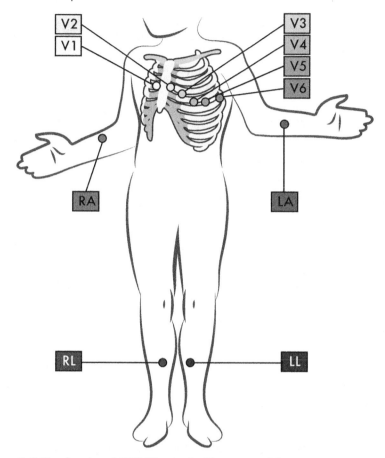

Figure 2.7. Twelve-Lead ECG Electrode Placement Diagram

Table 2.6. Twelve-Lead ECG Electrode Placement

Electrode	Placement
V1	Fourth intercostal space to the right of the sternum
V2	Fourth intercostal space to the left of the sternum
V3	Midway between V2 and V4
V4	Fifth intercostal space at the midclavicular line
V5	Anterior axillary line at the same level as V4
V6	Midaxillary line at the same level as V4 and V5
RA	Between right shoulder and right wrist
LA	Between left shoulder and left wrist

Table 2.6. Twelve-Lead ECG Electrode Placement (continued)

Electrode	Placement
RL	Above right ankle and below the torso
LL	Above left ankle and below the torso

- A 12-lead ECG includes 3 types of leads:
  - 3 bipolar (leads I, II, and III)
  - 3 unipolar (leads aVR, aVL, and aVF)
  - 6 precordial (leads V1 – V6)

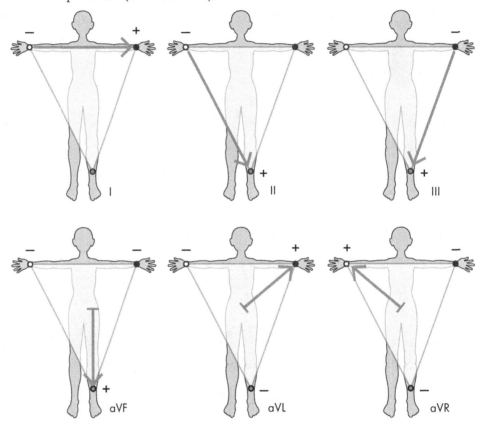

Figure 2.8. Bipolar and Unipolar Leads in a 12-Lead ECG

- The leads show activity in different areas of the heart:
  - The inferior portion of the heart can be seen through leads II, III, and aVF.
  - The anterior portion of the heart can be seen in leads V3 and V4.
  - The lateral portion of the heart can be seen in leads I, aVL, V5, and V6.
  - The septal region can be seen in leads V1 and V2.
- Additional leads may be used when the patient is suspected of having damage to the posterior of the heart or the right ventricle.
  - **Posterior leads** (V7, V8, and V9) are placed on the patient's back when a posterior infarction is suspected.

○ **Right-side leads** (V3R, V4R, V5R, and V6R) are placed on the patient's right side in a mirror image of V3 – V6 when a right ventricular infarction is suspected.

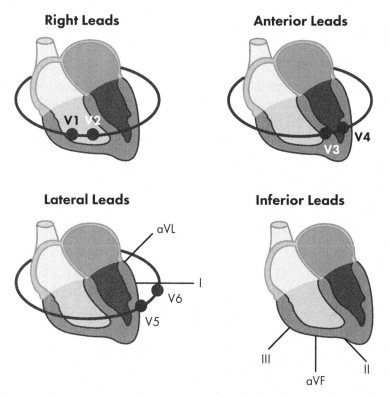

Figure 2.9. Portion of Heart Corresponding to ECG Leads

- Damage to coronary arteries can be seen in changes to specific leads (see Table 2.7).

Table 2.7. Lead Changes and Affected Coronary Artery by Location of MI

Location of MI	Lead with ST Changes	Affected Coronary Artery
anteroseptal	V1 – V4	LAD
anterior	V2 – V4	LAD
lateral	I, aVL, V5, V6	circumflex artery
inferior	II, III, aVF	RCA
posterior	V7 – V9	RCA
right ventricular	V4R – V6R	RCA

QUICK REVIEW QUESTION

12. A 12-lead ECG is performed on a patient with chest pain. The ECG shows ST elevations in leads II, III and aVF. Which medications are contraindicated for this patient?

- **P wave:** The P wave is the small bump seen before a QRS complex. This bump represents atrial depolarization and should measure 0.06 – 0.11 seconds.

- **PR interval:** The PR interval is measured from the start of the P wave to the start of the QRS interval. This segment represents the AV conduction time and should measure between 0.12 and 0.20 seconds.

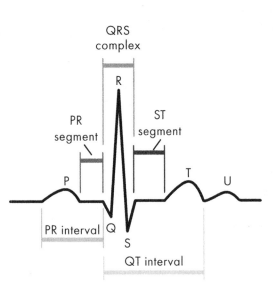

Figure 2.10. Waveforms and Intervals on an ECG

- **QRS complex:** The QRS complex is measured from the end of the PR interval until the end of the S wave. (Measure the spike.) This complex represents ventricular depolarization and should measure 0.08 – 0.10 seconds.

- **T wave:** The T wave is the small bump directly following the QRS complex and represents the repolarization of the ventricles.

- **U wave:** This is another small bump that, when visible, will follow the T wave.

- **QT interval:** The QT interval is measured from the beginning of the QRS complex until the end of the T wave. This segment represents the total time of ventricular activity (depolarization and repolarization). A normal QT interval should be 0.36 – 0.44 seconds.

- **ST segment:** The ST segment is measured from the end of the QRS complex to the start of the T wave. This segment shows the early part of ventricular repolarization.

- **RR interval:** The RR interval is the distance between QRS complexes.

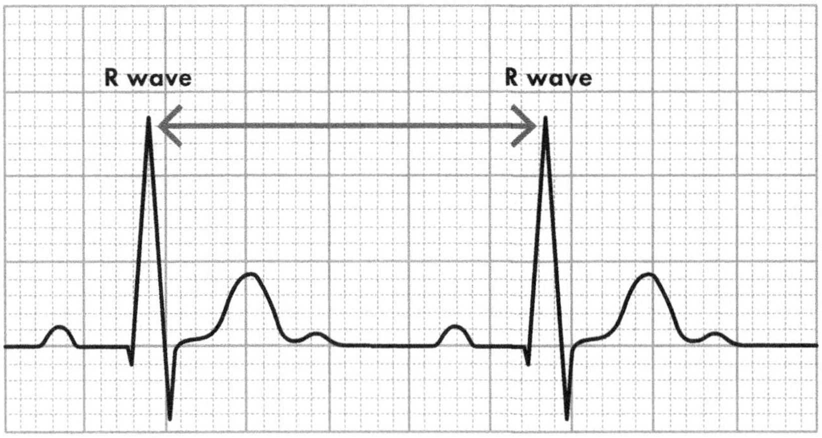

Figure 2.11. The RR Interval on an ECG

QUICK REVIEW QUESTION

13. If a rhythm is missing P waves or has an excessive number of P waves, which area of the heart is having difficulty conducting?

ANSWER KEY

1. Lower back pain is a symptom of ACS often seen in women and the elderly. Because the patient has a history of angina, the nurse should assess the patient for other s/s of ACS and expect to get an ECG.

2. The nurse's priority should be the patient's breathing. The nurse should elevate the head of the bed, apply oxygen, and notify the physician.

3. Low ABI values (≤ 0.9) indicate a likely arterial occlusion.

4. The patient is showing signs of an ischemic stroke, possibly caused by A-fib. The nurse should alert the medical provider and prepare for the patient to have an immediate noncontrast CT scan of the head.

5. The nurse should expect to hear decreased or absent breath sounds in the area of effusion. The nurse may also hear bronchial breath sounds and egophony.

6. S3 gallops are heard with heart failure.

7. Right-sided heart failure can cause edema in the extremities and abdomen. When fluid collects in the peritoneal cavity (ascites), it creates a dull sound during percussion of the abdomen.

8. The patient's foot is cyanotic and pulseless, which indicates arterial occlusion. The occluded artery has resulted in hypoxia in the patient's foot, giving it a blue color.

9. The nurse should focus on CVP as CVP is an indirect measure of right ventricular pressure and is highly influenced by fluid status. In sepsis, CVP is < 2 mmHg, because of profound systemic vasodilation. Both treatments would be expected to increase preload, thereby increasing CVP.

10. The patient will have decreased O_2 and increased CO_2 levels and will show signs of anemia, including dyspnea, fatigue, and palpitations.

11. Because a cardiac catheterization is performed by gaining access to a patient's artery, the procedure puts them at a high risk of bleeding. If bleeding occurs, the nurse should apply pressure at the catheterization site and notify the physician.

12. The symptoms indicate right-sided MI. When treating patients with right ventricular infarction, nitrates, diuretics, and morphine are to be avoided due to their preload-reducing effects.

13. The P wave shows atrial depolarization. If a rhythm shows abnormalities in the P waves, then the patient's atria are not functioning properly.

THREE: CARDIOVASCULAR PHARMACOLOGY

Administering Medications

There are seven "rights" to medication administration.

- Right Patient
  - Verify that the medication is for the patient about to receive it.
  - Use two patient identifiers (usually name and date of birth as these demographics are patient-specific).
  - Check the ID band to make sure it matches the patient's reported name and DOB.
  - Make sure the drug matches the patient's diagnosis.
  - Ensure that medication was ordered for the correct patient.
- Right Drug
  - Check that the medication to be delivered matches the order.
  - Have another nurse check the order if necessary; some high-risk medications require two nurses to check the order.
- Right Route
  - Assess if the patient can take the drug via the route ordered.
  - Administer the drug via the route ordered.
- Right Dose
  - Clarify the dose written by the provider and administer only that dose.
  - Verify drug calculations.
- Right Time
  - Determine how often to administer the medication, based on its duration of action.
  - Give the medication at the appropriate time so that the dosing schedule is undisrupted.

- Right Response
  - Monitor for the anticipated response of the drug.
- Right Documentation
  - If it is not documented, it is not done.

QUICK REVIEW QUESTION

1. During shift change, the oncoming nurse asks about the time of the last administration of PRN pain medication. How will the current assigned nurse verify the administration of the last dose of pain medication?

ACE Inhibitors (ACE-Is)

Mechanism of Action

- lowers SVR by blocking the angiotensin-converting enzyme (ACE) from converting angiotensin I to angiotensin II (a potent vasoconstrictor)
- lower levels of aldosterone, reducing retention of water and sodium
- lower blood pressure

Therapeutic Uses

- hypertension (first line)
- congestive heart failure (recommended when left ventricular ejection fraction < 40%)
- medical management following MI (reduces remodeling)
- diabetic nephropathy

Possible Adverse Reactions

- persistent dry cough (due to buildup of bradykinin)
- hypotension
- worsening renal function
- hyperkalemia
- angioedema
- neutropenia

Contraindications

- aortic and renal artery stenosis
- acute kidney injury
- hyperkalemia

- pregnancy

- persistent dry cough on ACE-I (switch to ARB)

- angioedema (considered an allergy to this drug class)

Common ACE Inhibitors (suffix –*pril*)

- lisinopril

- ramipril

- enalapril

- benazepril

QUICK REVIEW QUESTION

2. The nurse is preparing to administer lisinopril 10 mg. The patient has a blood pressure of 138/95 mm Hg and heart rate of 88 bpm. Labs show K+ 5.5 and Cr 1.7. What action should the nurse take?

HELPFUL HINT

Since 2012, Lisinopril (Prinivil, Zestril) has been one of the three most commonly prescribed medications in the United States (along with levothyroxine and atorvastatin [Lipitor]).

Adrenergic Group

ALPHA$_1$-ADRENERGIC AGONISTS

Mechanism of Action

- stimulate vascular smooth muscle, causing vasoconstriction and increased SVR and BP

Therapeutic Uses

- hypotension

- shock

Possible Adverse Reactions

- bradycardia

- hypertension

- headache

- vision deficits

- erythema multiforme

Contraindications

- CAD

- hypertension

- tachycardia

- acute renal failure
- thyrotoxicosis
- pheochromocytoma

Common Drugs

- methoxamine (Vasoxyl)
- midodrine (ProAmatine)
- phenylephrine (Neo-Synephrine)

QUICK REVIEW QUESTION

3. A patient presents with cardiogenic shock secondary to aortic stenosis. What medication is likely to be ordered for the patient?

ALPHA$_1$-ADRENERGIC BLOCKERS

Mechanism of Action

- block alpha$_1$-adrenergic receptor sites in vascular smooth muscle resulting in vasodilation and decreased tone of vasculature

Therapeutic Uses

- hypertension (fourth line)
- BPH (second line)

Possible Adverse Reactions

- orthostatic hypotension (especially after first dose)
- tachycardia
- dysrhythmias
- dizziness
- nausea
- diaphoresis
- weakness and fatigue

Contraindications

- hypotension
- heart failure
- renal failure
- pregnancy
- erectile dysfunction medications

Common Drugs (suffix –*zosin*)

- doxazosin

- prazosin

- terazosin

ALPHA$_2$-ADRENERGIC AGONISTS

Mechanism of Action

- bind to alpha$_2$-adrenergic receptors in the brain, which reduces the action of the sympathetic nervous system

- result in decreased heart rate, speed of cardiac contraction, and BP

Therapeutic Uses

- hypertension (fourth line)

- ADHD (third line)

Possible Adverse Reactions

- hypotension

- bradycardia

- heart failure

- drowsiness or fatigue

- constipation

Contraindications

- CAD

- renal failure

Common Drugs

- clonidine (Catapres)

- guanabenz (Wytensin)

- guanfacine (Tenex)

ALPHA$_2$-ADRENERGIC BLOCKERS

Mechanism of Action

- block alpha$_2$-adrengeric receptors, which disables the sympathetic response of peripheral blood vessels and results in decreased SVR and lowered BP

Therapeutic Uses

- hypertension (especially due to pheochromocytoma)
- hypertensive crisis (emergency-level reaction to anesthesia)

Possible Adverse Reactions

- orthostatic hypotension (especially after first dose)
- tachycardia
- dysrhythmias
- dizziness
- nausea
- peptic ulcer disease
- priapism

Contraindications

- recent MI
- renal failure
- CAD
- angina
- breastfeeding

Common Drugs

- phentolamine (Regitine)

BETA-ADRENERGIC ANTAGONISTS (BETA-BLOCKERS)

Mechanism of Action

- block beta-adrenergic receptors in the heart (beta$_1$) and blood vessels (beta$_2$), resulting in lowered BP and HR and decreased cardiac output

- block beta$_1$-adrenergic receptors in the kidneys that promote secretion of renin, reducing renin production and SVR

Therapeutic Uses

- post MI (first line)

- hypertension (second line)

- chronic angina

- cardiac dysrhythmias (A-fib, SVT)

- prophylactic treatment of migraines

- anxiety (off-label use)

Possible Adverse Reactions

- bradycardia

- heart block

- hypotension

- exacerbation of asthma (beta$_2$ blockade effect)

- fatigue

- memory loss and confusion

- masking of hypoglycemia

Contraindications

- bradycardia

- sick sinus syndrome without pacemaker

- second- or third-degree AV block (including Mobitz II)

- junctional rhythm

- dual BBB

- asthma (only beta$_1$-selective beta blockers should be used)

- COPD (only beta$_1$-selective beta blockers should be used)

Common Drugs (suffix −*olol*)

- metoprolol

- atenolol

- bisoprolol
- propranolol

QUICK REVIEW QUESTION

7. For which dysrhythmias are beta blockers contraindicated?

SYMPATHOMIMETICS

Mechanism of Action

- alpha- and beta-adrenergic agonists that activate $alpha_1$, $alpha_2$, $beta_1$, and/or $beta_2$ receptors
- result in vasoconstriction, increased force of cardiac contraction, or increased rate of cardiac conduction (depending on the affected receptors)
- dopamine: at lower doses acts on dopaminergic receptors to stimulate renal vasodilation and perfusion
- include endogenous catecholamines (e.g., epinephrine) and drugs that mimic endogenous catecholamines (e.g., dobutamine).

Therapeutic Uses

- hypotension
- heart failure
- cardiogenic shock
- cardiac arrest/asystole/PEA
- acute bronchospasm
- anaphylaxis

Possible Adverse Reactions

- hypertension
- tachydysrhythmias
- headache
- nausea and vomiting

Contraindications

- V-fib

Common Drugs

- epinephrine (Adrenalin)
- norepinephrine (Levophed)

- dobutamine (Dobutrex)

- dopamine (Intropin)

QUICK REVIEW QUESTION

8. The nurse is caring for a patient being administered Levophed to maintain a MAP greater than 60 mm Hg. The infusion is currently at the maximum dose and the patient has a MAP of 55 mm Hg. What does the nurse anticipate the physician will order for this patient?

Angiotensin II Receptor Antagonists (ARBs)

Mechanism of Action

- block angiotensin II receptor site, causing vasodilation and lowered BP

- have a similar mechanism of action to ACE inhibitors but cause fewer adverse effects (e.g., do not affect bradykinin levels)

Therapeutic Uses

- hypertension (second line if intolerant to ACE-Is)

- heart failure (recommended when left ventricular ejection fraction < 40%)

- medical management following MI (second line if intolerant to ACE-Is)

- diabetic nephropathy

Possible Adverse Reactions

- hyperkalemia

- acute kidney injury

- dizziness

- syncope

- headache

- angioedema (considered an allergy to the medication)

Contraindications

- hypotension

- acute renal failure

- pregnancy

- angioedema (considered an allergy to the medication)

HELPFUL HINT

NSAIDs, ARBs, and ACE inhibitors can cause or worsen prerenal disease and acute tubular necrosis.

Common Angiotensin II Receptor Antagonists (–*artan*)

- losartan

- irbesartan

- valsartan

QUICK REVIEW QUESTION

9. The nurse is completing medication reconciliation with a patient in clinic. The patient states that he was previously taking lisinopril for high blood pressure but the cardiologist recently switched his prescription to losartan. What is a likely reason that the patient's medication was switched?

Anticoagulants

Mechanism of Action

- increase clotting time via various mechanisms that disrupt production of clotting factors

- warfarin: disrupts the hepatic production of vitamin K clotting factors (II, VII, IX, X, proteins C and S)

- heparin: binds to the enzyme antithrombin III, catalyzing the inactivation of thrombin and other clotting factors

- low molecular weight heparins (enoxaparin): bind to the enzyme antithrombin III and accelerate activity, inhibiting thrombin and factor Xa

- direct Xa inhibitors (apixaban, rivaroxaban, edoxaban): inhibit action of factor Xa

HELPFUL HINT

Heparin is neutralized with protamine sulfate. Warfarin is neutralized with Vitamin K.

Therapeutic Uses

- known thrombosis (e.g., PE or DVT)

- prophylaxis of thrombosis (e.g., post A-fib, cardiac post-op procedures)

- antiphospholipid syndrome

- hypercoagulable states (protein C and S deficiencies)

- adjunct therapy in mechanical valve replacements, MI, and stroke

Possible Adverse Reactions

- hemorrhage

- nausea and vomiting

- headache

- thrombocytopenia (HIT)

- direct Xa inhibitors: false elevation in INR levels

HELPFUL HINT

Heparin-induced thrombocytopenia (HIT) causes platelet activation, significantly increasing risk of thrombosis (usually 5 – 10 days after exposure to heparin.) If HIT is suspected, heparin should be discontinued immediately and the patient should be placed on a different anticoagulant.

Contraindications

- active hemorrhage or suspected acute blood loss

- epidural or spinal anesthesia

- valvular disorders

- use with caution in patients > 65 who are at high risk for falls

- use with caution in patients with heart failure or fever

- pregnancy (only LMWH or heparin can be used safely)

Common Drugs

- warfarin

- apixaban (Eliquis)

- rivaroxaban (Xarelto)

- enoxaparin (Lovenox)

- heparin

QUICK REVIEW QUESTION

10. During morning rounds, the nurse receives orders to discontinue enoxaparin (Lovenox) injections and transition the patient to apixaban (Eliquis). It is 11:00 a.m. and the patient received the morning enoxaparin injection at 8:00 a.m. What is the appropriate time for the first dose of apixaban?

Antidysrhythmics

Mechanism of Action

- suppress cardiac dysrhythmias and restore normal cardiac conduction

Table 3.1. Classes of Antidysrhythmics

Class	Mechanism	Common Medications	Therapeutic Uses
Class IA	fast sodium-channel blockers	disopyramide	treats ventricular dysrhythmias
		procainamide	
Class IB	fast sodium-channel blockers	lidocaine	
		mexiletine	
Class IC	fast sodium-channel blockers	flecainide	chemical conversion of A-fib, prophylactic treatment of paroxysmal A-fib and atrial flutter, maintenance therapy for SVT, treats ventricular dysrhythmias

Table 3.1. Classes of Antidysrhythmics (continued)

Class	Mechanism	Common Medications	Therapeutic Uses
Class II	beta blockers (discussed in detail above)		
Class III	potassium-channel blockers	amiodarone	treats V-fib, A-fib, atrial flutter
Class IV	slow calcium-channel blockers	verapamil	treats A-fib and atrial flutter; can lower blood pressure
		diltiazem	treats A-fib and atrial flutter; can lower blood pressure
Class V	variable mechanisms	adenosine	restarts the heart; commonly used to treat SVT
		digoxin	treats A-fib, heart failure
		magnesium sulfate	treats V-tach, torsades de pointes, eclampsia, hypomagnesemia, and cerebral edema

Possible Adverse Reactions

- bradycardia
- subsequent lethal ventricular dysrhythmias
- hypotension
- cardiac arrest
- lidocaine: decreased seizure threshold

Contraindications

- hypotension
- heart block
- respiratory depression
- use caution in patients with bilateral BBB if pacemaker is not present
- use caution in patients with heart failure

QUICK REVIEW QUESTION

11. A patient presents to the ED complaining of shortness of breath and syncope. Once the patient is placed on telemetry, the nurse observes the following rhythm:

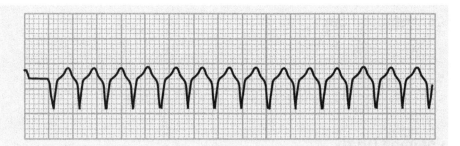

Which antidysrhythmic medication should the nurse anticipate being ordered by the physician?

Antiplatelets

Mechanism of Action

- decrease platelet aggregation and inhibit thrombus production via various mechanisms
- ADP receptor inhibitors: inhibit ADP receptor sites on platelets
- aspirin: prevents activation of platelets
- glycoprotein IIB/IIIA inhibitors: inhibit receptors on platelets that bind to fibrinogen

Therapeutic Uses

- PCI/stent placement for ACS
- treatment and prophylaxis for ischemic stroke
- unstable angina

Possible Adverse Reactions

- increased bleeding risks (may need to be held before major invasive procedures)
- headache
- nausea or other GI distress
- rash
- thrombocytopenia
- ticagrelor (Brilinta): mild, transient shortness of breath that typically resolves within a week
- aspirin: GI bleeding especially with dual antiplatelet therapy

Contraindications

- hypersensitivity
- active bleeding
- recent surgery (must be held for at least 4 hours post op)

Common Drugs

- clopidogrel (Plavix)
- ticagrelor (Brilinta)
- prasugrel (Effient)
- aspirin

QUICK REVIEW QUESTION

12. In preparation for major surgery, the nurse instructs a patient to stop taking clopidogrel (Plavix). The patient becomes concerned regarding coronary artery stents he had placed 18 months prior and asks if it is safe to stop taking clopidogrel. How should the nurse respond?

Diuretics

Therapeutic Uses

- hypertension
- heart failure
- edema
- osmotic diuretics: ICP

Possible Adverse Reactions

- electrolyte imbalances including hypokalemia, hyponatremia, and hyperuricemia
- metabolic alkalosis
- acute kidney injury related to overdiuresis
- dehydration
- hypotension

Contraindications

- hypotension
- acute renal failure
- dehydration
- use with caution in patients with dysrhythmias

Table 3.2. Types of Diuretics

Type of Diuretics	Mechanism of Action	Common Medications
Loop diuretics	prevent reabsorption of sodium, potassium, and chloride in the ascending loop of Henle and the distal renal tubule result in excretion of water, sodium, chloride, and large amounts of potassium	furosemide (Lasix) bumetanide (Bumex) torsemide (Demadex)
Thiazide diuretics	prevent reabsorption of sodium and chloride primarily in the distal convoluted renal tubule result in increased excretion of water, sodium, chloride, and moderate amounts of potassium	chlorothiazide hydrochlorothiazide
Potassium-sparing diuretics	block aldosterone-specific mineralocorticoid receptors in the distal convoluted renal tubule result in excretion of water and sodium, but potassium is retained	spironolactone triamterene
Osmotic diuretics	elevate glomerular filtrate osmolarity active in the loop of Henle and can be used to reduce fluid volume and ICP result in increased excretion of water and small amounts of sodium	mannitol

QUICK REVIEW QUESTION

13. A patient on a continuous furosemide (Lasix) drip starts to have bilateral lower extremity muscle cramps and non-sustained V-tach. What could potentially be causing these issues?

Inotropic Agents
CARDIAC GLYCOSIDES

Mechanism of Action

- increase intracellular calcium by inhibiting Na-K ATPase

- cause increased myocardial contraction, decreased heart rate, and slowed cardiac conduction

- increase cardiac output and renal perfusion (inotrope)

Therapeutic Uses

- atrial dysrhythmias (e.g., A-fib, third line)

- PSVT conversion

- heart failure

Possible Adverse Reactions

- heart block

- bradycardia

HELPFUL HINT

Digoxin toxicity presents with dysrhythmias, confusion, weakness, and/or GI symptoms (e.g., nausea, vomiting). It is treated with digoxin immune Fab (Digibind).

- dizziness

- headache

- nausea and vomiting

Contraindications

- V-fib

- acute MI

- hypertrophic cardiomyopathy

Common Drugs

- digoxin (Lanoxin)

QUICK REVIEW QUESTION

14. The nurse is caring for a patient admitted with an acute kidney injury, Cr 3.4 mg/dL. The patient has been taking digoxin as part of his treatment regimen for A-fib. The nurse understands digoxin is excreted by the kidneys. What is the nurse's best practice before administering a dose of digoxin?

PHOSPHODIESTERASE INHIBITORS

Mechanism of Action

- increase calcium concentrations in cardiac muscle cells by inhibiting cAMP phosphodiesterase

- cause increased myocardial contraction, resulting in decreased cardiac preload and afterload

Therapeutic Uses

- heart failure

Possible Adverse Reactions

- hypotension

- ventricular dysrhythmias

- headache

- worsening heart failure over long term

Contraindications

- aortic or pulmonic valve disease (severe)

- ventricular dysrhythmias

- acute MI

Common Drugs

- milrinone (Primacor)

QUICK REVIEW QUESTION

15. What is the difference in the mechanism of action between milrinone (Primacor) and dobutamine (Dobutrex)?

Other Vasodilators

NITRATES

Mechanism of Action

- vasodilators; relax vascular smooth muscle
- result in decreased venous return, which leads to decreased cardiac output
- cause decreased afterload and reduces work effort of LV

Therapeutic Uses

- treatment and prophylaxis of angina (outpatient setting)
- MI (MONA [morphine, oxygen, nitroglycerin, aspirin] treatment in ED)
- hypertension (critical care setting)

Possible Adverse Reactions

- hypotension
- tachycardia
- headache
- nausea

Contraindications

- phosphodiesterase inhibitors taken within 48 hours
- right ventricular infarction
- hypotension
- intracranial hemorrhage
- pregnancy

Common Drugs (often contain the roots *nitro* or *nitra*)

- nitroglycerin
- isosorbide dinitrate
- isosorbide mononitrate

- nitroprusside

- minoxidil

QUICK REVIEW QUESTION

16. A patient reports a headache after starting a nitro drip for chest pain. The patient asks the nurse why the medication helped his chest pain but caused a headache. How should the nurse respond?

CALCIUM CHANNEL BLOCKERS

Mechanism of Action

- Dihydropyridines hinder the movement of calcium into vascular smooth muscle and cardiac muscle, resulting in lower concentrations of intracellular calcium

- Non-dihydropyridines cause coronary vasodilation from smooth muscle relaxation, slowed cardiac conduction, decreased heart rate, decreased myocardial contraction, and prolonged AV node refractory period (class IV antidysrhythmic)

Therapeutic Uses

- hypertension

- Prinzmetal angina

- artery vasospasm

- non-dihydropyridines: cardiac dysrhythmias

Possible Adverse Reactions

- hypotension

- bradycardia

- dizziness

- light-headedness

Contraindications

- second- or third-degree heart block

- hypotension (SBP < 90 mm Hg)

- use with caution in patients with ventricular dysfunction

Common Drugs

- amlodipine (dihydropyridine)

- nicardipine (dihydropyridine)

- diltiazem (non-dihydropyridine)

- verapamil (non-dihydropyridine)

QUICK REVIEW QUESTION

17. What hemodynamic response should the nurse expect to observe in a patient after administration of diltiazem IV push?

ANTIHYPERTENSIVE VASODILATORS

Mechanism of Action

- act primarily on the arterioles in the peripheral vessels to cause vasodilation and relax smooth muscle

Therapeutic Uses

- hypertension (third line outpatient, can be first line IV in emergency situations)

- increase or sustain renal perfusion

Possible Adverse Reactions

- reflex tachycardia

- angina

- headache

- fatigue

Contraindications

- hypotension

- tachycardia

- acute MI

- acute hypertrophic cardiomyopathy

- mitral valvular rheumatic heart disease

- pregnancy

Common Drugs

- hydralazine

QUICK REVIEW QUESTION

18. What is the pathophysiology that produces the adverse reaction of reflex tachycardia in patients who have been given antihypertensive vasodilators?

Thrombolytics (Fibrinolytic Agents)

Mechanism of Action

- promote destruction of fibrin clots (thrombus) by activating the conversion of plasminogen to plasmin
- can be administered systemically via IV but are most effective if administered directly into the area of the clot

Therapeutic Uses

- MI when coronary angiography is unavailable (most effective if given within 6 hours of MI)
- acute CVA (most effective if given within 3 hours of CVA; time frame may extend up to 4.5 hours)
- massive pulmonary embolism
- restore blood flow in central venous catheters (1 – 2 mg doses; dwell time of 30 min – 2 hours)

Possible Adverse Reactions

- bleeding
- intracranial hemorrhage
- cardiac arrhythmias

Contraindications

- hypertension (SBP > 180)
- active bleeding
- recent stroke history
- recent intracranial surgery
- hepatic dysfunction in patients > 65

Common Drugs (suffix –*plase*)

- tPA or alteplase
- tenecteplase (TNKase)

QUICK REVIEW QUESTION

19. A patient is receiving tPA for the treatment of acute pulmonary embolism and the nurse is observing the patient. What types of adverse effects related to tPA could present during this time?

ANSWER KEY

1. The nurses will open the medication administration record and verify the documented time of the last administration.

2. The nurse should consider the potential to aggravate the current elevated K+ and Cr levels. The nurse should hold the dose and contact the physician to consider the safest option for the patient.

3. Phenylephrine is the first-line medication used to increase BP in patients with aortic stenosis.

4. The nurse should obtain the patient's blood pressure before administering the medication. If the patient is hypotensive, terazosin should be avoided.

5. Beta blockers can potentially cause bradycardia, so the combined effects of the two medications may cause harm if not monitored.

6. The mechanism of action and resulting effects of lowered blood pressure and heart rate can cause hemodynamic instability in patients with recent MI.

7. Contraindications to beta blockers include junctional rhythm, Mobitz II, and bilateral BBB. Administering beta blockers to these patients will increase the likelihood of dangerously low heart rates and possible hemodynamic compromise.

8. The nurse should anticipate an order for fluids (colloids or crystalloids). The vasopressor will constrict the blood vessels and increase SVR but will not add volume to the body. Additional fluids will need to be introduced into circulation.

9. The patient was likely experiencing side effects when taking an ACE inhibitor (e.g., a persistent dry cough), so his doctor prescribed an ARB.

10. Due to the duration of action of enoxaparin, the nurse should administer the first dose of apixaban approximately 12 hours following the enoxaparin injection.

11. The patient's ECG shows V-tach. The nurse can anticipate that the physician will order amiodarone. The IV administration and preceding bolus dosing can help chemically convert the patient or maintain normal sinus rhythm if the patient is cardioverted.

12. The nurse should inform the patient of the significant bleeding risk related to the antiplatelet action of clopidogrel. To minimize this risk, clopidogrel should be held at least 3 – 5 days before the procedure. Since the patient's coronary artery stents were placed more than 12 months ago, holding the medication will not compromise their patency.

13. Furosemide is a loop diuretic and removes potassium as well as magnesium from the body. It is possible that these serum levels could be low in the patient and causing the muscle cramps and non-sustained VT. Frequent lab monitoring is necessary to keep these electrolytes replaced and within normal serum levels.

14. The nurse should search the patient's lab work for a digoxin level. An acute kidney injury evidenced by elevated creatinine could indicate a decrease in glomerular filtration rate and subsequent decrease in digoxin excretion. The nurse needs to know if the patient has a toxic digoxin level before administering more digoxin.

15. Dobutamine creates vasodilation, which reduces afterload by lowering systemic vascular resistance. Milrinone creates more forward cardiac flow by stimulating cardiac receptors.

16. Nitroglycerin works as a vasodilator to open coronary arteries and increase blood flow. The increased blood flow to the heart decreases chest pain, but the vasodilation is systemic, causing venous pooling, and can increase the amount of blood in the brain, resulting in headache.

17. The nurse should anticipate a slower heart rate and lower blood pressure as a result of the negative dromotropic, chronotropic, and inotropic effects.

18. As antihypertensive vasodilators cause vasodilation, the systemic blood pressure is reduced. Subsequently, the decreased force in the arterioles activates baroreceptors, which elevate the heart rate as a compensatory mechanism.

19. The nurse should assess the patient for any signs consistent with internal bleeding. These signs include neurological changes that may indicate intracranial hemorrhage, hematuria, bright red blood per rectum, epistaxis, or acute drop in hemoglobin.

FOUR: CARDIOVASCULAR TECHNOLOGIES and PROCEDURES

Cardiac Monitoring

- An **event recorder** is a battery-operated portable device used to monitor a patient's heart rhythm.

  ○ **Loop recorders** are implanted devices that continuously monitor and record heart rhythms.

  ○ **Symptom event monitors** are handheld or worn on the patient's wrist. If the patient detects an abnormal rhythm, the patient places the device on the chest and presses a button so the device will start recording.

- A **Holter monitor** is a portable cardiac monitor that a patient wears for a short time, usually 24 – 48 hours. The patient does not have to press a button to activate recording.

- An **insertable cardiac monitor (ICM)** is a cardiac monitor inserted under the skin by a cardiologist or an electrophysiologist. They can last up to 5 years.

- **Mobile cardiac telemetry (MCT)** is the continuous monitoring of heart rhythms by means of a small sensor and monitor that a patient wears on the chest.

QUICK REVIEW QUESTION

1. For the third time in a month, a patient has been admitted to the hospital with complaints of chest pain, palpitations, and dizziness. No ECG abnormalities were found during the patient's hospital stay. What intervention does the nurse expect?

Care for Extremities

- **Sequential compression devices (SCD)** are wrapped around the calf areas of both legs and alternately inflate and deflate.

  ○ The compression device improves blood flow by preventing "pooling" of the blood in the legs and helps prevent DVT in patients with limited mobility.

- The nurse should ensure that the correct size is used. SCDs that are too tight may cause pressure necrosis, and those that are too large will be ineffective.
- **Thromboembolic deterrent (TED) stockings** are compression stockings worn by post-op or non-ambulatory patients to prevent DVT.
  - The nurse should assess for skin breakdown and pedal pulses when the TED stockings are in place.
  - The nurse should remove the TEDs at night, or for any part of the day that the patient is comfortable with, to give the patient relief from the pressure against the skin.
  - If removed at night, TEDs should be applied before the patient gets out of bed in the morning.
- An **Unna boot** is a compression dressing made from gauze infused with zinc, glycerin, or calamine.
  - Unna boots are used in the treatment of venous leg ulcers and lymphedema.
  - The dressing is contraindicated in patients with arterial insufficiency.

QUICK REVIEW QUESTION

2. Before placing an SCD or a TED stocking on a patient, what priority action should the nurse complete?

Cardiac Catheter Procedures
Catheter Procedure Pre-Op and Post-Op

- In **cardiac catheter procedures**, a catheter is inserted into a large blood vessel to diagnose and treat damage in the arteries, heart muscles, and valves.
- The CV nurse assists with procedures, administers medication, monitors the patient's vital signs, and documents the patient's condition before, during, and after the procedure.
- Pre-procedure nursing considerations:
  - Make sure that the patient has been NPO beginning at midnight before the procedure.
  - Ask the patient about current medications, including antiplatelets, anticoagulants, and insulin.
    - Warfarin should be stopped and replaced with LMWH 48 hours before the procedure.
    - Aspirin may be given before the procedure.
  - Ensure that baseline labs are drawn, including CBC, CMP, PT/INR, PTT, and type and cross (blood typing and cross-matching).
- Post-procedure complications:
  - retroperitoneal bleeding

HELPFUL HINT

Signs of retroperitoneal bleeding include hypotension; bradycardia; ecchymosis on the flank (Grey Turner's sign); and abdominal, back, or flank pain.

- cardiac ischemic pain
- excessive bleeding
- dysrhythmia
- hematoma
- neurovascular insufficiency (signs include pale limbs, an extremity that feels cool to the touch, and weak or absent pulses)

- Patient education:
  - The affected leg (for catherization through femoral artery) should be kept straight immediately after the procedure.
  - It is normal for the insertion site to show bruising or discoloration, and a small lump may be present.
  - The patient should refrain from strenuous physical activity and heavy lifting for approximately 3 – 4 days.
  - Patients should drink plenty of fluids to flush out the contrast dye.

Compression Devices

- A **femoral compression device** (FemoStop) is used to prevent further bleeding after the removal of femoral sheaths, venous sheaths, and intra-aortic balloon pumps (IABPs).
  - A plastic dome is used to apply pressure at the insertion site.
  - The nurse inflates the dome to prevent bleeding, and deflates the device once hemostasis has been achieved.

- **Radial compression devices** are used to achieve hemostasis and prevent arterial damage after a transradial procedure.
  - The device wraps around the patient's wrist to apply pressure at the insertion site.
  - While the device is in place, the nurse should place a pulse oximeter probe on the affected hand.

- Nursing considerations:
  - The nurse should monitor vital signs and peripheral pulses while the device is in place.
  - Numbness, tingling, cyanosis, or diminished pulse in the extremity may indicate that the pressure on the device should be reduced.

Angioplasty

- **Percutaneous transluminal angioplasty (PTA)** is used to widen arteries in patients with peripheral artery disease or stenosis in the carotid, renal, or coronary arteries.

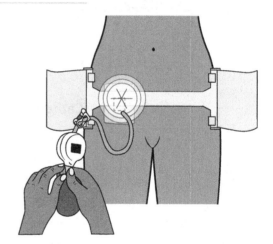

Figure 4.1. FemoStop Femoral Compression Device

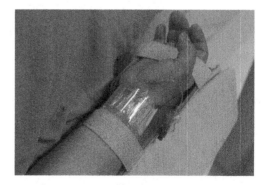

Figure 4.2. Radial Compression Device

- **Percutaneous coronary intervention (PCI)** (also called coronary angioplasty) is performed to revascularize the coronary arteries of the heart.
    - PCI is commonly performed for:
        - unstable angina or angina that does not respond to medication
        - acute coronary syndrome
        - patients who are not candidates for a coronary artery bypass graft (CABG)
    - During an angioplasty, a balloon is placed in the stenotic artery via a catheter and inflated. The inflated balloon applies pressure to the plaque occluding the artery and increases blood flow. A stent may also be placed to keep the artery open.

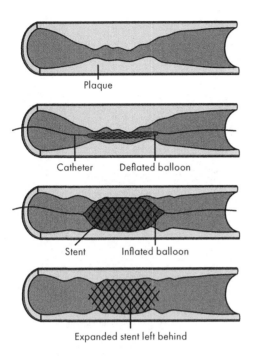

Plaque

Catheter   Deflated balloon

Stent   Inflated balloon

Expanded stent left behind

Figure 4.3. Angioplasty with Stent

Atherectomy

- During an **atherectomy**, plaque is removed from atherosclerotic arteries.

- The artery is accessed with a specialized catheter that cuts the plaque into small pieces that can be removed. Some types of atherectomies will cut the plaque into pieces small enough to be left in the vasculature.

Catheter Ablation

- **Catheter ablation** is performed to correct dysrhythmias, including atrial flutter, A-fib, SVT, and V-tach.

- An ablation is performed if the patient is not tolerating antidysrhythmic medications or is at high risk for cardiac arrest or V-fib.

- In the heart's electrical conduction systems, the tissue that is causing the dysrhythmia is ablated using heat (radiofrequency ablation) or cold (cryoablation).

- The procedure is performed percutaneously via bilateral groin access.

Intra-Aortic Balloon Pump (IABP)

- **Intra-aortic balloon pump (IABP) therapy** is used in patients with cardiogenic shock to increase coronary artery perfusion and raise blood pressure.

- The intra-aortic balloon is inserted into the ascending aortic arch via the femoral artery.
    - The balloon inflates during diastole and forces blood flow back into the coronary arteries.
    - During systole, the balloon deflates, which decreases afterload and increases CO.

- Contraindications for IABP include coagulopathies, aortic regurgitation, and dissecting/ruptured aortic aneurysm.

HELPFUL HINT
IABPs should only be paused briefly, as thrombus formation can occur quickly.

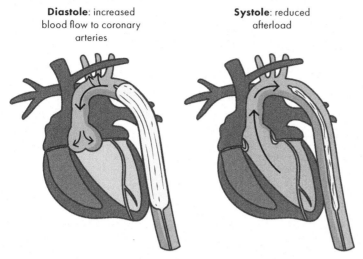

Diastole: increased blood flow to coronary arteries

Systole: reduced afterload

Figure 4.4. Intra-Aortic Balloon Pump (IABP) Therapy

QUICK REVIEW QUESTION

3. The nurse is caring for a patient who just returned from the cardiac catheterization lab. While assessing the patient on initial return, the nurse notes swelling at the groin site. At the 15-minute reassessment, the nurse notes increased swelling from the initial assessment and notifies the charge nurse and performing physician. What device could the nurse anticipate using as an intervention for this patient?

HELPFUL HINT
Around 30 percent of patients will require a blood transfusion after CABG.

Surgical Interventions
Coronary Artery Bypass Graft (CABG)

- A **coronary artery bypass graft (CABG)** revascularizes ischemic heart tissue by diverting blood through the left internal thoracic artery or by grafting a section of the great saphenous vein to the aorta.

- CABG is performed in patients with cardiac ischemia who cannot be treated with PCI.

- Post-procedure complications:
  ○ excessive bleeding or anemia
  ○ dysrhythmias (particularly A-fib): common postoperatively and may require medication or cardioversion; patient may be given prophylactic amiodarone
  ○ cardiac conditions, particularly perioperative MI and vasodilatory shock

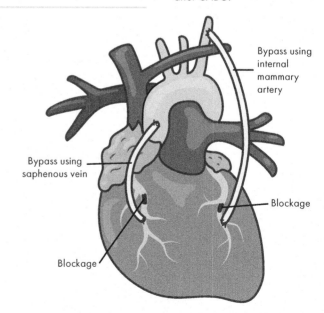

Bypass using internal mammary artery

Bypass using saphenous vein

Blockage

Blockage

Figure 4.5. Coronary Artery Bypass Graft (CABG)

- ○ post-pericardiotomy syndrome, which may present with fever, pericarditis, pericardial effusion, or tamponade

  - ○ neurological conditions, including stroke, post-cardiotomy delirium, and peripheral neuropathy

- Patient education:

  - ○ The patient should be enrolled in cardiac rehabilitation.

  - ○ The patient will require instruction on the prescribed mediation regimen, which will likely include a statin, a beta blocker, and ACE inhibitor.

  - ○ The patient should be instructed to avoid heavy lifting or other strenuous activity for approximately 8 weeks after surgery.

Arterial Bypass Graft

- During an **arterial bypass graft**, surgeons use harvested veins or synthetic grafts to reroute blood flow around obstructed arteries.

- The procedure is performed in patients with peripheral artery disease or aortoiliac disease.

- Bypass sites are named for the arteries being joined by the graft. Common sites for bypass include:

  - ○ aortobifemoral bypass (aortic to each femoral artery)

  - ○ axillobifemoral bypass (axillary to each femoral artery)

  - ○ fem-pop (femoral to popliteal artery)

  - ○ fem-fem (femoral to femoral)

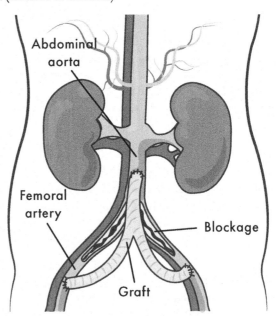

Figure 4.6. Aortobifemoral Bypass

- When taking baseline vitals, pay special attention to peripheral pulses, and regularly assess for tissue perfusion in extremities and adequate distal pulses.

- Post-procedure complications:
    - swelling of the extremities (patients may require vascular boot)
    - compartment syndrome (signs include intense pain and urinalysis consistent with rhabdomyolysis)
    - mesenteric ischemia

Aneurysm Repair

- Aortic and thoracic aneurysms can be surgically repaired if the risk of dissection is considered sufficiently high. Surgical repairs are the only treatment for a dissection that has already occurred.

- The majority of aneurysm repairs require surgery to open the aneurysm and place a graft.

- In some cases, the surgeon may perform an **endovascular aneurysm repair (EVAR)**, a less invasive procedure in which a catheter is used to place an endovascular stent graft across the aneurysm.

- Post-procedure complications:
    - cardiac complications (e.g., MI, dysrhythmias)
    - pulmonary complications (e.g., pulmonary embolism)
    - small-bowel obstruction
    - lower-limb ischemia
- Patient education:
    - Instruct patients on ways to prevent the aneurysm from rupturing, including smoking cessation, lowered BP, and lowered cholesterol.
    - Patients require CTs at 3- or 6-month intervals to monitor growth of aneurysms.

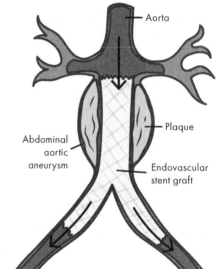

Figure 4.7. Endovascular Aneurysm Repair (EVAR)

Carotid Endarterectomy

- A **carotid endarterectomy** is a surgical procedure to remove plaque from carotid arteries in patients with carotid stenosis.

- The vascular surgeon surgically opens the affected carotid artery and removes the plaque from the vessel. The artery is then closed via suturing.

- Monitor for post-procedure complications.
    - Ensure that patient has frequent neurological assessments (at least every hour).
    - Assess cranial nerves, including the hypoglossal, facial, and vagal nerves, for impairment.
    - Monitor vital signs, especially blood pressure (important because of baroreceptors close to the carotid artery).

- Monitor patient for headache unrelieved by analgesics, because the headache may indicate intracranial bleeding.
- Monitor patient for dysrhythmias.

Heart Valve Repair and Replacement

- Damaged valves can be repaired or replaced.
- Replacement valves may be mechanical or bioprosthetic (bovine, porcine, or human).
  - Mechanical heart valves (MHV) are implanted surgically.
  - Bioprosthetic heart valves (BHV) can be implanted surgically or via transcatheter procedure.
- Surgical valve repair and replacement requires cardiopulmonary bypass.
- Post-procedure complications:
  - retroperitoneal bleeding
  - dysrhythmias
  - thromboembolism
  - bacterial endocarditis
- Patient education:
  - Patients with MHVs will require lifelong anticoagulation medication to prevent prosthetic valvular thrombosis.
  - All patients with heart valve repair or replacement require prophylactic antibiotics before dental and surgical procedures to prevent infective endocarditis.

Heart (Cardiac) Transplantation

- In an **orthotropic heart transplant**, the recipient's heart is removed and replaced with the donor heart.
- In a **heterotopic heart transplant**, the donor heart is placed alongside the recipient's heart, which remains in place.
- Heart transplantation is the last resort for patients with end-stage heart failure. Candidates for heart transplantation usually have a life expectance of < 1 year without the surgery.
- Very rarely, a heart transplant may be done on a patient with refractory V-tach in the absence of heart failure.
- Nursing care for heart transplant patients is specialized, complex, and intense. The patient will be closely monitored and treated for organ rejection, infection, graft dysfunction, and other serious complications.
- Signs and symptoms of organ rejection include:
  - fever, even low-grade

- weakness
- palpitations
- shortness of breath
- weight gain
- elevated WBC count

Surgical Thrombectomy

- Thrombus or emboli that result in acute arterial occlusion may be removed during a **surgical thrombectomy** to restore blood perfusion to tissues.

- During the procedure, the surgeon opens the blood vessel to remove the thrombus or embolus and then closes the vessel. A stent may also be placed.

- While open surgery is the most common form of thrombectomy, some patients may be candidates for the less invasive **mechanical thrombectomy**. This involves inserting a catheter into the groin and up to the location of the clot, and inserting a stent retriever to physically remove the clot.

- Post-procedure complications:
  - thromboembolism
  - compartment syndrome

QUICK REVIEW QUESTION

4. A patient presents to the ED with chest pain and the ECG shown below. What priority intervention should the nurse expect?

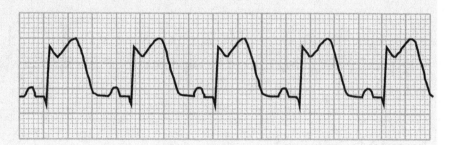

Devices
Pacemaker

- A **pacemaker** is a device that uses electrical stimulation to regulate the heart's electrical conduction system and maintain a normal heart rhythm.

- Conditions that commonly require a pacemaker include:
  - sinus node dysfunction
  - AV block, third- or second-degree
  - chronic or transient bifascicular block
  - post MI

HELPFUL HINT

Implantable cardiac devices, including pacemakers and ICDs, may lead to localized or systemic infections, including endocarditis.

○ neurocardiogenic syncope and hypersensitive carotid sinus syndrome

○ post cardiac surgery

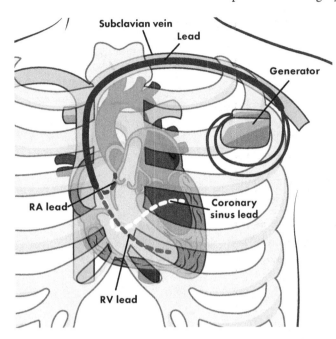

Figure 4.8. Lead Placement in Permanent Pacemaker

- Pacing can be permanent or temporary:

  ○ **Permanent pacemakers** are implanted subcutaneously, and the leads are then run through the subclavian vein into the heart. The device is battery operated and allows the physician to continuously monitor the patient's rhythm.

  ○ **Temporary pacemakers** can include transvenous leads or transcutaneous adhesive pads attached to the chest. Temporary pacemakers are controlled by an external pulse generator.

- Pacing can be single chamber (atrium or ventricle) or dual chamber.

- The pacemaker will have a set rate (number of times it fires per minute). **Rate-modulated** pacemakers use a physiological sensor to match the patient's heart rate to their activity level.

- The electrical activity of the pacemaker appears on the ECG as a **pacing spike**, a sharp vertical line that may appear below or above the isoelectric line.

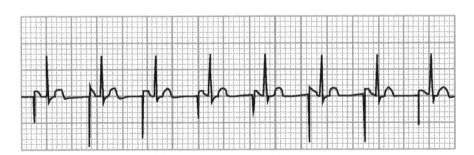

Figure 4.9. Pacing Spikes

- Pacemakers are classified with a 5-letter code. Because the last 2 letters are omitted if they are "O," many pacemakers are referred to using a 3-letter code.

Table 4.1. NASPE/BPEG Codes for Pacemakers				
I	**II**	**III**	**IV**	**V**
Chamber(s) paced	**Chamber(s) sensed**	**Response to sensing**	**Rate modulation**	**Multisite pacing**
O = None	O = None	O = None	O = None	O = None
A = Atrium	A = Atrium	T = Triggered	R = Rate modulation	A = Atrium
V = Ventricle	V = Ventricle	I = Inhibited		V = Ventricle
D = Dual (A+V)	D = Dual (A+V)	D = Dual (T+I)		D = Dual (A+V)

Table 4.2. Common Pacemaker Errors

Error	Description	Corrective Measures
Failure to pace (output failure)	Absence of needed pacing stimulus See Figure 4.10	Ensure device is turned on; check battery; check leads; ask patient about possible magnetic interference with pacemaker
Failure to capture	Device provides pacing stimulus when needed, but depolarization is not triggered (seen on ECG as pacing spike with no corresponding QRS complex) See Figure 4.11	Increase mA voltage
Oversensing	Device does not provide pacing stimulus when needed, because it detects noncardiac electrical activity (physiologic or nonphysiologic)	Reset sensitivity of device
Undersensing	Device provides pacing stimulus when not needed, because it cannot sense native cardiac activity	Reset sensitivity of device

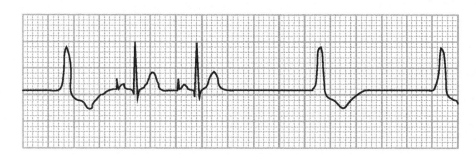

Figure 4.10. Failure to Pace (Output Failure)

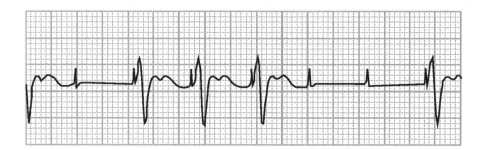

Figure 4.11. Failure to Capture

- Pacemaker malfunction procedures:
    - Notify physician.
    - Assess the pacemaker for mechanical issues. (See Table 4.2.)
    - Be prepared to provide temporary TCP.

HELPFUL HINT

Do not use the patient's carotid pulse to confirm mechanical capture, as the electrical impulses can be mistaken for the pulse.

- Patient education:
  - Signs of pacemaker malfunction include chest pain, palpitations, dizziness, syncope, and weakness.
  - Patients should avoid being near strong magnets, as they can reset the device settings.
  - Patients should be educated on device battery life (typically 5 – 10 years) and device interrogation schedule.
  - Patients may need long-term anticoagulant therapy to prevent stroke.

Implantable Cardioverter Defibrillator (ICD)

- An **implantable cardioverter defibrillator (ICD)** continuously monitors heart rhythms and emits an electric shock that terminates emergent dysrhythmias such as V-tach and V-fib, preventing cardiac arrest.

- A **transvenous ICD (TV-ICD)** is placed like a pacemaker. The device is implanted subcutaneously, and the leads run through the left subclavian vein and superior vena cava into the right atrium and ventricle.

- A **subcutaneous ICD (S-ICD)** is also implanted subcutaneously but does not include leads placed in the vasculature. Instead, the lead is placed subcutaneously along the rib cage.

- Nursing considerations and patient education for ICD patients are similar to those for patients receiving a permanent pacemaker.

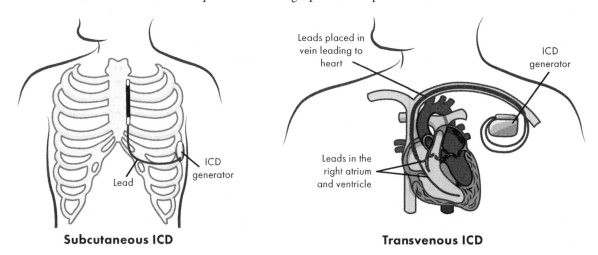

Figure 4.12. Implantable Cardioverter Defibrillator (ICD)

Left Ventricular Assist Device (LVAD)

- **Left ventricular assist devices (LVADs)** provide support for weakened left ventricles in patients with end-stage heart failure.

- This device is sometimes used as "bridge" treatment while a patient waits for heart transplantation.

- A mechanical pump is placed in the left ventricle. The pump moves blood from the left ventricle to the ascending aortic branch, from which it can be further circulated to the rest of the body.

- The LVAD is battery operated, and patients can remain on the device for months to years.

- Nursing considerations:
  - Monitor MAP closely, with the goal ranging from 60 – 90 mm Hg.
  - Monitor the patient's electrolytes to prevent dysrhythmias.
  - Monitor the patient for signs of pump thrombosis, which include shortness of breath, tachycardia, and hypotension.
  - Ensure that spare batteries are accessible.

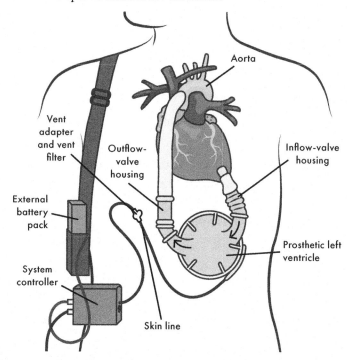

Figure 4.13. Left Ventricular Assist Device (LVAD)

- Patient education:
  - Patient should be taught how to change batteries and to perform daily self-tests to ensure that the device is functioning properly.
  - Patient should learn about the medications that may be prescribed, such as anticoagulants to prevent thrombosis and antihypertensives to control blood pressure.

QUICK REVIEW QUESTION

5. A patient presents to the clinic with complaints of a temperature of 101.3°F (38.5°C), night sweats, pain in the knees, cough, and bloody sputum. The patient recently had a permanent pacemaker implanted. What condition should the nurse suspect?

Cardioversion and Defibrillation

Cardioversion

- During **cardioversion**, electrical current or medications are used to reset the heart to a normal sinus rhythm.

- Cardioversion is indicated for:
  - narrow or wide QRS complex tachycardias (per ACLS guidelines)
  - SVT
  - V-tach with a pulse
  - A-fib
  - atrial flutter

- **Synchronized electrical cardioversion** uses electrical current supplied by external electrode pads placed on the anterior chest. Current is supplied during the R wave of the QRS complex.

- Electrical cardioversion can be monophasic (unidirectional current) or biphasic (bidirectional current).
  - Monophasic devices deliver current at a more consistent magnitude and are more effective at lower energies.

- The energy supplied during electrical cardioversion depends on the type of device and the underlying rhythm. General guidelines for biphasic devices are as follows:
  - narrow QRS, regular: 50 – 100 J
  - narrow QRS, irregular: 120 – 200 J
  - wide QRS, regular: 100 J
  - A-fib: 75 J

- **Pharmacologic cardioversion** uses antidysrhythmic medications, such as adenosine.
  - Adenosine should be administered via rapid IV push at 6 mg for the first dose, followed by 12 mg if needed for the second dose.

Defibrillation

- During **defibrillation**, also known as **unsynchronized cardioversion**, electrical current is used to reset the heart to a normal sinus rhythm.

- The electrical current is supplied randomly during the cardiac cycle, disrupting the heart's electrical rhythm and allowing the SA node's normal sinus rhythm to restart.

- Defibrillation is an emergent treatment for patients with:
  - pulseless V-tach
  - V-fib

HELPFUL HINT

Paddles should be placed away from implanted pacemakers and ICDs (most guidelines recommend about 1 inch distance).

- Common defibrillation doses start with 200 J, followed by 300 J for the second shock, with a maximum of 360 J.

QUICK REVIEW QUESTION

6. A patient presents to the ED with chest pain, dyspnea, and diaphoresis. The nurse finds a narrow complex tachycardia with a heart rate of 210 bpm, blood pressure of 70/42 mm Hg, and a respiratory rate of 18. The nurse should anticipate which priority intervention?

ANSWER KEY

1. The patient may need to have long-term cardiac monitoring since the patient's ECG has not shown any abnormalities during the hospital stay. The nurse should anticipate that the patient will receive an ICM such as a loop recorder to continuously monitor the heart rhythm so that the patient can be discharged home.

2. The nurse should make sure that there is no skin breakdown on the legs where the SCD or TED stocking is placed. Further restriction of an area of skin breakdown can worsen ulceration and necrosis. The nurse should also use the correct-sized device or stocking for the patient's leg to ensure efficacy.

3. The nurse should anticipate using a FemoStop on this patient. Because the patient is demonstrating signs of a developing hematoma at the insertion site, a FemoStop device applied can stop the hematoma from worsening and can help produce hemostasis for the patient.

4. The patient is experiencing a STEMI and needs immediate transport to the catheterization lab for PCI for reperfusion.

5. The patient is at increased risk for infective endocarditis because of the recent pacemaker implantation and is showing signs and symptoms of this infection (low-grade fever, arthralgias, night sweats, cough, and hemoptysis).

6. The patient is experiencing an unstable SVT (with BP of 70/42 mm Hg) and requires immediate synchronized cardioversion.

FIVE: CARDIAC and VASCULAR DISEASE

Risk Factors for Cardiovascular Disease (CVD)

ATHEROSCLEROSIS

Pathophysiology

Atherosclerosis, also called atherosclerotic cardiovascular disease (ASCVD), is a progressive condition in which **plaque** builds up in the tunica intima of arteries. Plaque deposits begin in childhood and may grow larger throughout adulthood. The initial stage of atherosclerosis includes **fatty streaks** composed of macrophages that have absorbed lipids. Over decades, more lipids are deposited and older cells become calcified, creating an **atheroma**. This atheroma, or plaque, may eventually become fibrous, creating **fibroatheroma** (also called fibrous plaque).

The presence of advanced atherosclerosis places patients at a high risk for several cardiovascular conditions.

- Arteries may become **stenotic**, or narrowed, limiting blood flow to specific areas of the body (e.g., carotid stenosis).

- When a plaque **ruptures**, the plaque and the clot that forms around it (superimposed thrombus) can quickly lead to complete occlusion of the artery (e.g., myocardial infarction [MI]).

- The clots or loosened plaque released by a rupture may also move through the bloodstream and occlude smaller vessels (e.g., ischemic stroke).

- Atherosclerosis is also a cause of **aneurysms** (widened arteries), which weaken arterial walls, increasing the risk of arterial dissection or rupture (e.g., abdominal aortic aneurysm).

Atherosclerosis can occur in any artery and is categorized according to the location of the plaque buildup.

- **coronary artery disease (CAD):** narrowing of the coronary arteries
- **peripheral artery disease (PAD):** narrowing of the peripheral arteries
- **renal artery stenosis:** narrowing of the renal arteries

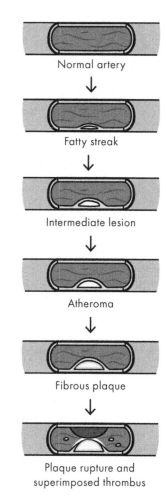

Normal artery

↓

Fatty streak

↓

Intermediate lesion

↓

Atheroma

↓

Fibrous plaque

↓

Plaque rupture and superimposed thrombus

Figure 5.1. Progression of Atherosclerosis

- **cerebrovascular disease:** dysfunction in the cerebrovascular system; most commonly caused by atherosclerosis

Demographics

- some degree of atherosclerosis common in people > 65
- more common in males
- 75% of all acute MIs caused by plaque rupture

Risk Factors

- dyslipidemia
- hypertension
- smoking
- diabetes
- obesity
- family history
- poor diet
- sedentary lifestyle

QUICK REVIEW QUESTION

1. A patient recovering from an atherectomy asks the nurse what to do to prevent further buildup of plaque in the arteries. What should the nurse tell the patient?

DIABETES

Pathophysiology

Diabetes mellitus is a metabolic disorder affecting insulin production and insulin resistance. It requires long-term management with insulin or oral hypoglycemic drugs. Diabetes mellitus is classified as type 1 or type 2.

- **Type 1 diabetes** is an acute-onset autoimmune disease predominant in children, teens, and adults < 30. Beta cells in the pancreas are destroyed and are unable to produce sufficient amounts of insulin, causing blood sugar to rise.

- **Type 2 diabetes** is a gradual-onset disease predominant in adults > 40, but it can develop in individuals of all ages. Type 2 diabetes is not an autoimmune disease. Instead, the person develops insulin resistance, which prevents the cellular uptake of glucose and causes blood sugar to rise.

Diabetes is highly correlated with CVD.

- At least 68% of people over age 65 with diabetes die from CVD.
- Approximately 16% of people over age 65 with diabetes die from stroke.
- People with diabetes develop CVDs at a younger age than do those without diabetes.

Demographics

- affects about 9% of US population

- can occur in any ethnicity but most common in African Americans

- type 1 most common in childhood

- type 2 most common in adults over age 40

Symptoms, Physical Findings, and Diagnostic Tests

- the 3 P's of diabetes:
  - polyuria
  - polydipsia
  - polyphagia

- elevated blood sugar: fasting blood glucose levels (> 126 mg/dL)

- elevated glucose tolerance test: (blood glucose level > 200 mg/dL)

- elevated HgbA1C (HbA1C)
  - normal (no diabetes): 4% – 5.6%
  - at risk for diabetes: 5.7% – 6.4%
  - diabetes: ≥ 6.5%

Management

- People with type 1 diabetes need insulin injections or continuous insulin infusions through a pump.

Table 5.1. Types of Insulin

Type of Insulin	Onset	Peak	Duration
rapid acting (insulin lispron injection [Humalog]; insulin aspart injection [Novolog])	15 – 30 minutes	1 – 2 hours	3 – 6 hours
short acting (regular insulin)	30 minutes – 1 hour	2 – 4 hours	3 – 6 hours
intermediate acting (neutral protamine Hagedorn insulin [NPH])	2 – 4 hours	8 – 10 hours	10 – 18 hours
long acting (insulin glargine [Lantus]; insulin detemir [Levemir])	1 – 2 hours	None	19 – 24 hours

- People with type 2 diabetes may be able to control the disease with lifestyle changes such as dietary improvements and exercise routines.

- People with type 2 diabetes may require medication management with oral hypoglycemic drugs, including:
  - sulfonylureas (e.g., glipizide, glimepiride)
  - meglitinides (repaglinide and nateglinide)

- ○ thiazolidinediones (pioglitazone and rosiglitazone)
- ○ metformin
- ○ alpha-glucosidase inhibitors (acarbose [Precose] and miglitol [Glyset])

QUICK REVIEW QUESTION

2. A patient with diabetes has a fasting blood glucose level of 98 mg/dL, but an HgbA1C of 7.0. The patient asks why the diabetes is not considered under control, since the fasting blood glucose is with the normal range. How should the nurse respond?

DYSLIPIDEMIA

Pathophysiology

Dyslipidemia is an abnormal level of lipids, including cholesterol and triglycerides, in the blood. The most common form of dyslipidemia is **hyperlipidemia**, or elevated lipids within the blood.

Dyslipidemia is usually asymptomatic but is correlated with heart disease. There are several types of cholesterol, each of which plays a different role in predicting CVD.

- High levels of **low-density lipoprotein (LDL)** are a risk factor for atherosclerosis. LDL is measured as LDL cholesterol (LDL-C).

- High levels of **high-density lipoprotein (HDL)** are inversely correlated with cardiovascular risk. HDL is measured as HDL cholesterol (HDL-C).

- High levels of **triglycerides** are correlated with cardiovascular risk related to atherosclerosis.

Demographics

- more common in Asian Indians, Filipinos, and Hispanics than in other ethnicities

- more common in males

- more common with advancing age

Risk Factors

- heredity

- chronic medical conditions (e.g., diabetes, renal failure)

- lifestyle factors (e.g., high-fat diet, smoking)

- medications (e.g., beta blockers, corticosteroids, antivirals)

Diagnostic Tests

- normal LDL-C: < 100 mg/dL

- normal HDL-C: > 60 mg/dL

- normal cholesterol: < 200 mg/dL

Management

- Dyslipidemia is initially managed through lifestyle changes, including weight loss, dietary changes, regular exercise, and smoking cessation.

- Medications are usually considered for patients with high cholesterol (> 200 mg/dL) or high LDL-C (> 190 mg/dL) levels that have not been lowered by lifestyle changes.

- Medications are also considered for patients with LDL-C > 70 mg/dL when the individual also has certain conditions (e.g., atherosclerosis, diabetes).

- **Statins** (e.g., atorvastatin [Lipitor], simvastatin [Zocor]) are a class of medications used to lower cholesterol.

- Nonstatin medications that may also be used to lower cholesterol include ezetimibe (Zetia) and fenofibrate (Fenoglide).

- Niacin may also be prescribed to increase HDL alongside other medications for hyperlipidemia.

QUICK REVIEW QUESTION

3. A patient diagnosed with hyperlipidemia tells the nurse that despite following a healthy diet, she has high cholesterol levels and wants to know why. How should the nurse respond?

HYPERTENSION

Pathophysiology

Hypertension is blood pressure > 120/80 mm Hg. Because blood pressure readings can vary, at least 2 readings on separate days must be taken to diagnose hypertension. **Primary (essential) hypertension** occurs with no known cause. Primary hypertension is highly correlated with lifestyle factors, including smoking, inactivity, obesity, high alcohol intake, and a high-sodium diet. **Secondary hypertension** has a known primary cause such as medication or an endocrine disorder. Persistent hypertension can cause organ damage and is a risk factor for other cardiac disease processes.

Table 5.2. Assessing for Hypertension

Category	Description
Elevated blood pressure	systolic BP 120 – 129 mm Hg diastolic BP < 80 mm Hg
Stage 1 hypertension	systolic BP 130 – 139 mm Hg diastolic BP 80 – 90 mm Hg
Stage 2 hypertension	systolic BP ≥ 140 mm Hg diastolic BP ≥ 90 mm Hg
Hypertensive urgency	systolic BP > 180/110 mm Hg without evidence of organ dysfunction
Hypertensive crisis	systolic BP > 180 mm Hg and/or a diastolic BP > 120 mm Hg, accompanied by evidence of impending or progressive organ dysfunction

Demographics

- affects > 30% of US population
- more common in African Americans than in other ethnicities
- more common in males < 50
- more common in females > 50

Management

- Initial management of chronic hypertension includes lifestyle changes:
  - decreased salt intake
  - DASH diet (high in fruits, vegetables, and lean meats; low in sugar and red meat)
  - increased exercise
  - weight loss
  - reduced caffeine intake
- First-line pharmacological treatments include ACE inhibitors, ARBs, calcium channel blockers, and thiazide diuretics.

HELPFUL HINT

Some OTC cold and cough medicines contain decongestants like pseudoephedrine, which may increase blood pressure.

QUICK REVIEW QUESTION

4. A patient has an initial blood pressure reading of 160/95 mm Hg and expresses concern about being diagnosed with hypertension and needing to be on lifelong hypertensive medications. What actions should the nurse take?

LIFESTYLE FACTORS

Certain lifestyle choices can increase a person's risk for CVD. These choices are referred to as **modifiable risk factors** because people can lower their risk by modifying their behavior. The main modifiable risk factors for CVD are discussed below.

Smoking

- Smoking is a strong risk factor for many cardiovascular conditions, including MI, stroke, atherosclerosis, and heart failure.
- Smoking increases mortality after cardiovascular catheterization and other surgical interventions.
- Smoking is estimated to account for one-third of all cardiovascular deaths in the United States.
- Smoking just 1 cigarette a day increases the risk of CVD by 50%.
- Cardiovascular risk increases with the duration and number of cigarettes smoked.
- All patients with acute or chronic cardiovascular conditions should be asked about tobacco use and offered support for smoking cessation.

Diet

- The relationship between diet and CVD is complex, and our understanding of it continues to improve.

- Across countries, increases in consumption of refined carbohydrates, trans fatty acids, and meat is linked to dramatic increases in CVD.

- Patients diagnosed with cardiovascular conditions should be educated on the components of a healthy diet that lowers CVD risk.

- A healthy diet:
  - includes foods with a low glycemic index
  - involves moderate alcohol consumption or abstinence
  - is high in fruits and vegetables
  - is high in lean protein
  - is high in fiber
  - is low in trans fatty acids
  - avoids red meat
  - avoids processed foods

- Patients with hypertension should be encouraged to follow a low-salt diet.

Exercise

- It is estimated that lack of physical activity increases the risk of CVD twofold.

- Potential cardiovascular benefits of exercise:
  - weight loss
  - increased overall cardiovascular fitness
  - increased HDL
  - reduced blood pressure

- Only moderate levels of exercise are needed to see cardiovascular benefits.

- Patients diagnosed with cardiovascular conditions should be educated on aspects of a healthy exercise program:
  - Adults should try to get 150 minutes of moderate aerobic activity or 75 minutes of intense aerobic activity every week.
  - Exercise programs should also include muscle-strengthening activities and activities to improve mobility.

- Patients with coronary heart disease should undergo **cardiac rehabilitation** under professional supervision to rebuild exercise tolerance.

Obesity

- linked to morbidity from many conditions (e.g., CVD, hypertension, stroke)
- categorized according to BMI (BMI = body weight [in kg] ÷ height [in meters]^2)

- underweight: < 18.5 kg/m²
- normal weight: 18.5 – 24.9 kg/m²
- overweight: 25.0 – 29.9 kg/m²
- obesity, class I: 30.0 – 34.9 kg/m²
- obesity class II: 35.0 – 39.9 kg/m²
- obesity class III: ≥ 40 kg/m² (also referred to as severe, extreme, or massive obesity)

- large waist circumference is considered a good indicator of cardiovascular risk
  - ≥ 102 cm (40 in) for males
  - ≥ 88 cm (35 in) for females

QUICK REVIEW QUESTION

5. A patient diagnosed with hypertension asks the nurse if a different diet could lower the risk of having a heart attack. How should the nurse respond?

Acute Coronary Syndrome (ACS)

Pathophysiology

Acute coronary syndrome (ACS) is an umbrella term for cardiac conditions in which thrombosis impairs blood flow in coronary arteries. **Angina pectoris** (commonly just called angina) is chest pain caused by narrowed coronary arteries and presents with negative troponin, an ST depression, and T wave changes.

- **Stable angina** usually resolves in about 5 minutes, is resolved with medications or with rest, and can be triggered by exertion, large meals, and extremely hot or cold temperatures.

- **Unstable angina** can occur at any time and typically lasts longer (> 20 minutes). The pain is usually rated as more severe than stable angina and is not easily relieved by the administration of nitrates.

- **Variant angina** (also called Prinzmetal angina or vasospastic angina) is episodes of angina and temporary ST elevation caused by spasms in the coronary artery. Chest pain is easily relieved by nitrates.

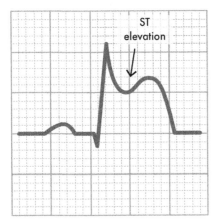
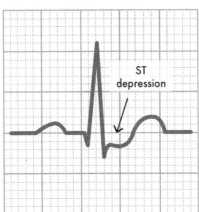
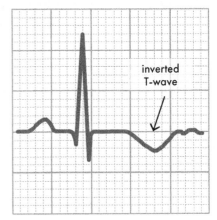

Figure 5.2. ECG Changes Associated with ACS

A **myocardial infarction (MI)**, or ischemia of the heart muscle, occurs when the coronary arteries are partly or completely occluded. MI is diagnosed via positive troponin and ECG changes; it is classified by the behavior of the ST wave. A **non-ST-elevation myocardial infarction (NSTEMI)** includes an ST depression and a T wave inversion. An **ST-elevation myocardial infarction (STEMI)** includes an elevated ST (> 1 mm), indicating a complete occlusion of a coronary artery. Signs, symptoms, and diagnostic findings for MI vary depending on which coronary artery is occluded.

- **anterior-wall MI**: occlusion of the LAD artery, which supplies blood to the anterior of the left atrium and ventricle
    - ST changes in V1 – V4
    - increased risk of left ventricular failure (and subsequent cardiogenic shock)
    - increased risk of second-degree, type II heart block and bundle branch blocks
    - increased risk of ventricular septal rupture (usually 2 – 7 days post-MI)
- **inferior-wall MI**: occlusion of the RCA, which supplies blood to the right atrium and ventricle, the SA node, and the AV node
    - ST changes in II, III, aVF
    - presents with bradycardia and hypotension
    - increased risk of AV heart blocks (e.g., first-degree AV block)
    - increased risk for papillary muscle rupture
    - cautious use of beta blockers and nitrates to avoid reducing preload
- **right ventricular infarction**: may occur with inferior-wall MI
    - ST changes in V4R – V6R
    - presents with tachycardia, hypotension, and JVD
    - treat with positive inotropes
    - avoid preload-reducing medications (beta blockers, diuretics, morphine, nitrates)
- **lateral-wall MI**: occlusion of the left circumflex artery, which supplies blood to the left atrium and the posterior/lateral walls of the left ventricle (ST changes may be seen in I, aVL, V5, or V6)
- **posterior-wall MI**: occlusion of the RCA or left circumflex artery, with ST elevation in V7 – V9 and ST depression in V1 – V4

Demographics

- angina
    - experienced by > 9 million individuals in the United States each year
    - more common in females, especially among African Americans
    - common in individuals with CAD
    - in males, most common between ages 55 and 65

- MI
    - more common in males
    - occurs most often in the early morning hours and on Mondays
    - in the United States, > 1.5 million MIs occur every year

Symptoms and Physical Findings

- continuous chest pain that may radiate to the back, arm, or jaw (possible Levine's sign)
- upper abdominal pain (more common in adults > 65, people with diabetes, and females)
- dyspnea
- nausea or vomiting
- dizziness or syncope
- diaphoresis and pallor
- palpitations

Diagnostic Tests

- elevated troponin (> 0.01 ng/mL)
- elevated CK-MB (> 2.5%)

Management

- 160 – 325 mg aspirin (chewed and swallowed); clopidogrel for patients who cannot take aspirin
- NSTEMI: continual monitoring; may require PCI; initially treated with medication:
    - nitroglycerin for vasodilatation of coronary arteries
    - beta blockers or calcium channel blockers to reduce myocardial oxygen demand
    - heparin to improve blood flow
    - morphine if pain is not relieved by nitroglycerin
- STEMI: immediate fibrinolytic therapy or PCI
    - goal for door to balloon time: 90 minutes
    - goal for door to fibrinolytic therapy: 30 minutes

QUICK REVIEW QUESTION

6. A patient with a new complaint of chest pain and left arm pain is found clutching his chest. He is in bed and appears pale and diaphoretic. His heart rate is 55 bpm. What priority interventions should the cardiac nurse take?

Arterial and Venous Disease
ABDOMINAL AORTIC ANEURYSM (AAA)
Pathophysiology

An **abdominal aortic aneurysm (AAA)**, often called a triple A, occurs when the lower aorta is enlarged. The AAA is the most common type of aneurysm. Other common aneurysms include thoracic aneurysms and thoracoabdominal aortic aneurysms.

An **aortic rupture**, a complete tear in the wall of the aorta, rapidly leads to hemorrhagic shock and death. An **aortic dissection** is a tear in the aortic intima; the tear allows blood to enter the aortic media. Both aortic rupture and dissection will lead to hemorrhagic shock and death without immediate intervention.

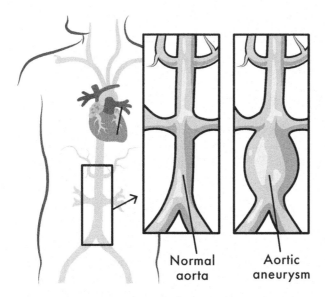

Normal aorta

Aortic aneurysm

Figure 5.3. Abdominal Aortic Aneurysm (AAA)

Demographics

- more common in males
- affects approximately 4 – 8% of US population
- most common in patients aged 60 and older
- more common in Caucasians than in other ethnicities

Symptoms and Physical Findings

- usually asymptomatic unless rupture or dissection occurs
- rupture or dissection:
  - sharp, severe pain in the chest, back, abdomen, or flank; often described as "tearing"
  - a blood pressure difference of ≥ 20 mm Hg between the left and right arms
  - new-onset murmur
  - signs and symptoms of hypovolemic shock

Diagnostic Tests

- CT scan, TEE, angiogram, or chest MRI

Management

- treatment determined by size of aneurysm
- small aneurysms: monitoring, medications, and/or lifestyle changes
    - maintain normal BP and low cholesterol
    - smoking cessation
    - beta blockers
    - follow-up CTs at 3- or 6-month intervals
- aneurysms > 5 cm or rapidly enlarging aneurysm: surgery or endovascular repair
- aneurysm dissection or rupture: emergency surgery

QUICK REVIEW QUESTION

7. A patient is in the cardiology clinic for monitoring of a previously diagnosed AAA that has remained 4 cm in size. The patient asks the nurse if the AAA will need to be surgically repaired. How should the nurse respond?

CAROTID ARTERY OCCLUSIVE DISEASE (CAOD)

Pathophysiology

Carotid artery occlusive disease (CAOD), or **stenosis**, is a narrowing or hardening of the carotid arteries, usually caused by atherosclerosis. The artery may be occluded, or plaque may break off and travel to the brain, causing a TIA or an ischemic stroke. Carotid artery stenosis may be asymptomatic and is usually diagnosed after a CVA. It is the most common cause of ischemic strokes.

Demographics

- more common in males
- more common in Native Americans and Caucasians than in other ethnicities

Symptoms and Physical Findings

- can be asymptomatic
- carotid bruits
- diminished carotid pulse
- dizziness
- blurry vision

Diagnostic Tests

- arteriography

- carotid ultrasound to examine blood flow

Management

- carotid artery < 50% blocked: lifestyle changes and medications
  - maintain normal BP and low cholesterol
  - antiplatelet or anticoagulant

- carotid artery > 50% blocked: surgical intervention (carotid artery angioplasty or carotid endarterectomy [CEA])

QUICK REVIEW QUESTION

8. A patient is diagnosed with carotid artery stenosis and asks the nurse why this condition puts a person at greater risk for having a stroke. How should the nurse respond?

CHRONIC VENOUS INSUFFICIENCY (CVI)

Pathophysiology

Chronic venous insufficiency (CVI) occurs when the veins within the legs do not move blood effectively, because of inadequate muscle pump function, damaged venous valves, or thrombosis. Blood then pools within the veins, and blood flow to the heart is diminished.

Demographics

- more common in females

- more common in adults > 50

- approximately 6 – 7 million Americans with CVI

Risk Factors

- immobility

- prolonged sitting or standing

- DVT

- obesity

- pregnancy

- family history

Symptoms and Physical Findings

- distended vessels
- varicose veins
- lower extremity edema
- pain that increases with movement
- a feeling of tightness or stretching of the legs
- itching feeling in lower extremities
- skin discoloration
- leg muscle cramps or spasms
- venous ulcers

Diagnostic Tests

- venous duplex ultrasound

Management

- most patients managed without medication or invasive procedures
  - elevation of legs to promote blood flow back to the heart
  - compression stockings to apply pressure to legs and keep blood flowing
  - exercise to increase circulation
  - higher-fiber diet to help control CVI
  - reduced-sodium diet to prevent excess fluid accumulation
- surgical or endovascular procedures (vein ablation or venous bypass) for patients who do not respond to noninvasive management

HELPFUL HINT

Patients with CVI should be educated on proper skin hygiene to prevent skin infections.

QUICK REVIEW QUESTION

9. The nurse is caring for a patient with CVI. What type of diet should the nurse teach the patient to follow?

DEEP VEIN THROMBOSIS (DVT)

Pathophysiology

A **deep vein thrombosis (DVT)** is the most common form of acute venous occlusion and occurs when a thrombus forms within a deep vein. DVT is most common in the lower extremities. Risk factors for acute venous occlusion include the following:

- Virchow's triad:
  - hypercoagulability (e.g., due to estrogen or contraceptive use or malignancy)
  - venous stasis (bed rest or any other activity that results in decreased physical movement)

- endothelial damage (damage to the vessel wall from trauma, drug use, inflammatory processes, or other causes)
- pregnancy, hormone replacement therapy, or oral contraceptives
- recent surgery

Demographics

- most common in adults > 45
- more common in males

Symptoms and Physical Findings

- pain localized to a specific area (usually the foot, ankle, or calf or behind the knee)
- unilateral edema, erythema, and warmth
- positive Homans sign

Diagnostic Tests

- elevated D-dimer
- venous duplex ultrasonography to diagnose

Management

- anticoagulants (first line)
- thrombolytics may be administered when anticoagulants are ineffective
- surgical or endovascular thrombectomy may be required
- inferior vena cava filter may be placed to avoid a pulmonary embolism in patients who cannot tolerate anticoagulants

QUICK REVIEW QUESTION

10. A patient diagnosed with a DVT complains of dyspnea. The nurse knows the priority intervention for this patient is what?

PERIPHERAL VASCULAR INSUFFICIENCY

Pathophysiology

Atherosclerosis that occurs in peripheral arteries leads to **peripheral vascular insufficiency** (also called peripheral arterial disease [PAD]).

Acute peripheral vascular insufficiency (also **acute arterial occlusion**) occurs when a thrombus or an embolus occludes a peripheral artery and causes ischemia and possibly the loss of a limb. This condition is a medical emergency requiring prompt treatment to prevent tissue necrosis.

Demographics

- approximately 10% of US population affected by lower extremity arterial disease
- more common in males
- more prevalent with age
- more prevalent in African Americans than in other ethnicities

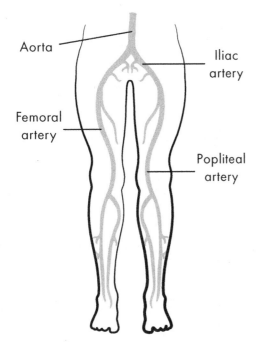

Figure 5.4. Common Locations of Acute Peripheral Vascular Insufficiency

Risk Factors

- valvular heart disease
- trauma
- fractures and compartment syndrome
- circumferential burns
- A-fib
- heart failure

Symptoms and Physical Findings

- the 6 Ps (hallmark signs) of an arterial occlusion:
    - pain (intermittent claudication)
    - pallor
    - pulselessness
    - paresthesia
    - paralysis
    - poikilothermia
- petechiae (visible with microemboli)
- ABI < 0.30 (indicating poor outcome of limb survivability)

Diagnostic Tests

- duplex ultrasonography, CT angiography, or catheter-based arteriography
- elevated D-dimer

Management

- pharmacological management: thrombolytics, anticoagulants (e.g., heparin), and antiplatelet agents
- other interventions: embolectomy, catheter-directed thrombolysis, or bypass surgery

- Nursing considerations for arterial occlusion:
  - frequent pulse and neurovascular checks to monitor for worsening of condition or other changes
  - do not elevate extremity or apply heat
  - thrombolytic therapy, typically for 4 – 24 hours; reevaluation via angiogram; monitoring for symptoms and physical findings of bleeding

QUICK REVIEW QUESTION

11. Catheter-directed thrombolysis is performed on a patient with an acute arterial occlusion in the lower right leg. What nursing interventions are the most important?

Cardiomyopathies

Cardiomyopathy is abnormal functioning of the heart muscles. Symptoms and physical findings of cardiomyopathy are similar to those of HF and vary with the location and degree of dysfunction. Types of cardiomyopathies include dilated, hypertrophic, and restrictive.

Table 5.3. Pathophysiology and Management of Cardiomyopathy

Type of Cardiomyopathy	Management
Dilated congestive cardiomyopathy (DCCM) occurs when damage to the myofibrils causes dilation in the ventricles, causing enlargement and systolic impairment (< 40% ejection fraction). DCCM has a high mortality rate: the 2-year survival rate is 50%, and most patients will die within 10 years of diagnosis. See Figure 5.5 page 88.	<ul><li>beta blockers, ACE inhibitors (ARBs if patient is ACE intolerant), and diuretics</li><li>implantable defibrillator or cardiac resynchronization therapy</li></ul>
Hypertrophic cardiomyopathy (HCM) is an inherited disorder characterized by left ventricular hypertrophy and diastolic dysfunction. In **obstructive HCM**, CO is decreased. The stiffening of the ventricle septum obstructs the left ventricle outflow tract and disrupts mitral valve function, resulting in a decreased preload and an increased afterload. Hypertrophic cardiomyopathy is one of the most common causes of sudden death in adolescent athletes. See Figure 5.6 on page 88.	<ul><li>beta blockers, calcium channel blockers, and antidysrhythmic agents</li><li>implantable defibrillator</li><li>**contraindicated**: ACE inhibitors, digoxin, vasodilators, and diuretics</li></ul>
Restrictive cardiomyopathy (RCM) occurs when fibrous tissue builds up within the ventricles, resulting in diastolic dysfunction and decreased CO. Systolic function is usually normal. Unlike other cardiomyopathies, in RCM the ventricles will not be enlarged or hypertrophic. See Figure 5.7 on page 88.	<ul><li>diuretics; beta blockers and calcium channel blockers used cautiously</li><li>**contraindicated**: digoxin, nitrates</li></ul>
Ischemic cardiomyopathy is impaired left ventricular functioning caused by CAD and the resulting ischemia and ventricular remodeling.	ACE inhibitors and beta blockers

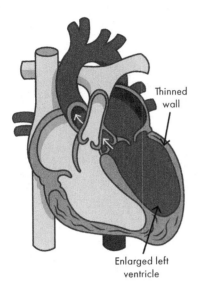

Figure 5.5. Dilated Congestive Cardiomyopathy

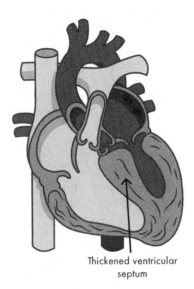

Figure 5.6. Hypertrophic Cardiomyopathy

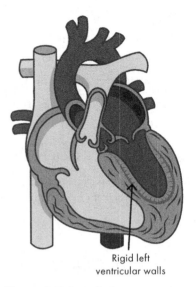

Figure 5.7. Restrictive Cardiomyopathy

QUICK REVIEW QUESTION

12. The nurse is completing a medication reconciliation on a patient admitted with HF symptoms and a history of HCM. The home medications include metoprolol, diltiazem (Cardizem), and digoxin. Which medication should the nurse be concerned about?

Cerebrovascular Accident (CVA)

A **cerebrovascular accident (CVA)**, also known as a stroke, is a neurological emergency where blood flow to the brain is stopped or blocked. There are 2 types of stroke: hemorrhagic and ischemic.

HEMORRHAGIC STROKE

Pathophysiology

A **hemorrhagic stroke** occurs when a vessel ruptures in the brain or when a brain aneurysm bursts. The blood that accumulates in the brain leads to increased ICP and edema, both of which damage brain tissue and cause neurological impairment. Hemorrhagic stroke is an emergent condition that requires immediate and aggressive care to prevent further bleeding.

Demographics

- more common in males

- accounts for approximately 10% – 20% of strokes

- more common in African Americans and Hispanics than in Caucasians

Risk Factors

- hypertension
- trauma
- blood thinners
- oral contraceptives
- excessive consumption of alcohol
- cocaine use

Symptoms and Physical Findings

- severe, sudden headache
- sudden onset of weakness
- difficulty speaking
- difficulty walking
- lethargy
- altered LOC, or coma (using Glasgow Coma Scale [GCS])

Diagnostic Tests

- immediate CT scan necessary to show location of bleed

Management

- protect patient's airway; intubation and mechanical ventilation may be required
- common complications: hypertension, increased ICP, seizures
- immediately discontinue and/or reverse anticoagulants and antiplatelets
- surgery or a thrombectomy may be needed
- contraindicated: NSAIDs, fibrinolytics, lumbar puncture

QUICK REVIEW QUESTION

13. What is the nursing priority for a patient experiencing a hemorrhagic stroke?

ISCHEMIC STROKE

Pathophysiology

An **ischemic stroke** occurs when blood flow within an artery in the brain is blocked, leading to ischemia and damage to brain tissue. The lack of blood flow can be caused by a thrombosis or an embolus.

Demographics

- accounts for approximately 80% of strokes
- twice as common in African Americans than in other groups
- more common in males

Risk Factors

- history of previous strokes or TIA
- atherosclerosis or CAD
- history of A-fib
- sickle cell disease
- cocaine and/or amphetamine use
- vasculitis

Symptoms and Physical Findings

- facial drooping, usually on one side
- numbness, paralysis, or weakness on one side of the body
- slurred speech or inability to speak
- confusion
- vision changes
- dizziness or loss of balance control
- sudden onset of severe headache
- arm drift possible
- **National Institutes of Health Stroke Scale (NIHSS)** to quantitatively measure the patient's neurological deficits:
  - lowest score: 0 (no deficits)
  - highest score: 42 (severe stroke)

Diagnostic Tests

- CT scan without contrast a priority to exclude hemorrhage
- bedside glucose test to rule out hypoglycemia as cause of symptoms

Management

- administer tPA (if CT scan is negative for hemorrhage)
  - within 3 – 4.5 hours of the last time patient was seen as normal

- o dosing: 0.9 mg/kg, with a maximum dose of 90 mg, with 10% of dose given as an IV push bolus and the remainder given through infusion

- o BP strictly controlled: < 185 mm Hg systolic and < 110 mm Hg diastolic

- o monitor for bleeding

- tPA contraindicated in patients with hemorrhagic stroke, head trauma, or recent neurosurgery or stroke

- frequent neurological checks

- possible thrombectomy to remove clot

QUICK REVIEW QUESTION

14. Upon entering a patient's room, the nurse notices a patient who previously had a GCS of 15 now has slurred speech, has a left-sided facial droop, and seems confused. What interventions should the nurse prioritize?

Congenital Heart Defects

Congenital heart defects are heart-structure abnormalities that exist at birth.

Table 5.4. Pathophysiology and Management of Congenital Heart Defects

Defect	Management
An **atrial septal defect (ASD)**, an abnormal opening in the atrial septum, results from a lack of formation of septal tissue. Oxygen-rich blood flows through the hole from the left atrium to the right atrium (left-to-right shunting) instead of flowing normally into the left ventricle. This shunting can lead to increased pulmonary hypertension and enlargement of the right atrium. The most common symptom in children is a midsystolic pulmonary flow or ejection murmur. See Figure 5.8 on page 92.	<ul><li>monitoring; intervention only required when symptomatic</li><li>defects < 6 mm: high likelihood of spontaneous closure</li><li>surgical or endovascular repair when ASD does not close</li><li>symptomatic patients: beta blockers, anticoagulants, diuretics, and digoxin</li></ul>
Patent ductus arteriosus (PDA) occurs when the fetal ductus arteriosus does not close within the first few weeks of life. Without closure, blood flows from the aorta to the pulmonary artery. This alteration in blood flow increases the workload of the left side of the heart and causes pulmonary congestion. Symptoms include murmur with a characteristic machine-like sound and poor feeding/weight gain. See Figure 5.9 on page 92.	<ul><li>preterm infants: indomethacin and ibuprofen to close patent ductus</li><li>monitoring; intervention only required when symptomatic</li><li>PDA closed surgically or percutaneously when infant is at safe weight</li></ul>
The foramen ovale is an opening that allows oxygen-rich blood to move from the right to left atrium in the fetus, bypassing the fetus's lungs (which are nonfunctional). The foramen ovale normally closes after birth because of increased blood pressure from the left side of the heart. A **patent foramen ovale (PFO)** is when this hole fails to close.	<ul><li>do not normally need to be closed; managed with medication to prevent blood clots</li><li>catheter closure when necessary</li></ul>

Table 5.4. Pathophysiology and Management of Congenital Heart Defects (continued)

Defect	Management
Tetralogy of Fallot consists of 4 defects within the heart (**PROVE** mnemonic): • pulmonic stenosis • right ventricular hypertrophy • overriding aorta • ventricular septal defect Patients may experience transient cyanotic episodes (tet spells). See Figure 5.10.	• open surgery before 1 year of age • pharmacological management of cyanosis and HF symptoms before surgery
Transposition of the great arteries, sometimes called dextro-transposition of the great arteries, occurs when the vessels that carry blood from the heart to the lungs are reversed. The aorta is attached to the right-sided ventricle instead of the left, and the pulmonary artery is attached to the left-sided ventricle instead of the right. This type of heart defect is cyanotic in nature, meaning that deoxygenated blood is pumped into circulation.	• immediate pharmacological or surgical intervention to ensure adequate oxygenation • surgery (atrial switch procedure) when infant is 3 – 5 days old
A **ventricular septal defect (VSD)** is an abnormal opening or hole between the right and left ventricles. Blood flows through the opening into the pulmonary artery. The increased blood volume into the lungs can cause increased pulmonary vascular resistance. See Figure 5.11.	• monitoring and possible closure (as with ASD) • pharmacological management for symptoms • high-calorie nutrition for infants

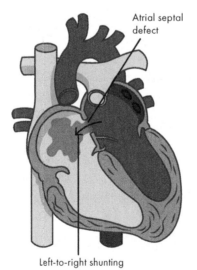

Figure 5.8. Atrial Septal Defect (ASD)

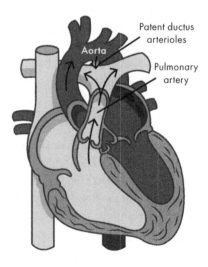

Figure 5.9. Patent Ductus Arteriosus (PDA)

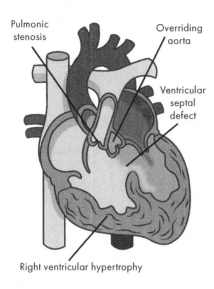

Pulmonic stenosis	Overriding aorta
	Ventricular septal defect
Right ventricular hypertrophy	Ventricular septal defect

Figure 5.10. Tetralogy of Fallot   **Figure 5.11. Ventricular Septal Defect (VSD)**

QUICK REVIEW QUESTION

15. The parents of a child diagnosed with a large ASD ask why their child will need a catheter procedure even though the child has no symptoms. How should the nurse respond?

Dysrhythmias

A cardiac **dysrhythmia** is an abnormal heartbeat or rhythm. Dysrhythmias are typically caused by a malfunction in the heart's cardiac conductions system. Most dysrhythmias of clinical importance are caused by **reentry**: the re-excitation of the heart by an electrical impulse that did not die out. Reentry dysrhythmias include A-fib, atrial flutter, V-tach, and V-fib.

Treatment is based on whether the patient is deemed hemodynamically stable or unstable.

- stable patients: noninvasive interventions or drugs to correct an abnormal rhythm

- unstable patients: appropriate electrical therapy

HELPFUL HINT

When treating dysrhythmias, medical staff should always consider a hypotensive patient unstable.

BRADYCARDIA

Pathophysiology

Bradycardia is a heart rate of < 60 bpm. It results from a decrease in the sinus node impulse formation (automaticity). Bradycardia is normal in certain individuals and does not require an intervention if the patient is stable. Symptomatic patients, however, need immediate treatment to address the cause of bradycardia and to correct the dysrhythmia. Symptoms of bradycardia may include hypotension, syncope, confusion, or dyspnea.

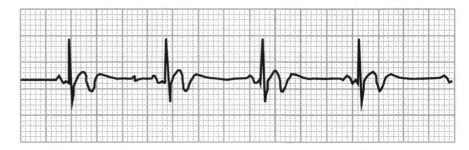

Figure 5.12. ECG: Bradycardia

Management

- stable, asymptomatic patients: no intervention required; may be monitored for development of symptoms

- symptomatic, hemodynamically stable patients: monitor while determining underlying cause

- symptomatic, hemodynamically unstable patients: medication:
    - first line: atropine 0.5 mg for first dose, with a maximum of 3 mg total
    - second line: dopamine or epinephrine if atropine is ineffective or if maximum dose of atropine already given and patient is still stable
    - patients with bradycardia and who have had a heart transplant: administer isoproterenol (Isuprel); atropine is ineffective in these patients

- unstable patients who do not respond to medication: TCP

QUICK REVIEW QUESTION

16. A patient presents with complaints of confusion, dizziness, and dyspnea. The patient's blood pressure is 72/40 mm Hg, with a heart rate of 32 bpm and O_2 saturation of 92% on room air. What priority intervention should the nurse prepare for?

NARROW-COMPLEX TACHYCARDIAS

Pathophysiology

Narrow-complex tachycardias (also **called supraventricular tachycardia [SVT]**) are dysrhythmias with > 100 bpm and a narrow QRS complex (< 0.12 seconds). The dysrhythmia originates at or above the bundle of His (supraventricular), resulting in rapid ventricular activation. Narrow-complex tachycardias are often asymptomatic. Symptomatic patients may have palpitations, chest pain, hypotension, and dyspnea.

Management

- first line treatment for SVT: vagal maneuvers

- rapid bolus dose of adenosine (6 mg) to restore sinus rhythm if dysrhythmia continues; second dose (this time 12 mg) may be administered if chemical cardioversion does not occur within 1 – 2 minutes

- for refractory SVT:
  - stable patients: calcium channel blockers, beta blockers, or digoxin may also be given

  - unstable patients and patients for whom medications are ineffective: synchronized cardioversion required

QUICK REVIEW QUESTION

17. A patient in SVT is unresponsive to vagal maneuvers. What intervention is likely to be ordered next?

ATRIAL FIBRILLATION AND FLUTTER

Pathophysiology

Atrial fibrillation (A-fib) is an irregular narrow-complex tachycardia. During A-fib, the heart cannot adequately empty, causing blood to pool and clots to form, increasing stroke risk. The irregular atrial contractions also decrease CO. The ECG in A-fib will show an irregular rhythm with no P waves and an undeterminable atrial rate (Figure 5.13).

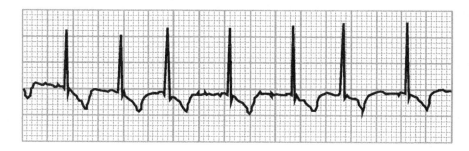

Figure 5.13. ECG: Atrial Fibrillation (A-fib)

During **atrial flutter**, the atria beat regularly but too fast (240 – 400 bpm), causing multiple atrial beats in between the ventricular beat. Atrial flutter can be regular or irregular. The ECG in atrial flutter will show a saw-toothed flutter and multiple P waves for each QRS complex (Figure 5.14).

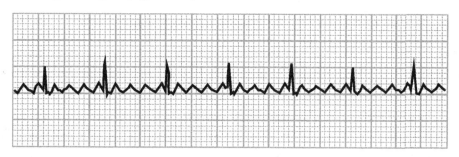

Figure 5.14. ECG: Atrial Flutter

HELPFUL HINT

A-fib is the most common cardiac dysrhythmia. It occurs in approximately 2 – 6 million individuals in the United States annually.

Management

- adenosine: slows the rhythm so that it may be identified, but will not convert dysrhythmia to a sinus rhythm

- hemodynamically stable patients:
  - calcium channel blockers, beta blockers, or cardiac glycoside to slow the rhythm
  - antidysrhythmics may be administered to convert to sinus rhythm

- hemodynamically unstable patients: cardioversion required

- anticoagulants to lower risk of stroke

- cardiac ablation may be used to correct A-fib and atrial flutter

---

QUICK REVIEW QUESTION

18. A patient presents with A-fib. Vital signs are as follows:

BP	125/80 mm Hg
HR	150 bpm
RR	23

What intervention should the nurse anticipate?

VENTRICULAR TACHYCARDIA AND FIBRILLATION

Pathophysiology

Ventricular tachycardia (V-tach) is tachycardia originating below the bundle of His, resulting in slowed ventricular activation. During V-tach, ≥ 3 consecutive ventricular beats occur at a rate > 100 bpm. V-tach is often referred to as a **wide-complex tachycardia** because of the width of the QRS complex.

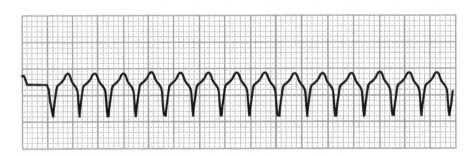

Figure 5.15. ECG: Monomorphic Ventricular Tachycardia (V-tach)

HELPFUL HINT

Torsades de pointes, a type of V-tach with irregular QRS complexes, occurs with a prolonged QT interval. It can be congenital or caused by antidysrhythmics, antipsychotics, hypokalemia, or hypomagnesemia.

Because the ventricles cannot refill before contracting, patients in this rhythm may have reduced CO, resulting in hypotension. V-tach may be short and asymptomatic, or it may precede V-fib and cardiac arrest.

During **ventricular fibrillation (V-fib)** the ventricles contract rapidly (300 – 400 bpm) with no organized rhythm. There is no CO. The ECG will initially show **coarse V-fib** with an amplitude > 3 mm (Figure 5.16). As V-fib continues, the amplitude of the waveform decreases, progressing through **fine V-fib** (< 3 mm) and eventually reaching asystole.

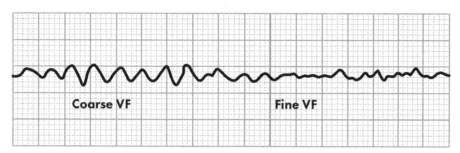

Figure 5.16. ECG: Ventricular Fibrillation (V-fib)

Management

- priority intervention for V-tach: check for pulse
  - for pulseless V-tach: follow ACLS protocols
  - for V-tach with a pulse, patient stable: administer amiodarone
  - for V-tach with a pulse, patient unstable (hypotensive): synchronized cardioversion
  - patients with recurrent V-tach: may require implantable defibrillator or radiofrequency ablation
- for V-fib: follow ACLS protocols
  - immediately initiate high-quality CPR at 100 – 120 compressions per minute
  - defibrillation ASAP, before administration of any drugs
  - defibrillation doses: 200 J → 300 J → 360 J (biphasic)
  - ≥ 2 defibrillation attempts should be made for patients in V-fib before giving any medications
  - first line: epinephrine 1 mg every 3 – 5 minutes
  - shock-refractory V-fib: amiodarone (300 mg as first dose and 150 mg for second dose)

QUICK REVIEW QUESTION

19. The nurse is participating in a cardiac resuscitation attempt of a patient found in V-fib. A total of 2 defibrillation attempts have been made, and 1 dose of epinephrine has been given 2 minutes earlier. What priority action should the nurse take next?

PULSELESS ELECTRICAL ACTIVITY (PEA)/ASYSTOLE

Pathophysiology

Pulseless electrical activity (PEA) is an organized rhythm in which the heart does not contract with enough force to create a pulse. **Asystole**, also called a "flat line," occurs when there is no electrical or mechanical activity within the heart (Figure 5.16). Both PEA and asystole are nonshockable rhythms with a poor survival rate.

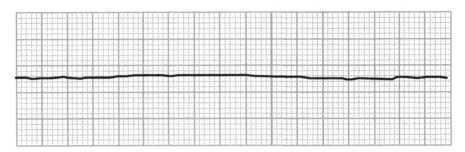

Figure 5.17. ECG: Asystole

Management

- immediate high-quality CPR

- epinephrine 1 mg every 3 – 5 minutes until circulation returns or a shockable rhythm emerges

- immediate attempts to determine and treat underlying cause, particularly H's and T's (common causes of PEA and asystole):
  - hypovolemia
  - hypoxia
  - hydrogen ion (acidosis)
  - hyperkalemia/hypokalemia
  - hypothermia
  - toxins
  - tamponade
  - tension pneumothorax
  - thrombosis (coronary or pulmonary)

QUICK REVIEW QUESTION

20. A patient is found in bed and is unresponsive to commands. The person appears cyanotic, and the nurse determines there is no pulse and no breathing present. What should the nurse do first?

Heart Failure (HF)
Pathophysiology

Heart failure (HF) occurs when either one or both of the ventricles in the heart cannot efficiently pump blood, resulting in decreased CO. The condition is typically due to another disease or illness, most commonly CAD. **Acute decompensated heart failure**

is the sudden onset or worsening of HF symptoms. The American Heart Association classifies HF into four stages:

- **Stage A**: high risk of developing heart failure
- **Stage B**: diagnosis of left systolic ventricular failure with no symptoms
- **Stage C**: diagnosis of heart failure, with symptoms
- **Stage D**: advanced symptoms that have not improved with treatment

HF is classified according to the left ventricular ejection fraction. Impairment of systolic function results in **heart failure with reduced ejection fraction (HFrEF, or systolic HF)**, classified as an ejection fraction of < 50%. **Heart failure with preserved ejection fraction (HFpEF, or diastolic HF)** is characterized by an ejection fraction of > 50% and diastolic dysfunction.

Table 5.5. Systolic Versus Diastolic Heart Failure

Systolic HF (HFrEF)	Diastolic HF (HFpEF)
reduced ejection fraction (< 50%)	normal ejection fraction
dilated left ventricle	no enlargement of heart
S3 heart sound	S4 heart sound
hypotension	hypertension

HF can also be categorized as left-sided or right-sided, depending on which ventricle is affected. **Left-sided HF** is usually caused by cardiac disorders (e.g., MI, cardiomyopathy) and produces symptoms related to pulmonary function. **Right-sided HF** is caused by right ventricle infarction or pulmonary conditions (e.g., PE, COPD) and produces symptoms related to systemic circulation. Unmanaged left-sided HF can lead to right-sided HF.

HELPFUL HINT

Cor pulmonale, or impaired functioning of the right ventricle, is caused by pulmonary disease or pulmonary hypertension.

Demographics

- in the United States, > 500,000 new cases of HF every year
- more common in African Americans than in other ethnicities
- equally common in males and females

Risk Factors

- CAD
- MI
- congenital heart disease
- cardiomyopathy
- alcohol abuse

Symptoms and Physical Findings

Table 5.6. Symptoms and Physical Findings of Right- and Left-Sided Heart Failure (HF)

Left-Sided HF	Right-Sided HF
<ul><li>increased LVEDP and left atrial pressures</li><li>increased PAP</li><li>dyspnea or orthopnea</li><li>pulmonary edema</li><li>tachycardia</li><li>bibasilar crackles</li><li>cough, frothy sputum, hemoptysis</li><li>left-sided S3 sound</li><li>diaphoresis</li><li>pulsus alternans</li><li>oliguria</li></ul>	<ul><li>increased right ventricular end-diastolic pressure (RVEDP) and right atrial pressures</li><li>increased CVP</li><li>increased PAP</li><li>dependent edema (usually in lower legs); ascites</li><li>JVD</li><li>hepatomegaly</li><li>right-sided S3 sound</li><li>weight gain</li><li>nausea, vomiting, abdominal pain</li><li>nocturia</li></ul>

Diagnostic Tests

- BNP > 100 pg/mL
- echocardiogram to assess ejection fraction, ventricular hypertrophy, valve dysfunction
- chest X-ray to show cardiomegaly or pulmonary congestion

Management

- patient needs for pharmacological and surgical interventions vary, depending on the type and degree of HF
- improve CO and CI
- medications:
  - inotropics
  - vasodilators
  - ACE inhibitors, ARBs
  - digoxin
  - diuretics
  - beta blockers (decreases risk of sudden cardiac death)
- other interventions: ICD, a permanent pacemaker, an IABP, a ventricular assist device (VAD), or a transplant

Hypertensive Crisis

Pathophysiology

Hypertensive crises include hypertensive urgency and hypertensive emergencies. **Hypertensive urgency** occurs when BP is > 180/110 mm Hg without evidence of organ dysfunction. A **hypertensive emergency** occurs when systolic BP is > 180 mm Hg or when diastolic BP is > 120 mm Hg and when either of these is accompanied by evidence of impending or progressive organ dysfunction. Hypertensive crises increase the risk of cerebral infarction, and prolonged hypertension can lead to heart or renal failure.

Symptoms and Physical Findings

- usually asymptomatic
- headache
- blurred vision
- dizziness
- dyspnea
- retinal hemorrhages
- epistaxis
- chest pain

Management

- blood pressure reduction: limited to a decrease of ≤ 25% within the first 2 hours to maintain cerebral perfusion
- labetalol, hydralazine, clonidine, or metoprolol (first-line medications)
- quiet, nonstimulating environment for relaxation
- oxygen administration

Infective Endocarditis

Pathophysiology

Infective endocarditis occurs when an infection causes inflammation of the endocardium. The inflammation impairs valve function and may also disrupt the electrical conduction system. The most common cause of infection is bacterial, but the infection may also be fungal or viral. *Staphylococcus aureus* and *Streptococcus* account for about half of all cases. Infective endocarditis can occur secondary to surgical valve replacement; these cases have a high mortality rate.

Demographics

- more common in males
- more common in Caucasians than in other ethnicities
- affects > 30,000 individuals each year in the United States

Risk Factors

- heart-valve problems or surgery involving heart valves
- recent implantation of cardiac device
- immunocompromised individuals
- poor dental health or recent dental work
- central venous line access
- rheumatic heart disease
- IV drug abuse

Symptoms and Physical Findings

- general signs and symptoms of infection (e.g., fever, chills, anorexia)
- petechiae
- splinter hemorrhages under fingernails
- Janeway lesions, Osler nodes, or Roth spots
- arthralgias
- dyspnea

Diagnostic Tests

- ECG may show dysrhythmias (A-fib or AV block most common)
- echocardiogram to assess valves
- blood cultures showing bacteria present in the bloodstream
- WBC may be elevated

Management

- aggressive treatment with IV antimicrobials

- pharmacologic management of symptoms: antipyretics, diuretics, or dysrhythmics

- surgical repair of valves if necessary

QUICK REVIEW QUESTION

23. A patient is admitted with signs of infective endocarditis. What priority interventions should the nurse expect to perform?

Myocardial Conduction System Defects
ATRIOVENTRICULAR BLOCKS
Pathophysiology

An **atrioventricular (AV) block** is the disruption of electrical signals between the atria and ventricles. The electrical impulse may be delayed (first-degree block), intermittent (second-degree block), or completely blocked (third-degree block).

A **first-degree AV block** occurs when the conduction between the SA and the AV nodes is slowed, creating a prolonged PR interval. A first-degree AV block is a benign finding that is usually asymptomatic, but it can progress to a second-degree or third-degree block.

The ECG in a first-degree AV block will show a prolonged PR interval of > 0.20 seconds (Figure 5.18).

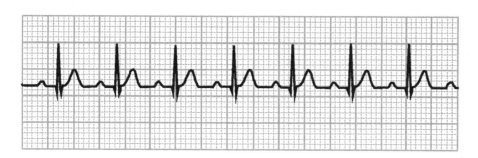

Figure 5.18. ECG: First-Degree Atrioventricular (AV) Block

A **second-degree AV block, type 1** (Wenckebach or Mobitz type 1), occurs when the PR interval progressively lengthens until the atrial impulse is completely blocked and does not produce a QRS impulse. This dysrhythmia occurs when the atrial conduction in the AV node or bundle of His is either being slowed or blocked. This type of block is cyclic; after the dropped QRS complex, the pattern will repeat itself.

The ECG in second-degree AV block, type 1, will show progressively longer PR intervals until a QRS complex completely drops (Figure 5.19).

A **second-degree AV block, type 2** (Mobitz type 2), occurs when the PR interval is constant in length but not every P wave is followed by a QRS complex. This abnormal

HELPFUL HINT

If the R is far from *P*, then you have a **first degree**.

Longer, longer, longer, *drop*, this is how you know it's a *Wenckebach*.

If some Ps just don't go *through*, then you know it's a **type 2**.

If Ps and Qs don't agree, then you have a **third degree**.

rhythm is the result of significant conduction dysfunction within the His-Purkinje system.

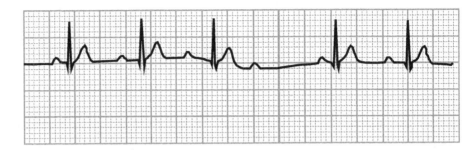

Figure 5.19. ECG: Second-Degree AV Block, Type 1

The ECG in second-degree AV block, type 2, will show constant PR intervals and extra P waves, with dropped QRS complexes (Figure 5.20).

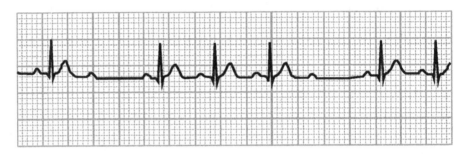

Figure 5.20. ECG: Second-Degree AV Block, Type 2

A **third-degree AV block**, sometimes referred to as a complete heart block, is characterized by a complete dissociation between the atria and the ventricles. There are effectively 2 pacemakers within the heart, so there is no correlation between the P waves and the QRS complexes. The most common origin of the block is below the bundle of His, but the block can also occur at the level of the bundle branches of the AV node.

The ECG for third-degree AV block will show regular P waves and QRS complexes that occur at different rates. There will be more P waves than QRS complexes, with P waves possibly buried within the QRS complex (Figure 5.21).

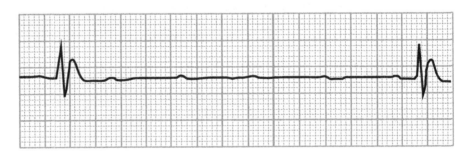

Figure 5.21. ECG: Third-Degree AV Block

Symptoms and Physical Findings

- first- and second-degree AV blocks usually asymptomatic
- may show symptoms of reduced CO (e.g., hypotension, dyspnea, chest pain)
- bradycardia

Management

- symptomatic patients: TCP possibly needed to manage symptoms
- implantable pacemaker if underlying cause cannot be resolved
- hypotensive patients: dopamine or epinephrine may be needed
- discontinue medications that slow electrical conduction in the heart (e.g., anti-dysrhythmic drugs)

QUICK REVIEW QUESTION

24. A patient begins to complain of dizziness and weakness and appears diaphoretic. The nurse notes from the telemetry monitor that the patient is in a third-degree AV block, and the blood pressure reads 71/55 mm Hg, with a heart rate of 30 bpm. What interventions does the nurse expect?

SINUS NODE DYSFUNCTION (SND)

Pathophysiology

Sinus node dysfunction (SND), also known as sick sinus syndrome (SSS), refers to dysrhythmias caused by a dysfunction in the SA node. An individual with SND can have bouts of bradycardia or tachycardia or can alternate between the two. SND can also arise from an SA block or sinus arrest. Because of these irregular and usually unpredictable signals, most people with SND will need a permanent pacemaker. The ECG for SND will show alternating bradycardia and tachycardia and sinus arrest (Figure 5.22).

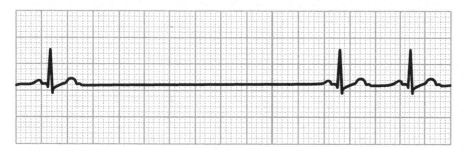

Figure 5.22. ECG: Sinus Arrest

Symptoms and Physical Findings

- syncope
- fatigue
- dyspnea

- palpitations
- confusion

Management

- hemodynamically unstable patients: atropine and temporary pacing to correct bradycardia

- stable, asymptomatic patients: monitoring only

- symptomatic patients with recurrent episodes of bradycardia: implantable pacemaker required

HELPFUL HINT

Use non-dihydropyridine calcium channel blockers, beta blockers, and antidysrhythmic drugs with caution because they may worsen SA node dysfunction.

QUICK REVIEW QUESTION

25. A patient with recurring episodes of bradycardia due to SND tells the nurse that they do not want to have surgery for a pacemaker, since they currently have no symptoms. What is the nurse's best response?

BUNDLE BRANCH BLOCK (BBB)

Pathophysiology

Right bundle branch block (RBBB) and **left bundle branch block (LBBB)** are interruptions in conduction through a bundle branch. Bundle branch blocks (BBB) usually occur secondary to underlying cardiac conditions, including MI, hypertension, and cardiomyopathies. LBBB in particular is associated with progressive underlying structural heart disease and is associated with poor outcomes post-MI. However, both RBBB and LBBB may occur in the absence of heart disease.

HELPFUL HINT

LBBB may mask the characteristic signs of MI on an ECG.

Ischemic heart disease is the most common cause of both RBBB and LBBB. LBBB can also arise from other heart diseases, hyperkalemia, or digoxin toxicity. Other causes of RBBB include cor pulmonale, pulmonary edema, and myocarditis.

If the patient with a BBB is asymptomatic, no treatment is necessary. Patients with syncopal episodes may need to have a pacemaker inserted.

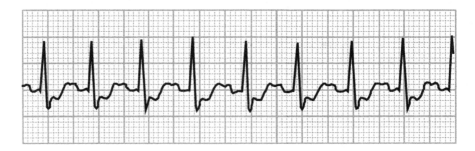

Figure 5.23. ECG: Bundle Branch Blocks (BBB)

QUICK REVIEW QUESTION

26. A patient with HF develops a new-onset LBBB. What medication would be important to consider as a possible cause of the LBBB?

- **Wolff-Parkinson-White syndrome**, caused by an early excitation of an extranodal accessary pathway, results in tachycardia.

  - asymptomatic, or presents as sudden A-fib or paroxysmal tachycardia (HR > 150)

  - ECG: short PR interval (< 0.12 seconds) with slurred QRS upstroke and wide QRS (> 0.12 seconds)

  - treatment: synchronized cardioversion; unstable patients may require catheter ablation

  - contraindications: adenosine, digoxin, amiodarone, beta blockers, calcium channel blockers

- **Long QT syndrome** is a cardiac electrical disturbance that causes a prolonged ventricular repolarization (seen as a QT interval > 0.44 seconds on ECG).

  - asymptomatic, or presents with dysrhythmias (especially torsades de pointes), syncope, seizure, or sudden cardiac death

  - management: beta blockers and placement of an ICD

  - contraindications: medications likely to prolong the QT interval

- **Brugada syndrome** is a genetically inherited cardiac electrical pathway syndrome that is linked to 4 – 12% of all sudden cardiac deaths.

  - characteristic ECG findings with sudden cardiac arrest, ventricular tachy-dysrhythmias, or syncopal episodes to diagnose

  - ECG: pseudo-RBBB and persistent ST-segment elevation

  - ECG abnormalities may be unmasked by sodium channel blockers

  - treat with medication (quinidine or flecainide) or ICD placement

  - contraindications: medications likely to prolong the QT interval

HELPFUL HINT

Caution should be exercised when administering antipsychotics, antidepressants, and anticonvulsants if the QT is > 0.45 seconds.

QUICK REVIEW QUESTION

27. A combative patient with schizophrenia develops torsades de pointes in the ICU. What medications may have caused this dysrhythmia?

Pericarditis

Pathophysiology

Pericarditis is the inflammation of the **pericardium**, the lining that surrounds the heart. When inflammation occurs, fluid can accumulate, resulting in **pericardial effusion**. When the effusion is large enough to impair the ability of the heart to pump blood sufficiently, the condition is called **pericardial tamponade**.

Pericarditis can be classified into 3 categories: acute, subacute, or chronic. Acute pericarditis occurs quickly (< 6 weeks), subacute pericarditis usually occurs over a few months, and chronic pericarditis occurs for > 6 months.

Demographics

- more common in males
- more common in individuals 20 – 50 years old
- more common in African Americans than in other ethnicities

Risk Factors

- mostly idiopathic
- secondary to MI, cardiac surgery, or thoracic trauma

Symptoms and Physical Findings

- chest pain
  - sudden and severe
  - increases with movement, lying flat, and inspiration
  - decreases by sitting up or learning forward
  - radiates to neck
- pericardial friction rub
- tachycardia (usually the earliest sign)
- tachypnea or dyspnea
- fever, chills, and cough

Diagnostic Tests

- ECG
  - ST elevation possible, usually in all leads except aVR and V1
  - tall, peaked T waves
- chest X-ray showing "water bottle" silhouette in pericardial effusion
- echocardiogram may show pericardial effusion, thickening, or calcifications

Management

- manage symptoms:
  - pain not relieved by nitroglycerin or rest
  - NSAID (e.g., ibuprofen or indomethacin [Indocin])
  - place patient in comfortable position (e.g., leaning over a bedside table)
  - bed rest
  - oxygen
- treat underlying conditions (e.g., antibiotics, steroids, or corticosteroids)
- pericardiocentesis or pericardial window if effusion needs to be drained

- complications: dysrhythmias, cardiac tamponade, heart failure

QUICK REVIEW QUESTION

28. A patient with acute pericarditis complains of sudden chest pain, and a pericardial friction rub can be heard on auscultation. What interventions should the nurse expect to perform to treat this patient?

Pulmonary Edema

Pathophysiology

Pulmonary edema is characterized by fluid accumulation in the lungs and is caused by extravasation of fluid from pulmonary vasculature into the interstitium and alveoli of the lungs. The fluid impairs respiration and may lead to acute respiratory failure.

Cardiogenic pulmonary edema develops secondary to a decrease in left ventricular function. The decrease in left-side function increases pulmonary venous pressure and capillary pressure in the lungs, forcing fluid from the vasculature into interstitial spaces. Common causes of **acute cardiogenic pulmonary edema (ACPE)** include acute decompensated HF, MI, severe dysrhythmias, hypertensive crises, valvular disease, or complications of cardiopulmonary bypass.

Symptoms and Physical Findings

- severe, sudden onset of dyspnea
- blood-tinged sputum
- orthopnea (requiring high-Fowler's positioning)
- anxiety, irritability, or restlessness
- tachycardia
- inspiratory fine crackles, rales, or wheezing
- other symptoms and physical findings of right-sided HF

Diagnostic Tests

- chest X-ray shows intestinal edema
- PAOP > 25 mm Hg

Management

- immediate objective: to improve oxygenation and reduce pulmonary congestion
- O_2 therapy: noninvasive (e.g., BiPAP) preferred; intubation may be required
- morphine to reduce anxiety and afterload
- diuretic therapy (e.g., furosemide [Lasix]) to reduce fluid overload
- vasodilator therapy (e.g., nitroglycerin) to reduce preload and afterload

- medication to improve contractility (digoxin, dopamine, dobutamine)

- aminophylline to prevent associated bronchospasm (may increase risk of tachycardic dysrhythmias)

- identification and treatment of the underlying cause

> ### QUICK REVIEW QUESTION
>
> **29.** A patient being treated for refractory V-tach develops severe orthopnea and dyspnea, and the lung sounds are coarse, with rales throughout. What is the probable cause of these symptoms and physical findings, and what testing is likely to be ordered to confirm the diagnosis?

Pulmonary Hypertension (PH)

Pathophysiology

Pulmonary hypertension (PH) is a mean pulmonary arterial pressure > 25 mm Hg at rest or > 30 mm Hg while exercising. (A normal pulmonary arterial pressure is 15 mm Hg.) PH is caused by increased pulmonary vascular resistance and increased pulmonary venous pressure. These increases can lead to right ventricular hypertrophy, which can ultimately cause heart failure.

PH is classified by the World Health Organization into 5 groups based on etiology.

- Group I: **pulmonary arterial hypertension (PAH)** that is inherited or caused by congenital disorders, drug use, or conditions not included in other groups.

- Group II: PH associated with left-sided heart disease

- Group III: PH associated with lung disease or hypoxemia

- Group IV: PH associated with chronic thrombotic or embolic disease

- Group V: PH with an unidentified etiology

Demographics

- more common in females

- much more common in Caucasians than in other ethnicities

- symptoms most commonly begin at age 30 – 50 years

Symptoms and Physical Findings

- dyspnea, worsening with activity

- dizziness

- syncope

- fatigue

- poor appetite

- right upper quadrant pain due to liver involvement

- possible hoarseness due to compression of laryngeal nerve by pulmonary artery
- JVD
- edema of lower extremities and abdomen
- midsystolic ejection murmur
- S4 sound

Diagnostic Tests

- right heart catheterization
- echocardiogram may be needed to visualize heart chambers and blood flow

Management

- diuretics to reduce edema and congestion
- vasodilators (e.g., epoprostenol) to improve blood flow
- anticoagulants to prevent blood clots
- sildenafil (Viagra) or tadalafil (Cialis) to expand the blood vessels within the lungs
- calcium channel blockers to relax blood vessel walls

QUICK REVIEW QUESTION

30. A patient is diagnosed with PAH and is prescribed sildenafil (Viagra). The patient questions this medication, knowing that it is used for erectile dysfunction. How should the nurse respond to the patient's question?

Rheumatic Heart Disease (RHD)
Pathophysiology

Rheumatic heart disease (RHD) is an autoimmune reaction to rheumatic fever. It is triggered by infections of group A beta hemolytic streptococci, most commonly from untreated strep throat. RHD is characterized by carditis and valvulitis, especially in the mitral and aortic valves. Having RHD greatly increases the risk of developing mitral stenosis because of valve damage.

Demographics

- common cause of HF in developing countries; rare in populations with access to high-quality health care
- globally, > 30 million individuals have RHD
- more common in females
- rheumatic fever most common in children 5 – 15 years old
- RHD symptoms usually appear in adults between ages 20 and 50

Symptoms and Physical Findings

- fatigue
- dyspnea
- tachycardia
- chest pain
- joint pain
- cardiomegaly
- syncope
- murmurs related to mitral or aortic regurgitation

Diagnostic Tests

- echocardiogram

Management

- antibiotics to treat infected heart valves (possibly long term)
- anti-inflammatories to reduce heart-valve inflammation
- heart valve replacement if necessary

QUICK REVIEW QUESTION

31. What combination of physical findings and medical history should cause a nurse to suspect RHD?

Shock

CARDIOGENIC SHOCK

Pathophysiology

Cardiogenic shock, a cyclical decline in cardiac function, results in decreased CO in the presence of adequate fluid volume. A lack of coronary perfusion causes or escalates ischemia/infarction by decreasing the ability of the heart to pump effectively. The heart rate increases in an attempt to meet myocardial oxygen demands. However, the reduced pumping ability of the heart reduces CO and CI, and demands for coronary or tissue perfusion are not met. LVEDP increases, which leads to stress in the left ventricle and an increase in afterload. This distress results in lactic acidosis. Cardiogenic shock is most commonly seen after an MI but can be associated with trauma, infection, or metabolic disease.

HELPFUL HINT

Left ventricular dysfunction caused by an anterior MI is the most common cause of cardiogenic shock.

Symptoms and Physical Findings

- tachycardia and sustained hypotension (SBP < 90 mm Hg)
- oliguria (< 30 mL/ hr or < 0.5 mL/kg/hour output)

- crackles
- tachypnea and dyspnea
- pallor
- JVD
- altered LOC
- cool, clammy skin
- S3 heart sound possible

Diagnostic Tests

- CI < 2.2 L/min/m^2
- PAOP > 15 mm Hg
- elevated SVR, CVP
- decreased SvO$_2$, MAP
- elevated lactate
- ABG shows metabolic acidosis and hypoxia

Management

- main treatment goal: to identify and treat underlying cause, reduce cardiac workload, and improve myocardial contractility
- immediate IV fluids
- medications:
    - dobutamine or norepinephrine (to increase contractility and CO)
    - antiplatelet drugs (e.g., aspirin or clopidogrel)
    - thrombolytic drugs (e.g., alteplase [Activase] or reteplase)
    - morphine
    - nitroprusside (Nipride)
- other interventions:
    - IABP to reduce afterload and increase coronary perfusion
    - cardiac catheterization to improve myocardial perfusion and increase contractility
    - LVAD
- monitor patient for cardiac dysrhythmias

QUICK REVIEW QUESTION

32. A patient presents with tachycardia, pallor, JVD, and crackles after emergent PCI for anterior MI. What hemodynamic findings for this patient would indicate cardiogenic shock?

Pathophysiology

Hypovolemic shock (hypovolemia) occurs when rapid fluid loss decreases the circulating blood volume and cardiac output, resulting in inadequate tissue perfusion. **Hemorrhagic shock** is a type of hypovolemic shock is which blood is lost rapidly.

Risk Factors

- most common cause of hypovolemic shock: trauma

- in cardiac care setting, most common causes of hypovolemic shock: postoperative bleeding and diuresis

Symptoms and Physical Findings

- tachycardia

- hypotension

- tachypnea

- oliguria

- dizziness

- confusion

- weakness

- headache

- nausea

- diaphoresis

- cool, clammy skin

HELPFUL HINT

Patients in early shock are often normotensive. Narrowed pulse pressure can be a better indicator of the patient's level of shock.

Diagnostic Tests

- electrolyte imbalances
  - ○ hyperkalemia
  - ○ increased magnesium
  - ○ hypernatremia
- increased BUN/creatinine
- increased lactate
- increased urine specific gravity and urine osmolality

Management

- oxygen

- volume resuscitation with isotonic crystalloid (i.e., normal saline or lactated Ringer's)

- transfusion of blood products for hemorrhagic shock

- dopamine, epinephrine, norepinephrine, or dobutamine for refractory hypotension

- monitor for cardiac dysrhythmias

QUICK REVIEW QUESTION

33. A patient recovering from a CABG begins to show signs of hemorrhagic shock, including tachycardia, tachypnea, hypotension, and oliguria. What interventions should the nurse expect?

Valvular Heart Disease

- In **aortic stenosis (AS)**, blood flow from the left ventricle to the aorta is impeded.

  - The pressure load on the left ventricle is increased, eventually leading to left ventricular hypertrophy and decreased CO and HF.

- **Aortic regurgitation (AR)** occurs when blood flows backward from the aorta to the left ventricle.

  - Volume overload in the left ventricle leads to left ventricular hypertrophy and systolic dysfunction with a lowered ejection fraction.

- In **mitral stenosis (MS)**, blood flow from the left atrium to the left ventricle is impeded, resulting in an enlarged atrium.

  - Almost all cases of mitral stenosis are caused by rheumatic heart disease, with most patients showing symptoms $\geq$ 15 years after the initial infection.

- **Mitral regurgitation (MR)** occurs when the blood flows backward from the left ventricle to the left atrium.

  - This backward flow increases the preload and decreases the afterload.

- Aortic and mitral valve disease presents with symptoms and physical findings similar to HF; they include dyspnea, exercise intolerance, angina, and dizziness or syncope.

- Symptomatic patients will require surgical valve repair or replacement (e.g., transcatheter aortic valve replacement).

HELPFUL HINT

Diuretics, beta blockers, and vasodilators should be avoided in patients with AS because they can worsen symptoms.

QUICK REVIEW QUESTION

34. What heart sound is associated with aortic stenosis?

1. The nurse should tell the patient that some lifestyle choices can slow the progression of atherosclerosis. Topics to discuss with the patient include a healthy diet and exercise regimen, smoking cessation, and the management of dyslipidemia.

2. The nurse should explain that a blood glucose result gives an accurate representation of the blood sugar at that specific moment but an HgbA1C result shows how well controlled the blood sugar has been over approximately 3 months. Therefore, the best way to determine compliance and the plan of care is based on the HgbA1C result.

3. The nurse should inform the patient that diet is only one risk factor for dyslipidemia. Lack of exercise or a sedentary lifestyle, along with smoking or excessive alcohol use, can also contribute to dyslipidemia. Additionally, some individuals have a genetic predisposition for dyslipidemia and may have elevated cholesterol levels even with regular exercise and a healthy diet.

4. The nurse should make sure that the correct cuff size is being used and should check the blood pressure a second time, preferably on the opposite arm unless contraindicated. The nurse can also inform the patient that a diagnosis of hypertension must be made after 2 separate elevated blood pressures are confirmed on 2 separate days.

5. The nurse should provide the patient with educational materials on how to build a healthy diet. The patient should be encouraged to try a diet low in fat and red meat and high in fruits, vegetables, lean protein, and fiber. The nurse should also tell the patient that reducing sodium intake can help lower blood pressure.

6. The main priority for this patient is obtaining a 12-lead ECG to rule out a STEMI. Additional priorities include obtaining labs, specifically a troponin and electrolyte panel; monitoring the patient's vital signs; applying oxygen if the person is hypoxic; and placing the patient on telemetry to continuously monitor cardiac rhythm.

7. The nurse should explain that an AAA that remains at 4 cm has a low risk of rupture and does not need surgical intervention. The medical provider will likely recommend surgical repair if the aneurysm grows to > 5 cm or if it begins to enlarge rapidly.

8. The nurse should explain that the plaque within the carotid artery can become dislodged and travel through the vessels to the brain, where pieces of plaque can block blood vessels. This blockage prevents blood flow to the brain, causing a stroke.

9. The patient with CVI should follow a low-sodium, high-fiber diet to reduce fluid buildup.

10. Patients with DVT and dyspnea should immediately have a CT scan ordered to rule out a PE. A PE is an emergent condition that needs immediate treatment.

11. The nurse should ensure strict bedrest and make sure that the affected extremity is kept straight. The nurse should also assess the site frequently and notify the physician for bleeding, coldness, increased pain, or decreased pulse. NPO status should be initiated 8 hours before reevaluation.

12. Digoxin is contradicted with HCM, as the medication is a positive inotropic and can reduce LV filling and increase obstruction of the left ventricular outflow tract. The medication should be verified with the patient, and the admitting physician should be notified immediately.

13. The nursing priority is to manage complications from the stroke (especially hypertension, ICP, and seizures) and to prepare the patient for possible surgery.

14. The nurse should prioritize preparing the patient for an immediate CT scan to rule out a hemorrhagic stroke and to see if the patient meets the criteria for tPA administration.

The nurse should also assess the patient's neurological deficits using the NIHSS. The patient's blood pressure and heart rhythm should also be closely monitored.

15. The nurse should explain that the hole between the atria allows oxygenated blood to flow back into the right atrium. The increased blood volume in the right atrium causes the muscles of the heart to enlarge. While the child has no symptoms now, an enlarged heart will eventually lead to dysrhythmias and heart failure when the child is an adult. Closing the hole early allows the heart muscle to regain normal size and prevents future symptoms.

16. This patient is hemodynamically unstable because of bradycardia. The nurse should prepare to push IV atropine.

17. If the patient in SVT does not respond to vagal maneuvers, the patient will likely be administered 6 mg of adenosine to terminate the dysrhythmia.

18. The nurse should expect a hemodynamically stable patient with A-fib to receive calcium channel blockers, beta blockers, or cardiac glycosides to decrease the heart rate.

19. After 2 defibrillation attempts and the first dose of epinephrine has been given, the nurse should prepare the first dose of amiodarone (300 mg) to be given next.

20. The nurse should activate the code team and begin high-quality compressions immediately. (CPR should not be delayed to administer epinephrine.)

21. A BNP lab value of > 100 pg/mL indicates HF.

22. After confirming that the BP reflects a hypertensive crisis, the nurse should administer an antihypertensive medication but should aim for a reduction of no more than 25% within the first 2 hours.

23. The nurse should expect orders to get an ECG and draw labs to monitor the patient's WBC count, sedimentation rate, and C-reactive protein and to collect at least 2 sets of blood cultures. The nurse should also expect to administer antibiotics after the blood cultures have been drawn.

24. The nurse should prepare the patient for TCP. Dopamine and epinephrine may be appropriate medications to administer for a third-degree block as they will increase the overall heart rate.

25. The nurse should explain that the absence of symptoms does not mean that underlying conditions are gone. Without the pacemaker, the patient risks developing additional dysrhythmias or could go into sudden cardiac arrest without warning.

26. Digoxin, often administered for treatment of HF, has a narrow therapeutic index. Digoxin toxicity may manifest itself as an LBBB. Labs would need to be drawn to assess for digoxin toxicity.

27. There is a strong association between antipsychotic medication use and torsades de pointes in patients with prolonged QT. The patient may have been administered haloperidol, which is one of the most commonly used medications in the ICU associated with torsades de pointes.

28. The nurse should obtain a 12-lead ECG and then have the patient sit up and lean forward, a position that can help reduce the pain. The nurse can also administer an NSAID such as ibuprofen or indomethacin to assist with pain control and reduce inflammation.

29. Because of the patient's dysrhythmia and the presented symptoms, pulmonary edema should be suspected. Confirmation through a chest X-ray will reveal anomalies, especially pleural effusions and basal congestion due to accumulation of fluid within the alveolar space.

30. The nurse should explain that sildenafil (Viagra) can be used to treat erectile dysfunction but that it is also used to treat PAH because it relaxes and widens the blood vessels within the lungs, which allows for better activity tolerance.

31. A patient with RHD will have a history of untreated rheumatic fever and usually will have had untreated strep throat. The patient will also show symptoms and physical findings related to valve dysfunction, including fatigue, dyspnea, and regurgitation murmurs.

32. Cardiogenic shock is characterized by symptoms and physical findings of hypoperfusion combined with a systolic BP of < 90 mm Hg, a CI of < 2.2 L/min/m^2, and a normal or elevated PAOP (> 15 mm Hg).

33. The nurse should expect to provide IV fluids or blood products to the patient and to prepare the patient to return to the operating theater.

34. In aortic stenosis, an S4 heart sound may be heard. This extra heart sound, heard before S1, is caused by the atrial contraction of blood into a noncompliant ventricle.

SIX: PLANNING, IMPLEMENTATION, and OUTCOME EVALUATION

Developing an Individualized Plan of Care

- A **nursing care plan** is a comprehensive overview of a patient's condition and required nursing care.

- The cardiac vascular nurse is responsible for initiating and updating the plan of care for patients from arrival through discharge.

- The **ADPIE model** is used to develop nursing care plans.

    - **Assessment**: gather data about the client's physiological, psychological, and emotional condition

    - **Diagnosis**: use clinical judgment to identify the patient's condition and medical needs

        - **NANDA-I diagnoses**: guide clinical care planning for patients under the care of the cardiac vascular nurse

        - While it is not in the cardiac vascular nurse's scope of practice to diagnose a specific disease or ailment, it is within the scope to identify a general cause of symptoms. For example, a patient with congestive heart failure may have shortness of breath, fatigue, and swelling. The cardiac vascular nurse would choose NANDA-I diagnoses related to those symptoms, such as decreased CO.

    - **Planning**: set measurable goals and outcomes for the patient and identify nursing interventions aimed to meet them

    - **Intervention**: implement the care plan

        - The nurse's role in the implementation phase may include both oversight of and action on interventions.

    - **Evaluation**: determine if the goals and outcomes from the planning stage have been achieved

        - Care and outcomes should be continuously monitored, and the care plan should be modified per the patient response.

- **Concept mapping** is a way of organizing and planning the course of the patient's care. It is a visual tool that addresses each element of the ADPIE and provides a path to outcomes assessment.
- **Discharge planning** is the process of planning for the patient's exit from the health care facility.
  - begins when a patient is admitted to an inpatient, rehab, procedural, or surgical setting
  - considers the patient's ability to care for themselves independently, medical equipment or care needed in the home, referrals, available social support, and available community resources
  - includes **discharge teaching** relevant to the patient's care plan
- Patient education, including health promotion and lifestyle changes, should be included in the care plan and is a key responsibility of the cardiac vascular nurse. (See chapter 7, "Education and Health Promotion," for more information on patient education.)
- **Nursing diagnoses** should be prioritized with consideration for Maslow's hierarchy of needs. (Most nursing diagnoses will fall in the first two levels of the hierarchy.) The needs, in order of importance, are as follows:
  - physiological needs: food, water, rest, health
  - safety: security of body, security of resources
  - love and belonging: friendship, intimacy, family
  - esteem: feelings of accomplishment
  - self-actualization: achieving one's full potential
- Cardiac vascular nursing requires critical thinking and prioritization to meet a patient's needs based on severity of symptoms or potential for harm.
  - planning includes triaging the patient's clinical presentation of diagnoses from those with the most potential to cause harm to those with the least
  - top priority: manage or prevent the occurrence of life-threatening symptoms
  - sources of potential harm that should be addressed as high priority include:
    - symptomatic dysrhythmias
    - decreased O_2 levels
    - lack of palpable or Doppler pulses
    - acute changes in patient's pain level
    - acute changes in blood glucose level
    - changes from baseline in critical labs

QUICK REVIEW QUESTION

1. The nurse is reviewing the care plan for a patient with congestive HF who is currently on BiPAP for fluid volume overload. The patient's labs return with a potassium of 2.9 mEq/L. The patient's morning medications are due, and the nurse is also being called by another patient who requires insulin before eating breakfast. What is the nurse's priority?

Coordinating Care Across the Continuum

- The cardiac vascular nurse is a member of an **interdisciplinary health care team**, which includes health care providers from different fields who work together to provide care for the patient.

- The members of a patient's health care team largely depend on the client's chief complaint, diagnosis, and treatment goals. Generally, the team will include the following:

  - physician: may be an internist, family practitioner, or cardiologist (depends on the organization); provides a medical diagnosis and contributes to the plan of care

  - CV nurse: contributes to the plan of care for the patient, the management of the patient's disease, and discharge planning

  - technicians/aides: act under the delegated authority of the physician and the nurse. Other technicians that may participate in the care of the cardiac patient include echocardiography technicians, radiological technicians, or ultrasound technicians.

  - case manager: responsible for coordinating care throughout the patient's stay and beyond; a key player in the discharge planning process

  - social worker: may participate on the care team if patient support needed (e.g., counseling, meal services) after inpatient care

- The goal of **care coordination** is to achieve safe, effective care through the deliberate organization of patient care activities within the interdisciplinary health care team. Some examples of care coordination include:

  - sharing knowledge within the health care team

  - managing care transitions

  - aligning resources with patients' medical, emotional, and social needs

  - setting patients up with community resources

- As the member of the health care team that spends the most one-on-one time with the patient, the cardiac vascular nurse is a key component of successful care coordination.

- Care coordination can significantly impact the efficacy and economics of health care.

  - Patients who receive high-quality care coordination have better health outcomes: they are less likely to miss follow-up appointments and less likely to be re-hospitalized.

  - Care coordination ensures that resources are being efficiently allocated and can minimize the cost of care for the patient and health care provider.

  - Care coordination ensures that the standard of care is met for every patient, which is necessary for some insurance reimbursements.

2. A patient who requires an ongoing milrinone infusion is being discharged. What are some considerations and services that must be in place before the patient leaves the facility?

Creating a Safe and Therapeutic Environment

- Cardiac vascular nurses are responsible for creating a safe, therapeutic environment that minimizes the risk of physical and emotional harm to the patient.

- **Patient safety** is the responsibility of each member of the interdisciplinary team. Considerations for patient safety that are the specific responsibility of the CV nurse include:

  ○ Preventing **medication errors**: These errors are more common in emergency situations or resuscitation efforts, which can occur regularly in cardiac care units. Drills and practice in these situations will increase nurses' confidence and efficiency in administering emergency drugs.

  ○ Preventing **falls**: Patients receiving cardiac care are often at high risk of falling. Communication with the patient, provision of call lights, and hourly rounding are good ways to mitigate the risk of patient falls.

  ○ **Communicating** effectively: The CV nurse is responsible for clearly and promptly communicating information about changes in the patient's condition to other members of the health care team.

  ○ Following **protocols**: The CV nurse should know and follow the protocols for their unit.

- **Environment of care** refers to the environment in which care is provided to patients. Nurses are part of the interdisciplinary team responsible for maintaining the safety within the environment of care.

  ○ **Inpatient care** settings are those in which a patient remains hospitalized for at least one day. Inpatient care settings often house patients with complex medical issues that have a high risk of complications.

  ○ **Procedural care** environments are where patients receive same-day procedures and are then discharged to their home. Nurses are responsible for providing clear, accurate, and comprehensive discharge instructions to the patient to prevent post-procedure complications.

  ○ **Surgical care** settings are those in which patients receive operative procedures that require them to remain as an inpatient. Safety concerns for CV nurses in a surgical setting include wrong-site surgeries, infection prevention, DVT prevention, and reactions to anesthetic agents.

  ○ **Rehabilitation** environments are often designed to more closely resemble the home environment, presenting unique safety concerns. Rehabilitation environments often house patients that are considered high risk for falls, infection, and pressure ulcers.

- The cardiac vascular nurse is responsible for identifying the severity and nature of the safety risks for each patient and initiating appropriate interventions within the plan of care to mitigate the risks.

- The **therapeutic environment** refers to the physical, psychological, and social environments in which patients receive care.

- Different patients require different therapeutic considerations, and the nurse is responsible for determining the patient's needs.

- The CV nurse's goal is to create a therapeutic environment that is physically and emotionally healing. This environment should:
  - support and practice excellence in treating the patient
  - have positive, measurable patient outcomes
  - have positive staff effectiveness
  - anticipate and support the patient's psychosocial and spiritual needs
  - anticipate the family's needs

QUICK REVIEW QUESTION

3. The nurse is caring for a patient who is admitted to the telemetry unit. The patient discloses that he has fallen several times at home before admission. What safety interventions should the nurse include in this patient's care plan?

Changes in Patient Condition

- The CV nurse is responsible for monitoring patients for acute changes in condition and communicating these changes to the appropriate member of the health care team.

- The CV nurse must know how to recognize changes in the patient's condition, no matter how minute, and react accordingly. Failure to do so can result in harm of the patient.

- Communication of changes in a patient's condition will depend on the acuity and level of concern related to the change in condition.
  - Improvement in patient condition requires an update of the plan of care. The provider should be notified so they can re-evaluate the care and discharge plans.
  - A decline in the patient's status requires rapid and precise communication to the provider using the SBAR method (see chapter 8).

- CV nurses should be continually assessing patients based on their needs. These assessments may include:
  - ongoing assessment of patient condition
  - re-assessment after intervention
  - continuous cardiac monitoring and telemetry

- Examples of changes in patient condition that require immediate communication to the provider may include:
  - ECG changes (changes from the baseline measurement such as STEMI/ NSTEMI)
  - respiratory distress or arrest
  - cardiac arrest
  - acute changes in mental status
  - new onset of chest pain
  - diaphoresis and nausea
  - vital signs changes of 20% from baseline

QUICK REVIEW QUESTION

4. A cardiac vascular nurse is caring for a patient on continuous cardiac monitoring in the CV unit. He notices the patient's heart rhythm has changed to SVT with a rate of 210 bpm. The patient's current medication has had no effect. What action should the nurse take next?

Outcomes Evaluations

- An **outcome** is a change in a patient's status. Outcomes are used to evaluate the effect of an intervention or nursing practice on a patient.
- Outcomes should be developed based on the care plan, the patient's needs, and the health care team's goals for the patient.
- Outcomes should be SMART:
  - Specific
  - Measurable
  - Attainable
  - Realistic
  - Time-restricted
- Common patient outcomes include:
  - objective data (e.g., blood pressure, blood sugar)
  - symptoms (e.g., dizziness, pain)
  - functional status (e.g., ADLs, employment)
  - lifestyle factors (e.g., diet, exercise)
- If the patient cannot maintain the interventions required for an outcome, then the nurse should modify the outcome so that the patient can sustain it.
- In an inpatient setting, plans of care are evaluated twice or more per day. The care plan is updated at every shift, when outcomes are met, or when goals change.

- Professional associations, both medical and nursing, have prepared evidence-based guidelines for care of certain patient populations. These associations include:
  - American Heart Association (AHA)
  - American Association of Cardiovascular and Pulmonary Rehabilitation (AACVPR)
  - Society for Vascular Nursing (SVN)
  - Joint National Committee on Prevention, Detection, Evaluation, and Treatment of High Blood Pressure (JNC)
  - National Heart, Lung, and Blood Institute (NHLBI)
  - National Institutes of Health (NIH)

Situation	A patient comes to the hospital with high blood pressure. He is a smoker and does not eat well or exercise.
Nursing diagnosis	decreased cardiac output r/t hypertension
Outcomes/SMART goals	<ul><li>The patient's SBP and DP will be maintained within a range of 110/75 to 130/90 per protocol and physician's orders.</li><li>The patient will verbalize the importance of smoking cessation by day 2.</li><li>The patient will verbalize the importance of following up with a cardiologist in 1 week.</li><li>The patient will demonstrate the ability to select a lunch that complies with a cardiac diet by day 3.</li><li>The patient will verbalize how exercise affects the body by day 3.</li></ul>
Nursing interventions	The nurse will assess the patient's blood pressure at least hourly or per unit protocol, administer ordered medication, and titrate drips as needed to maintain range. The nurse will educate the patient on hypertension and its effects on the body by day 2. The nurse will assist the patient in selecting appropriate foods for a cardiac diet by day 3. The nurse will assist the patient in obtaining smoking cessation materials by day 2.

Figure 6.1. Example Care Plan With Outcomes

QUICK REVIEW QUESTION

5. A cardiac vascular nurse is caring for a patient with the nursing diagnosis of acute pain related to myocardial ischemia. What are some possible outcomes the nurse could include in the care plan for this patient?

1. The nurse should focus on the patient that requires BiPAP, as this patient has a higher potential for serious harm. The nurse should review the patient's medications for any that would be potassium wasting (e.g., furosemide [Lasix]) which would be an expected treatment for this patient population. Unless contraindicated, morning medications should be administered followed by a call to the physician for further orders on holding diuretics and/or potassium replacement therapy.

2. Care coordination outside the facility must be in place. An assessment of the patient's ongoing access to care and medications will identify any needed interventions before the patient goes home. The nurse should ensure that future visits with the primary care physician and follow-up with cardiology are arranged. The patient will need home infusion equipment at discharge and have an appointment scheduled with the visiting infusion nurse. The patient and family should be given resources and contacts to ensure that they know what to do in case of any complications.

3. The nurse should consider the patient a high fall risk and update the plan of care to reflect the risk for falls. Appropriate safety interventions include initiating fall precautions, notifying the health care team, clearing the room of any obstacles, and discussing fall risk education with the patient.

4. The nurse should contact the cardiologist and prepare to intervene appropriately based on the patient's condition, which may include a 12-lead ECG, administration of adenosine, or direct current cardioversion.

5. Possible outcomes for this diagnosis include: the patient will report a decrease in chest pain at less than 3/10 on the pain scale, serial troponins will be drawn every 6 hours a total of 3 times with abnormal values reported to the cardiologist, systolic BP will remain between 110 and 130 for the duration of the patient's stay.

SEVEN: 7 EDUCATION and HEALTH PROMOTION

The Learning Process
CHARACTERISTICS OF ADULT LEARNERS

- Adult learners have several distinct traits that cardiac vascular nurses should consider while developing patient education plans.

  - Adult learners are **independent** and **self-directed**. Nurses should actively engage them in the learning process and encourage them to help develop their health plans.

  - Adult learners are **results-oriented** and **practical**. Nurses should give them information that they can apply immediately.

  - Adult learners may be **resistant to change** and will require justification for new behaviors.

  - Adult learners may **learn more slowly** than younger learners. However, they may be more skilled at integrating new knowledge with previous experience.

- Psychologist Benjamin Bloom described three domains of learning:

  - The **cognitive domain** includes collecting, synthesizing, and applying knowledge.

  - The **affective domain** involves emotions and attitudes, including the ability to be aware of emotions and to respond to them.

  - The **psychomotor** domain relates to motor skills, including the ability to perform complex skills and create new movement patterns.

- The "knowledge, skills, and attitude" discussed in nursing education align with the three learning domains: **knowledge** is cognitive learning, **skills** are psychomotor learning, and **attitude** is affective learning.

- Patient education plans should address all three learning domains. For example, a patient who is learning about smoking cessation may need to be taught about the negative health impacts of smoking (cognitive domain), how to manage negative emotions related to quitting (affective domain), and how to correctly apply a nicotine patch (psychomotor domain).

- A person's **learning style** is their preferred method of receiving new information.
  - **Visual** learners do best with pictures, diagrams, and modeling.
  - **Auditory** learners should be taught using spoken language, mnemonic devices, and music.
  - **Kinesthetic** (physical) learners should be taught using bodily motion.
  - **Social** learners learn best when interacting with other people.
  - **Solitary** learners prefer to learn on their own.

QUICK REVIEW QUESTION

1. A nurse is teaching a patient how to take their own blood pressure. While the patient is trying to apply the cuff, the nurse asks the patient to state their target blood pressure range. The patient becomes visibly frustrated and claims to not know. How can the nurse's teaching style meet this patient's needs?

HEALTH LITERACY

- **Health literacy** is the degree to which an individual has the ability to obtain, process, and understand basic health information needed to make personal health decisions.

- A patient's health literacy depends on many factors, including:
  - communication skills and ability
  - cultural considerations
  - knowledge of health topics
  - situation or context of the information delivery

- Health literacy has a critical impact on the delivery of health care and educational initiatives.

- Health literacy is measured as one of the components of the National Assessment of Adult Literacy.
  - The assessment categorizes people's health literacy as Below Basic, Basic, Intermediate, and Proficient.
  - Only a small percentage of adults in the United States have proficient health literacy, meaning they have the knowledge and skills to effectively manage their health.

- The US Department of Education's National Center for Education Statistics reports that the following populations are vulnerable to poor health literacy:
  - people > 65
  - minorities
  - people with mental illness
  - immigrants
  - people with low incomes

- Health care providers who are communicating with patients through speaking or writing should consider the patient's level of health literacy.
  - Health literacy assessments include the Rapid Estimate of Adult Literacy in Medicine (REALM), the Test of Functional Health Literacy in Adults (TOFHLA), and the Newest Vital Sign (NVS) screening tool.
  - Nurses should use available tools to measure the reading level of print material.
- Interventions for patients with low health literacy include:
  - asking patients questions to assess their current knowledge
  - using plain language and short sentences
  - limiting important points to three or fewer
  - using teach-backs to confirm the patient's understanding (see "Patient Education Strategies")
  - using visual materials such as videos or models
  - discussing issues in terms of short time spans (< 10 years)
  - being consistent when discussing numeric values (e.g., units, risk, dosage)
  - simplifying procedures and regimens as much as possible

HELPFUL HINT
Patient health literacy improves as patients become more involved in their own care.

QUICK REVIEW QUESTION

2. A nurse is meeting with a clinic patient who was recently diagnosed with hypertension and hyperlipidemia. During the interview, the nurse discovers that the patient is confused by the medication labels and so has not been taking the medications. What can the nurse do to help this patient adhere to the medication regimen?

CONDITIONS FOR LEARNING

- Patients' willingness and ability to learn depend on their motivation, readiness, and functional status.
- **Motivation** is the driving force behind people's actions.
- The cardiac vascular nurse should assess patients' source of motivation in the context of managing their health in order to better educate, encourage, and advocate for them.
  - **Intrinsic motivation** is the desire to achieve a goal, seek challenges, or complete a task that is driven by enjoyment and personal satisfaction (e.g., exercising because it is enjoyable).
  - **Extrinsic motivation** is the desire to accomplish a goal that is driven by external rewards or punishment (e.g., exercising to prevent cardiac vascular disease).
  - Patients with an **external locus of control** will attribute their success or failure to outside forces.
  - Patients with an **internal locus of control** will attribute their success or failure to themselves.

- Patients' **readiness to learn** can be shaped by many factors, including:
    - openness to new information
    - emotional response to illness (e.g., denial, anxiety)
    - religious and cultural beliefs
    - social support systems
- Assessing patients' readiness to learn will allow the cardiac vascular nurse to deliver educational information to patients when they will be most receptive.
- Patients' **functional status**—their ability to perform basic cognitive and physical tasks—will affect their ability to learn.
    - Patients with **physical impairments** may lack the strength, coordination, or sensory abilities to learn new skills.
    - **Cognitive impairments** may disrupt patients' ability to process new knowledge and maintain emotional stability.
- Functional status can be measured by assessing patients' ability to perform daily activities:
    - **activities of daily living (ADLs)**: personal care activities such as toileting, bathing, dressing, and eating
    - **instrumental activities of daily living (IADLs)**: activities necessary for independent living such as shopping and doing housework
- The cardiac vascular nurse must assess the functional status of a patient before developing an education plan for that patient. Doing so ensures that the plan aligns with the patient's abilities and capacity to learn.

QUICK REVIEW QUESTION

3. A nursing student asks a cardiac vascular nurse why she became a nurse. The nurse replies that she truly enjoys helping people and finds the medical field fascinating. What type of motivation does the nurse have?

PATIENT EDUCATION STRATEGIES

- Strategies for teaching include the following:
    - **Lectures** (groups or one-on-one) are effective for conveying cognitive knowledge, particularly to auditory learners.
    - **Group discussions** in which patients can ask questions are effective for social learners and can help with affective learning (e.g., changing attitudes).
    - **Role-playing** is a good way to teach affective skills (e.g., responding to peer pressure).
    - **Demonstrations** or modeling are useful for teaching psychomotor skills.
    - **Instructional materials** such as films or pamphlets may be used as part of a larger education plan. However, they may be ineffective if patients are disengaged or the material does not match patients' needs and learning abilities.

- Strategies for assessing patient understanding include the following:
  - During a **teach-back**, patients state what they've learned in their own words. These are often used at discharge but can be used while teaching as an ongoing measure of patient understanding.
  - **Oral** or **written tests** may be used to measure patient understanding, but many patients find these intimidating.
- Some specific strategies to engage patients and families in the learning process include the following:
  - Link new information to current behavior; new learning is better received when it focuses on what the patient already knows.
  - Be clear, explicit, and specific when speaking with patients.
  - Involve other health providers (e.g., dieticians) to engage patients and reinforce learning.
- Use technology to engage patients and connect them to providers and support communities.
  - **Webinars** or **live events** are often available in the community and are geared toward specific patient populations (e.g., parents).
  - Patients can often find support groups for specific conditions on **social media**. Nurses should caution patients to join such groups for support, not medical advice.
  - Nurses should instruct patients on how to use **patient care interfaces** if they are available. These allow patients to send secure messages to providers and receive timely replies to questions.

QUICK REVIEW QUESTION

4. A 50-year-old patient with cardiac vascular disease attends a group class on self-management of hypertension. The nurse notices that the patient is not participating in the group session. What can the nurse do to better meet the patient's needs?

Education Plans
COMPONENTS OF AN EDUCATION PLAN

- The cardiac vascular nurse should develop an **education plan** tailored to the learning needs of each patient.
- Patient education plans should be comprehensive and adaptable to patients' changing needs.
- Education plans should address the following topics:
  - procedures
  - risk factor modification
  - disease management
  - health promotion

- **Procedural education** should be included if a patient is going to or already has undergone a procedure that they will have to recover from. Such education should include:
  - details about the procedure
  - what the patient can expect after the procedure
  - the responsibilities of the patient in their own care after the procedure
- **Risk factor modification** should be included when a patient needs to make lifestyle changes to promote healthy outcomes, such as smoking cessation or following a restricted diet.
- **Disease management education** should focus on the patient's role in managing their chronic condition. Topics may include:
  - knowledge of the disease process
  - management of disease symptoms
  - diet and exercise recommendations
  - medication administration
  - management of medication side effects
- **Health promotion education** includes ways that patients can prevent deterioration in their health, including diet, exercise, and managing stress.

QUICK REVIEW QUESTION

5. The cardiac vascular nurse is providing patient education after a patient returns from a percutaneous transluminal coronary angioplasty (PTCA) procedure. The patient appears anxious. What should the nurse include in the teaching plan?

DEVELOPING TEACHING OBJECTIVES

- **Objectives** or expected outcomes are short-term outcomes that support a long-term goal.
- Every education plan should have measurable objectives that allow the cardiac-vascular nurse to identify a patient's ongoing needs and gauge the success of the education plan.
- Objectives can address cognitive, affective, or psychomotor knowledge and skills.
- Both the nurse and the patient should understand how the objective will be measured (e.g., teach-back, verbalization of understanding, compliance with the care plan).
- Measurable objectives in patient education must address the ultimate goals of the educational activity or plan. Possible goals fall into several broad categories:
  - increasing the patient's knowledge and skills
  - increasing adherence to or effectiveness of treatment
  - increasing self-efficacy and self-management
  - reducing physical morbidity and risk of mortality

- reducing stress and anxiety
- enhancing self-esteem and decision-making capacity
- improving quality of life
- Objectives should explicitly state:
  - **what** the patient will do
  - **how** it will be measured
  - **when** it should be accomplished
- Some examples of specific measurable objectives are:
  - The patient will be able to demonstrate how to take their blood pressure prior to discharge.
  - The patient will be able to verbalize how much weight gain to report to their provider one day before discharge.
  - The patient will be able to identify three signs and symptoms of heart failure to monitor for and report to their provider by the end of the shift.

QUICK REVIEW QUESTION

6. A cardiac vascular nurse is preparing an education plan for a patient recently diagnosed with congestive heart failure who will need to measure their weight daily at home. One of the nurse's teaching objectives is for the patient to be able to use a scale accurately by discharge. Which elements should the nurse include in the education plan to help the patient meet this objective?

Population Health

RISK MANAGEMENT

- **Cardiac risk factors** may lead to development of cardiac vascular diseases.
- **Modifiable risk factors** can be controlled by the patient with healthy lifestyle changes and decisions. (See chapter 5 for more information on managing modifiable risk factors.)
- Modifiable risk factors include:
  - smoking
  - diet
  - exercise
  - cholesterol levels
  - hypertension
  - diabetes
- **Non-modifiable risk factors** cannot be controlled by the patient.
- Non-modifiable risk factors include:
  - **Race:** Non-Hispanic blacks have higher rates of cardiac vascular disease (particularly hypertension) and higher age-adjusted mortality rates. Native

Americans/Alaskan Natives also die from cardiac vascular disease at a much younger age than other populations.

- ○ **Gender:** Heart disease (including MI, heart failure, and other cardiac-vascular conditions) is the leading cause of death for both men and women. However, onset of cardiac vascular diseases in women occurs on average about 10 years later than in men.

- ○ **Age:** People aged 65 or older are at greater risk of dying from cardiac-vascular disease.

- ○ **Family history:** Cardiac risk increases in patients with first-degree family members who developed cardiac vascular disease early in life.

- A patient's risk of cardiac vascular disease is usually calculated as a 10-year risk or a lifetime risk.

  - ○ A 10-year risk > 20% is classified as high-risk, and < 5% is classified as low-risk.

  - ○ High-risk patients are treated aggressively, even if they have not had a cardiac event.

  - ○ Low-risk patients are monitored and educated on disease prevention.

  - ○ Treatment guidelines vary for patients at intermediate risk.

  - ○ The American College of Cardiology (ACC) website includes a calculator for estimating cardiac risk based on specific patient characteristics (https://tools.acc.org/ASCVD-Risk-Estimator-Plus/).

  - ○ Calculators based on the Framingham Heart Study are also available.

- The level of prevention is based on the level of cardiac vascular disease.

  - ○ **Primary prevention** aims to prevent the occurrence of disease (e.g., smoking cessation, maintaining a healthy diet).

  - ○ **Secondary prevention** is the early identification of disease (often before symptoms appear) to alter the disease process (e.g., management of hypertension before a cardiac event occurs).

  - ○ **Tertiary prevention** is treatment of disease to mitigate further harm (e.g., cardiac rehabilitation after an MI).

QUICK REVIEW QUESTION

7. A cardiac vascular nurse is planning to discharge a 68-year-old obese patient newly diagnosed with PVD. The patient states, "Since I have the nicotine patch, I can still occasionally smoke if I remove it." What modifiable and non-modifiable risk factors should the nurse review with the patient?

HEALTH AGENCIES AND COMMUNITY RESOURCES

- The cardiac vascular nurse should be knowledgeable about community resources available to patients.

- The nurse may also partner with providers of community resources to ensure the most up-to-date information is available and provided to patients.

- **Cardiac rehabilitation** programs are available for qualified patients who need intensive outpatient follow-up for behavior modification and disease management. Cardiac rehabilitation has three phases:
  - Phase I occurs in the hospital and includes referrals, assessment of exercise capability, and education.
  - Phase II occurs in an outpatient setting and includes education about lifestyle changes along with monitored exercise.
  - Phase III also occurs in an outpatient setting. Patient education continues, and exercise is supervised but not monitored.
- **Mobile clinics** are available in rural or other areas that have limited access to cardiac care.
- **Home health services** are available to qualified patients with a medical necessity for home health visits.
- **Telehealth services** can increase access to care for patients in underserved areas. They may also be used with patients who require frequent monitoring (e.g., patients with heart failure).
- **Faith community nurses** are specialty practitioners who integrate spiritual care with medical treatment. They are usually attached to a specific church or religious organization and provide services such as screenings, referrals, and education.
- **Navigators** are cardiac vascular nurses who assist patients with the transition from the hospital to the home. These nurses also assist patients with self-care related to their disease process.

QUICK REVIEW QUESTION

8. An 80-year old patient with cardiac vascular disease is scheduled to attend cardiac rehabilitation. What should the cardiac vascular nurse tell the patient will be included in the rehabilitation program?

HEALTH PROMOTION AND DISEASE PREVENTION STRATEGIES

- The US Office of Disease Prevention and Health Promotion creates 10-year objectives—Healthy People initiatives—for improving the health of Americans.
- **Healthy People 2020** aims to reduce death from heart disease and stroke by focusing on:
  - management of hypertension and dyslipidemia
  - improved patient education on symptoms and response to MI and stroke
  - increased use of prophylactic aspirin
  - increasing the proportion of patients who receive artery-opening therapy
- A complete list of cardiac vascular and stroke objectives for Healthy People 2020 can be found at https://www.healthypeople.gov/2020/topics-objectives/topic/heart-disease-and-stroke/objectives.

- Healthy People 2020 also provides an up-to-date repository of evidence-based practice in the care of the cardiac vascular patient.

- Many communities and health care organizations arrange educational activities to increase community knowledge and understanding of cardiac vascular disease.

  ○ **Health fairs** are events that provide education and health care products to community members. They are often held at offices, churches, or schools, and may be part of a partnership with local health care providers.

  ○ Health fairs may offer **screenings** to identify health risk in asymptomatic patients. Screenings may include blood pressure, weight, BMI, cholesterol, and A1C.

QUICK REVIEW QUESTION

9. One of the Healthy People 2020 objectives is to increase the number of people who have had their blood cholesterol checked within how many preceding years?

ANSWER KEY

1. Psychomotor skills require concentration. When the nurse asked the patient about a BP target while the patient was trying to apply the cuff, the nurse disturbed the patient's focus on this skill. The nurse should help the patient learn to apply the cuff, and once that skill has been mastered, the nurse can ask questions from the cognitive domain.

2. The nurse should develop an education plan to help the patient better understand how to manage the medications. The nurse might use models or visual aids to teach the patient how to read the medication labels or could suggest that the patient use aids such as pillboxes or calendar alerts. The nurse might also work with the patient and provider to simplify the medication regimen and align it with the patient's current schedule.

3. The nurse is intrinsically motivated—she is doing something that is personally rewarding.

4. The nurse should determine why the patient is not engaging in the group discussion and then develop a new education strategy. For example, if the patient is uncomfortable in social settings, the nurse could suggest a webinar. If the patient lacks the foundational knowledge necessary to actively participate in a group discussion, the nurse could provide one-on-one teaching. The nurse should also consider the possibility that the patient's functional status prevents active participation and provide necessary accommodations.

5. To reduce the patient's anxiety, the nurse should explain that he is being monitored after the procedure. The nurse should say something like, "We will be checking your vital signs and heart rhythm frequently to assess for any changes." The nurse should not give the patient false reassurance or provide results of the procedure.

6. The nurse should demonstrate how to use the scale the patient will have at home and ask for a return demonstration. The nurse should ensure the patient understands what information is needed each day and where to find that information on the scale. The patient should also be given a point of contact for questions or for troubleshooting equipment if necessary.

7. The nurse should educate the patient on several risk factors for a cardiac event. The patient's age is non-modifiable, but other risks, including weight and smoking, are modifiable and can contribute to the management of PVD. The patient education plan should include information on smoking cessation, a healthy diet, and exercise, as well as how to effectively manage PVD.

8. Cardiac rehabilitation includes exercise counseling and training, managing dietary changes that need to be made, and stress reduction techniques.

9. Objective HDS-6 is to "increase the proportion of adults who have had their blood cholesterol checked within the preceding 5 years."

EIGHT: PROFESSIONAL ROLE

Communication
COMPONENTS OF COMMUNICATION

- **Therapeutic communication** is a set of communication techniques that address the physical, mental, and emotional well-being of patients.

- Therapeutic communication used should be tailored to the situation or context. The cardiac vascular nurse should consider the patient's age, language, any barriers to communication, and the nature of the information being communicated.

Table 8.1. Dos and Don'ts of Patient Communication

Do	Don't
Make eye contact with the patient	
Introduce yourself and use the patient's name	Use medical jargon
Speak directly to the patient when possible	Threaten or intimidate the patient
Ask open-ended questions	Lie or provide false hope
Speak slowly and clearly	Interrupt the patient
Show empathy for the patient	Show frustration or anger
Be silent when appropriate to allow patients time to think and process emotions	Make judgmental statements

- Some techniques used for therapeutic communication include the following:
  - **Active listening** includes facing the client, being attentive to what they are saying, and maintaining eye contact if culturally appropriate.
  - **Sharing observations** may open the conversation up to how the patient is feeling.
  - **Empathy**, or trying to understand and accurately perceive the patient's feelings and experiences, can make the patient more comfortable.

- o **Using touch**, such as a gentle hand on the shoulder or arm, when appropriate or welcome, can offer comfort.

- o **Silence** allows the patient a moment to absorb or process information given.

- o **Summarizing and paraphrasing** information back to a patient helps ensure or confirm understanding.

- o **Asking relevant questions** that pertain to the situation helps the nurse gather information for decision-making.

- Communication includes both verbal and nonverbal components.

  - o **Verbal communication** is the use of language to convey information. Characteristics of verbal communication include tone, volume, and word choice.

  - o **Nonverbal communication** includes behavior, gestures, posture, and other non-language elements of communication that transmit information or meaning.

QUICK REVIEW QUESTION

1. What elements of therapeutic communication should the nurse use when sharing news that may be troubling to a patient?

BARRIERS TO COMMUNICATION

- **Barriers to communication** can prevent effective communication between the nurse and patient. These barriers include language differences, sensory impairments, cognitive impairments, time constraints, and personality conflicts.

- **Language barriers** can occur when a nurse does not speak the patient's primary language or speaks it as a second language.

  - o When an interpreter is required, the organization should provide professional interpretation services for the patient.

  - o It is not appropriate for staff to act as interpreters.

- **Sensory impairments** include hearing or vision loss either as a result of heredity, disease, or injury.

  - o Patients with sensory impairments should be offered interpretation services when needed.

  - o Whenever possible, the nurse should ask the patient what their preferred method of communication is.

- **Cognitive impairments** can often result from trauma or injury, particularly stroke. In these cases patients may not be able to speak due to motor impairments, or they may have neurological impairments that prevent them from processing communication.

  - o The nurse should determine the method of communication that works best for the patient.

  - o Nurses should be aware of changes in a patient's cognitive status.

HELPFUL HINT

When treating patients who are blind or have low vision, describe what actions are being taken throughout assessment and treatment so that the client understands what is occurring.

- **Time constraints** are common in all care settings and can be the result of understaffing, high-acuity patient loads, or unanticipated emergencies.
  - When the nurse is speaking with patients and their families under time constraints, the nurse should share this issue with the patient. Being clear with patients will prevent misunderstandings.
- **Personality conflicts** can occur between two people with different communication or work styles. These issues are often outside the control of the patient or the nurse.
  - If the conflict is infringing on the quality of patient care, arrangements should be made to mitigate the issue whenever possible (e.g., reassigning nurses).

QUICK REVIEW QUESTION

2. A patient is admitted to the cardiac vascular ward and the nurse realizes that the patient is a native speaker of Spanish, but understands some English. What should the nurse do?

INTERVIEW TECHNIQUES

- **Patient interviewing** is a skill cardiac vascular nurses must develop so they can gather the information needed to perform a comprehensive assessment and create a plan of care. General interviewing techniques include:
  - **Active listening:** This means concentrating on the patient and responding appropriately to what they say.
  - **Adaptive questioning:** This is the use of guided questions that get progressively more specific, while allowing the patient to provide information in an uninterrupted narrative.
  - **Echoing:** Repeating words used by the patient in the form of a question can elicit more information.
  - **Open-ended questioning:** Yes-no questions do not actively elicit information. Patients should be encouraged to expand on their answers.
  - **Empathy:** Showing concern and understanding when the patient is speaking can make the patient feel comfortable.
  - **Validation:** The patient needs to know that their emotions and experiences are real and valid.
  - **Reassurance:** The patient needs to know that their concerns are being heard.
- **Motivational interviewing** is used to elicit a patient's personal reasons for changing behavior patterns to promote health. Nurses can use motivational interviewing to guide the plan of care and education given to the patient.

QUICK REVIEW QUESTION

3. How does motivational interviewing contribute to the overall plan of care for the cardiac vascular patient?

DOCUMENTING COMMUNICATION

- **Documentation of communication** should occur whenever information is passed from the patient to the nurse or from the nurse to the patient. Such communication includes:
  - patient contribution to assessment details (subjective)
  - notification of change in condition from patient
  - updates in care plan from nurse to patient
  - concerns or questions expressed by the patient
  - education provided to the patient by the nurse
  - confirmation of patient understanding of information given

QUICK REVIEW QUESTION

4. A patient calls the nurse to their room to explain that their chest pain has increased and they now feel nauseous. What should the nurse document after this interaction?

PROFESSIONAL COMMUNICATION

- Professional communication includes:
  - comprehensive handoff communication between nurses
  - professional interdisciplinary communication
  - conflict resolution in a variety of circumstances

- **SBAR** (**S**ituation, **B**ackground, **A**ssessment, and **R**ecommendations) handoff is a reporting tool used during shift change, when a patient is being admitted, or when an acute change in the patient's condition needs to be communicated to the care team.
  - **Situation:** nurse's name, patient's name and location, any current problems
  - **Background:** diagnosis, history, and current care plan
  - **Assessment:** relevant vital signs and diagnostic testing
  - **Recommendation:** recommendations for further testing, changes to care plan, or transfers

- **Interdisciplinary communication** is communication among disciplines (e.g., other medical staff, nursing staff, consultative services, ancillary services, and support staff). Such communication should be:
  - mutually respectful
  - timely
  - patient-focused

- **Conflict resolution** should be used in circumstances in which conflict within the interdisciplinary team is interrupting patient care. Conflict resolution strategies include:

- Accommodating: The goal of accommodating is to preserve harmony and relationships within the care team. It can be used to promote goodwill, but should be used sparingly.

- Compromising: Compromising involves concessions on both sides in order to preserve the interdisciplinary relationship. This may be used as a temporary solution to a complex issue.

- Collaborating: Collaborating is true problem solving, in which the goal is to come to a mutual solution that is acceptable for all parties.

- Avoiding: Avoiding is generally not the best approach in the context of patient care. It can be a temporary solution but should not be the final strategy used to resolve a particular conflict.

- Competing: Generally viewed as a negative way to manage conflict, competing is a strategy in which one party "wins." It may be useful when quick, decisive action is necessary.

QUICK REVIEW QUESTION

5. A nurse in the cardiac vascular intensive care unit is preparing to hand off a patient recovering from a CABG. What information should the nurse be prepared to provide?

Patient and Family Support
FACTORS THAT INFLUENCE CARE

- Factors that influence the care of the cardiac vascular patient include:
  - family dynamics
  - cultural considerations
  - religious considerations
  - socioeconomic factors
  - diverse health practices

- The cardiac vascular nurse should ask patients and families directly about such factors when possible, ideally during the admission assessment.

- Family dynamics may facilitate or impede patient care. It is important to determine the patient's preferences with regard to family involvement with care.

- Cultural considerations should be taken into account if the patient or patient's family shares specific cultural practices that are important to the patient.

- Religious considerations should be taken into account if the patient or the family indicates that certain interventions should be avoided.

- Socioeconomic factors should be considered when making plans for discharge. Socioeconomic status may affect patients' ability to meet discharge requirements such as physical therapy or rehabilitation, or patients may be unable to miss work for follow-up care.

HELPFUL HINT
Never ask family members to monitor or care for patients who are agitated, delirious, violent, or suicidal. This places an undue burden on the family. They may choose to provide support, but the nurse should ensure that appropriate monitoring or restraints are in place.

- **Diverse health practices** should be considered if the patient discloses them. Such practices include preferences for alternative therapies or the desire to avoid certain interventions.

QUICK REVIEW QUESTION

6. The spouse of a patient who is approaching the end of life shares that the couple would like a priest to come to the bedside to give last rites. The nurse does not share the same religion as the patient and family. What should the nurse do?

SUPPORT SYSTEMS

- Ancillary services and support systems may be available to assist directly or indirectly with the care of the cardiac vascular patient. The cardiac vascular nurse's responsibility is to understand the scope of responsibility and roles of these care support systems.

- Volunteers
  - Volunteers can be used as ancillary support in the event the nurse needs supplies or basic support.
  - Volunteers do not routinely provide patient care.

- Transportation
  - Transportation services include moving patients within the care facility as well as transporting patients outside the facility.
  - Transportation services should be chosen based on the acuity of the patient.
  - The nurse should travel with the patient within the facility when the patient requires monitoring during transport.

- Support groups
  - Support groups are usually available to patients with similar diagnoses or disease processes in order to cope with illness or to support required behavioral changes.

- Medication assistance
  - Financial assistance for medication may be available to patients, depending on socioeconomic status and level of need. The nurse should engage appropriate resources in order to get such support for patients.

- Community support
  - The cardiac vascular nurse can provide information on community resources that can help patients and their families with basic needs related to their illness or disease process.
  - Such resources include support groups, rehab services, meal services, and others.

HELPFUL HINT

Pastoral counseling integrates a faith-based perspective and spiritual guidance with psychology. It is offered by a trained minister or other clergyperson.

QUICK REVIEW QUESTION

7. A cardiac vascular nurse is caring for three patients with moderate acuity. One of the patients is scheduled to undergo a stress test in 30 minutes in the cardiac clinic. How can the nurse arrange for the patient to be transported to the appointment?

COPING STRATEGIES AND DEFENSE MECHANISMS

- The cardiac vascular nurse may encounter patients and families experiencing the diagnosis of a chronic or terminal illness. Such circumstances will elicit varied reactions and coping strategies from patients and families.

- Coping strategies are psychological efforts to manage stress and negative emotions.

  - **Active coping** is characterized by solving problems, seeking support, seeking professional consultation, and planning activities.

  - **Passive coping** is characterized by a feeling of helplessness in the face of stress or change. It generally involves withdrawal and wishful thinking.

  - **Avoidance** is considered maladaptive and involves changing behavior to avoid thinking about or feeling sad about uncomfortable things.

  - **Denial** gives the patient time to adjust to a distressing situation. It is acceptable for a short time, but can interfere with treatment if it continues.

- Patients may choose to suspend aggressive interventions and opt for palliative care or hospice in the face of terminal illness.

- **Palliative care** is an approach to care that improves the quality of life for patients and families experiencing terminal or life-threatening illness.

  - Palliative care focuses on the prevention and relief of suffering through assessment and early identification of pain and other physical and mental concerns related to the illness.

- **Hospice** is an approach to care for patients nearing the end of life.

  - Interventions include palliative care but are extended to the patient in a place of comfort, most often the patient's home, in the presence of family.

QUICK REVIEW QUESTION

8. A patient has just been diagnosed with moderate cardiovascular disease. The patient's spouse begins seeking medical advice from specialists and has hired a nutritionist for the family. How is the spouse coping with the new information regarding the patient?

The Work Environment

LEADERSHIP

- Nurses are expected to be leaders in the care setting. There are several leadership styles, but those commonly found in the nursing profession include transactional, transformational, and authoritarian leadership.

- **Transactional leadership** is an approach in which leaders promote compliance from followers through the use of rewards and punishments.

  - This leadership style is typically effective for the short term but does not create a positive long-term work environment.

- **Democratic leadership** is a style that allows members of the group to participate in decision-making.
  - This leadership style works well in settings that have already established shared governance practices, such as Magnet hospitals.
- **Laissez-faire leadership** is characterized by a hands-off approach in which staff is allowed to make decisions without input from leadership.
  - This type of leadership generally leads to low productivity among group members and is not ideal in nursing settings.
- **Transformational leadership** promotes change in individuals and systems.
  - Valuable and positive interaction with team members results in transforming followers into leaders.
  - It is often considered an ideal leadership approach for nursing leaders.
- **Authoritarian leadership**, also known as autocratic leadership, includes little input from staff, with the majority of decisions made by the leader.
  - Authoritarian leadership does not follow a model of shared governance and does not provide opportunities for input or advice from team members, resulting in low morale.
- Cardiac vascular nurses can assume the role of preceptor, mentor, clinical resource, or change agent.
- **Preceptors** are registered nurses who act in the dual role of nurse and educator for a newly hired or newly graduated nurse.
  - Preceptors are generally subject matter experts and leaders within the nursing unit.
- **Mentors** are experienced nurses whose role includes guidance, education, and support of nursing practice and career decisions for new nurses.
  - Mentors are usually assigned on a volunteer basis and are matched with mentees based on personality and similarity in career goals or paths.
- **Clinical resource nurses** are recognized as subject matter experts and are available to nurses within a unit.
  - Some organizations may employ clinical resource nurses as nurse educators or clinical nurse specialists, with a focus on acting as a resource for other nursing staff. Other organizations may use this role as a resource for patients.
- **Change agents** are recognized nurse leaders within units who encourage and enable change.
  - Change is usually brought about as a result of an evidence-based practice/process improvement project.

HELPFUL HINT

Evidence-based practice refers to scientifically tested methods and processes that have yielded consistent outcomes.

QUICK REVIEW QUESTION

9. The charge nurse on a unit is known to reward nurses who comply with directives by allowing them to have preference in daily assignments. What type of leadership does this charge nurse display?

WORKING AS A TEAM

- Healthy nursing work environments are built upon professional relationships, civility, team building, and shared governance.

- An absence of positive relationships, mutual respect, and good communication can result in a negative or toxic work environment.

- Nurses have a responsibility to contribute to a positive work environment by working toward:
  - professional relationships
  - workplace civility
  - team building
  - diversity
  - shared governance
  - appropriate delegation of tasks

- **Professional relationships** with the care team and interdisciplinary team result from good communication and mutual respect.

- **Workplace civility** is achieved through professionalism, respect, courtesy, and a general awareness of the feelings of others.

- **Team building** contributes to overall organizational effectiveness and civility within the work environment. Team building is usually prompted by nurse leaders or nurse managers.

- A healthy work environment is one that is accepting and welcoming of all **diverse** individuals, including those of different races, genders, ethnic groups, ages, religions, and sexual orientations.

- **Shared governance** provides the opportunity for team members to work together to make decisions that affect practice and the work environment.
  - Unit or clinical nursing practice councils are one way for team members to participate in shared governance.
  - Shared governance follows the constructs of a professional practice model.

- **Delegation of tasks** is governed by local organizational policies, state nurse practice acts, and professional association practice guidelines.
  - State nurse practice acts outline specific scopes of practice for all licensed personnel working in health care settings. Registered nurses in the clinical setting may delegate tasks to the following licensed personnel:
    - LPNs/LVNs
    - medical assistants
    - nursing assistants
    - technicians
  - Delegation does not take away the nurse's responsibility for completion of the task and its outcome.
  - The nurse should have in mind the scope of practice as well as the skills and abilities of the individual to whom they are delegating tasks.

QUICK REVIEW QUESTION

10. What can a CV nurse do in order to contribute to a work environment that promotes shared governance?

QUALITY IMPROVEMENT AND RISK MANAGEMENT

- Quality and process improvement are the assessment and critique of processes and systems within a health care organization.

- **Quality improvement** uses data to monitor the outcomes of care processes and improve the quality and safety of health care systems.

  ○ Cardiac vascular nurses are responsible for participating in quality improvement initiatives.

  ○ Cardiac vascular nurses who believe processes are not efficient or conducive to safe, high-quality patient care should make recommendations to the quality management team.

- **Risk management** is the assessment and mitigation of risk in a health care setting.

  ○ The role of a **risk manager** is to work to prevent situations that can result in losses or liability stemming from the care of patients.

  ○ Risk managers investigate adverse or sentinel events or any patient complaint or concern that may possibly lead to litigation.

  ○ Risk managers get case referrals from many sources, including:
    - medical or nursing quality councils
    - patient-safety reporting systems used internally
    - nurse or provider referrals
    - reports of adverse or sentinel events
    - patient referrals through patient-relations channels

- Quality improvement and risk management practices are often governed by regulatory or accrediting agencies such as the Centers for Medicare and Medicaid Services and the Joint Commission.

QUICK REVIEW QUESTION

11. A cardiac vascular nurse identifies a process that could be improved to be more efficient. What can the nurse do with that information?

Legal and Ethical Considerations
ETHICAL ISSUES

- The American Nurses Association (ANA) established the **Nursing Code of Ethics**. The code of ethics has nine provisions that span the following ethical constructs:

  ○ compassionate and respectful care

- commitment to the patient holistically
- patient advocacy
- responsibility in practice
- promotion of patient and self-health
- promotion of ethical practice
- participation in research
- collaboration with the health care team
- professional practice

- The **core ethical principles** include autonomy, beneficence, non-maleficence, justice, and veracity.
  - **Autonomy:** Acknowledging that a patient is a unique individual with the right to have their own opinions, values, beliefs, and perspectives.
  - **Beneficence:** Acting with the intent of doing the right thing or the most good. The nurse has an obligation to act in the best interest of the patient, regardless of other competing interests.
  - **Non-maleficence:** Do no harm. This principle addresses the nurse's responsibility to keep the patient from harm in the care setting.
  - **Justice:** Provision of equitable access to care. This principle covers providing care to all patients regardless of socioeconomic status, demographic category, or insurance coverage.
  - **Veracity:** The practice of complete truthfulness with patients and families.

- The **patient's bill of rights** may vary among medical organizations and professional nursing organizations. However, the core bill of rights originates from the Centers for Medicare and Medicaid, and includes:
  - the right to make decisions regarding care
  - the right to accept or refuse treatment
  - the right to formulate or establish advance directives
  - the right to accurate, easy-to-understand information about the health plan
  - the right to choose providers
  - the right to access emergency services
  - the right to confidentiality
  - the right to respect and non-discrimination
  - the right to a fair review of any complaint made with regard to health plan or care

- **Ethical dilemmas** are circumstances that require health care providers to make medical decisions using ethical principles such as those found in the Code of Ethics.

- Ethical dilemmas found in the setting of cardiac vascular nursing include advance directive actions, decisional capacity determination, and refusals of care.

- In situations where the cardiac vascular nurse is faced with an ethical dilemma, the nurse should remember the following:
  - The patient has a right and responsibility to be an active participant in their care, and should be treated with dignity and respect regardless of their choices.
  - The role of the nurse is to be a patient advocate.
  - The nurse has an obligation to clearly communicate such issues to the health care team and document them in the medical record objectively.

QUICK REVIEW QUESTION

12. A patient admitted to the inpatient ward does not want to be resuscitated in the event their heart stops beating again. The patient worries that their spouse will try to reverse the decision if the patient is unable to communicate. What should the nurse do?

REGULATORY ISSUES

- Regulatory considerations for the cardiac vascular nurse include knowing and understanding scope of practice and eligibility for board certification.
- Both the ANA and the state where the nurse practices dictate scope of practice.
  - It is the obligation of the cardiac vascular nurse to know the scope of practice and to practice within the limits of that scope.
  - Individual organizations may have more restrictive scopes of practice. Nurses employed by such organizations must operate under the scope of that organization, as long as it does not violate the state or ANA scope.
- Nurses are eligible for **board certification** if they meet the following criteria:
  - have practiced nursing for at least two years
  - hold an active, unencumbered nursing license
  - have completed 30 hours of continuing education in cardiac vascular nursing within the last three years
  - have a minimum of 2,000 hours of clinical practice in cardiac vascular nursing within the last three years

QUICK REVIEW QUESTION

13. Where can the cardiac vascular nurse find information regarding the scope of practice under which they are regulated?

LEGAL ISSUES

- Legal issues that may present in the context of cardiac vascular nursing include intentional and unintentional torts, negligence, privacy violations, and the application of advance directives.
- **Intentional torts** are actions that result in harm to the patient. The harm is not necessarily intentional, but the act that resulted in harm is.

- A typical example of an intentional tort is the act of forcing unwanted medical care on a patient.

- An **unintentional tort** is the result of unintended harm or injury to someone in a situation where a care provider should have known harm would result. Unintentional torts are most often characterized as negligence in the context of nursing.

  - An example of negligence would be a significant delay in care such as giving a medication several hours later than scheduled, resulting in harm or injury to a patient.

- The **Health Insurance Portability and Accountability Act (HIPAA)** requires that individual health care providers and health care organizations make every attempt to safeguard the **protected health information (PHI)** of the patient.

- PHI is defined as any information that concerns the past, present, or future mental or physical health of the patient, along with the treatments of such health conditions and the methods of payment for health services rendered.

- Organizations are required to take measures to protect all PHI on electronic platforms or in electronic formats.

- HIPAA is based on the **minimum necessary requirement**; i.e., the minimum amount of PHI needed to accomplish a task should be shared.

- Sharing of PHI with patient's family, friends, or others is only possible with the patient's consent.

- Sharing of PHI is permissible under HIPAA in the following contexts:

  - activities involving reimbursement or payment for care premiums, determining coverage or provision of benefits, etc.

  - health care operations such as quality improvement activities

  - competency assurance

  - audits of medical records for legal or competency reviews

  - insurance use

  - business planning, development, or management

- PHI may also be released for the following reasons:

  - public health reporting

  - fraud reporting

  - abuse and neglect reporting

  - organ and tissue donation

  - law enforcement proceedings

  - crime reporting

  - military and veterans' health and national security

- **Advance directives** are written statements of individuals' wishes with regard to medical treatment decisions such as resuscitation, intubation, and other interventions. They are made to ensure the wishes of the individual are carried out in the event the person is unable to express those wishes at the time of care.

- They are used to provide answers to difficult questions or decisions needing to be made in the context of end-of-life care. States and organizations may have policies that guide the establishment and use of advance directives.

- Advance directives must be valid, up to date, and documented before they can be honored in the clinical setting. In order to honor an advance directive, the physician must see the paperwork, validate the paperwork, and place an order that indicates the advance directive status of the patient.

- Advance directives generally dictate the level of lifesaving measures to be taken in certain circumstances.
  - **Do not resuscitate (DNR)** typically indicates that no heroic measures should be taken to sustain the patient's life.
  - **Do not intubate (DNI)** indicates that the patient does not wish to be intubated if the need presents.
  - **Allow natural death (AND)** indicates the patient does not want any intervention that may sustain life or prevent a natural progression to death.

- Any combination of DNR, DNI, and AND may be requested, as can other directives present in the documentation if applicable to the patient's circumstance.

- DNR, DNI, and AND all allow for palliative care and comfort measures.

- **Living wills** are used in situations where a patient may have a terminal illness or is acutely in a vegetative state.
  - Living wills allow an individual to state which treatments they would like in the event they are unable to express such at the time of illness.
  - The document must be present and valid in order to be applied to care in the clinical setting.

- **Durable power of attorney** (also called medical power of attorney or health care proxy) may be appointed to make health care decisions for a patient when they do not have the capacity to do so.
  - It may be general or very specific regarding the range of decisions the surrogate can make.
  - It must be present and valid in order to be used for decisions in care.

- In the absence of legal documentation to guide such decisions, a multidisciplinary approach should be taken to inform patients and families of options for these decisions.

QUICK REVIEW QUESTION

14. A patient's family member calls the unit to ask for an update on the patient's condition. What should the nurse do before providing the information?

ANSWER KEY

1. When delivering troubling news, the nurse should use communication skills such as active listening, empathy, touch, and silence where appropriate to assist the patient with processing the information.

2. The nurse should arrange for an interpreter to complete the admission assessment and to communicate any pertinent information between the patient and the care team. It would not be appropriate to try to communicate with the patient in a language other than Spanish.

3. Information gathered from a motivational interview can be used to assist a patient with making behavioral and lifestyle changes that can have a positive impact on their disease progression.

4. The nurse should document that the patient called to notify the nurse of a change in condition. The documentation should include the date, time, and nature of the change, any resulting assessment findings such as the nature and quality of the pain, the nature of the nausea, and other pertinent findings. The nurse should also document any intervention or action taken as a result of the change in condition.

5. The nurse should be prepared to provide an SBAR report that describes the situation, background, assessment, and recommendations. For this patient, the SBAR report may include:

   - **situation:** patient's name, location, and attending physician
   - **background:** diagnosis, date of surgery, relevant medical history
   - **assessment:** code status, vital signs, recent abnormal assessments, recent medications or procedures
   - **recommendation:** any recommended changes to care plan

6. The nurse should facilitate the presence of the requested clergy at the bedside if possible. The nurse's personal beliefs should not influence the care of the patient.

7. The nurse should understand the role of and availability of ancillary services, and what can and cannot be delegated to them. In this situation it would be appropriate to arrange for transport services within the hospital to bring the patient to the appointment so the nurse can stay with the other two patients.

8. The patient's spouse is actively coping with the diagnosis by seeking appropriate information and support.

9. This nurse is displaying a transactional leadership approach by using a rewards-based system.

10. The nurse can join a unit-level or hospital-level nursing practice council to participate in practice and policy discussions and change.

11. The nurse can bring that information, and any recommended solution, to the quality management team for consideration for a process improvement project. The nurse can play a role in supporting and implementing that change.

12. The cardiac vascular nurse is responsible for understanding the patient's advance directive preferences and communicating and documenting those preferences in the medical record. In the event that the advance directive must be used, the nurse must act as an advocate for the patient's end-of-life decisions. The nurse should inform the physician of the patient's preference for the advance directive and should document the discussion in the medical record.

13. The cardiac vascular nurse should review the ANA scope of practice, the scope of practice of the state in which they work, and the organizational scope of practice, if established.

14. The nurse should first determine if the patient has given permission to disclose medical information to family members, and which family members specifically. If the patient has given permission, the nurse must confirm the identity of the patient on the phone through the use of a HIPAA password or other method.

NINE: PRACTICE TEST

DIRECTIONS: READ THE QUESTION, AND THEN CHOOSE THE MOST CORRECT ANSWER.

1. The nurse is assessing a patient who was hit in the chest by the steering wheel during a car accident. The patient has a blood pressure of 88/40 mm Hg, a heart rate of 140 bpm, and has labored breathing at 30/min. Which injury is the patient MOST likely experiencing?

    A. myocardial contusion

    B. aortic dissection

    C. cardiac tamponade

    D. pulmonary embolism

2. A patient who just had an ICD placed is concerned about upcoming travel plans and going through airport security screenings with the device. The cardiac vascular nurse should tell him that he must

    A. cancel his travel plans, as he cannot fly for a period for 6 months after the procedure.

    B. inform airport security that he has an ICD before going through metal detectors.

    C. take a strong magnet with him so he can deactivate the ICD before flying.

    D. travel how he normally does without any modifications.

3. A patient presents to the ED with severe chest pain. The nurse knows which of the following would be a contraindication to administering nitrates?

    A. presence of ST elevation on the ECG

    B. recent phosphodiesterase use

    C. anterior wall infarction

    D. use of beta blockers

4. Dopamine (Intropin) is ordered for a patient with heart failure because the drug

    A. lowers the heart rate.

    B. opens blocked arteries.

    C. prevents plaque from building up.

    D. increases the amount of oxygen delivered to the heart.

5. According to the National Heart, Lung, and Blood Institute (NHLBI), which of the following can be a trigger for a heart attack?

    A. stress

    B. abrupt smoking cessation

    C. moderate exercise

    D. caffeine

6. Which of the following is a Healthy People 2020 objective for improving heart disease?

    A. decrease the proportion of adults with hypertension whose blood pressure is under control

    B. increase the number of hospital admissions with heart failure as the primary diagnosis

    C. reduce the proportion of persons in the population with hypertension

    D. raise the number of adults diagnosed with high total blood cholesterol levels

7. Which of the following can BEST help reduce hospital readmission rates?

    A. having the patient complete a discharge survey to address concerns

    B. ensuring collaborative care

    C. providing the patient with comprehensive information regarding diagnosis

    D. keeping patients with chronic illnesses an additional day in the hospital

8. While giving discharge instructions to an adult patient, which material BEST ensures health literacy?

    A. material that is only text, with no distracting photos

    B. material that is written in a large font

    C. material that is written at an eighth-grade level

    D. as much material as possible on the patient's diagnosis

9. After a patient has been diagnosed with A-fib, the cardiac vascular nurse knows he understands his risk factors when he states he is at greater risk for which of the following?

    A. arthralgia

    B. influenza

    C. DIC

    D. stroke

10. A patient diagnosed with heart failure needs to be started on a new medication. The patient speaks only Spanish and does not understand English. What should the cardiac vascular nurse do before administering the new medication?

   A. ask a family member who speaks both fluent English and Spanish to translate information regarding the reason for the medication and side effects

   B. find a hospital employee who speaks fluent English and Spanish to translate the information

   C. use a language line to translate the conversation with an interpreter

   D. wait until change of shift to administer the new medication so the patient can be assigned a Spanish-speaking nurse to explain the plan of care

11. The nurse is reviewing the history of a patient with heart failure. Which of the following coexisting health problems will cause an increase in the patient's afterload?

   A. diabetes

   B. endocrine disorders

   C. hypertension

   D. Marfan syndrome

12. The registered CV nurse can delegate tasks to all of the following staff members EXCEPT

   A. a licensed practical nurse (LPN).

   B. a patient care tech.

   C. a respiratory therapist.

   D. a medical assistant.

13. The cardiac vascular nurse is precepting a student nurse on her first day on the unit. A patient with heart failure begins to experience respiratory distress. Which task is MOST appropriate to assign to the student nurse?

   A. drawing an arterial blood gas

   B. applying oxygen to the patient

   C. calling the attending physician for orders

   D. preparing an IV infusion of normal saline

14. A patient's ECG shows torsades de pointes, and magnesium sulfate is ordered STAT. The nursing priority is to

   A. monitor patient for bradycardia and respiratory depression.

   B. prepare patient for synchronized cardioversion.

   C. monitor patient for tachycardia and hyperventilation.

   D. prepare patient for Swan-Ganz catheter.

15. The nurse reviews a 12-lead ECG from a patient complaining of crushing chest pain. The ECG reveals ST elevation in leads II, III, and aVF. Which area of the heart is being affected?

    A. anterior

    B. lateral

    C. inferior

    D. posterior

16. The cardiac vascular nurse is educating a patient following a PTA procedure. The patient appears anxious. Which of the following is an appropriate response from the nurse?

    A. "Your procedure went well, so you have nothing to worry about."

    B. "Would you like some medication for your anxiety?"

    C. "We will be monitoring your vital signs and heart rhythm frequently to assess for any changes."

    D. "The physician will be in soon to discuss the rest of your treatment plan."

17. A 75-year-old patient complains of fatigue, weakness, and visual disturbances. The cardiac vascular nurse reviews the patient's medication history and finds they have been taking digoxin (Lanoxin), a potassium supplement, and amlodipine. What is the patient MOST likely experiencing?

    A. ineffective dosing of digoxin

    B. digoxin toxicity

    C. hypercalcemia

    D. hypotension

18. When providing a hospitalized cardiac patient with a therapeutic environment, what should the nurse consider?

    A. assigning the same nurse to the patient each day

    B. restricting friends and family visitation hours

    C. administering all medications within an appropriate time frame

    D. ensuring the patient's psychosocial and spiritual needs are met

19. Which of the following is an example of a SMART goal for a cardiac patient?

    A. "I will walk for 10 minutes, 3 times a day, for 5 days this week."

    B. "I will increase my physical activity this week."

    C. "I will begin a moderate walking program by the end of the month."

    D. "I will record a log of each time I exercise this week."

20. Advance directives are applicable in which of the following patient situations?

   A. an alert and oriented patient being admitted for heart failure

   B. a patient who is post–cardiac arrest and remains unconscious with a poor prognosis

   C. a stable patient being extubated after open heart surgery

   D. any patient who is discharged to a long-term care facility

21. A patient arrives in the ED with midsternal chest pain radiating down the left arm and left jaw. He slumps to the floor and is unresponsive, pulseless, and apneic. High-quality compressions are started, and the patient's ECG shows the following rhythm. What is the priority nursing intervention?

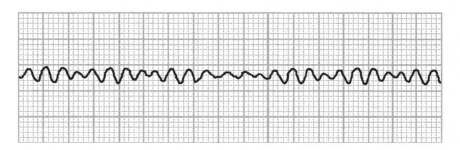

   A. administer a fluid bolus of 1 L normal saline

   B. defibrillate with 200 J

   C. administer 1 mg epinephrine IV

   D. insert an advanced airway

22. The cardiac vascular nurse enters a patient's room and finds them to be unresponsive. The nurse is aware that the patient has a DNR order in place. Which of the following would be the MOST appropriate action for the nurse to take?

   A. begin chest compressions immediately

   B. apply the AED pads and deliver an unsynchronized shock

   C. administer oxygen via non-rebreather mask and notify the physician

   D. prepare equipment for the physician to intubate

23. The nurse assists a patient in creating a measurable goal during the shift. Which of the following is an appropriate goal?

   A. The patient will take all scheduled pain medication.

   B. The patient will have a pain level of 5 or less on a scale of 1 – 10 by the end of the shift.

   C. The patient will be pain-free by the end of the shift.

   D. The patient will take less pain medication than during the previous shift.

24. A patient in the ED is diagnosed with a right ventricular infarction with hypotension. The nurse should prepare to administer which of the following to treat the hypotension?

   A. NS fluid boluses 1 to 2 L

   B. dopamine (Intropine) at 10 mcg/kg/min

   C. D5W fluid boluses titrate 3 L

   D. furosemide drip at 20 mg/hr

25. The cardiac vascular nurse is caring for a patient with STEMI. Which home medication would the nurse report to the physician as being contraindicated with an ordered dose of nitroglycerin?

   A. phosphodiesterase inhibitors

   B. antihypertensives

   C. statins

   D. beta blockers

26. When evaluating the effect of nitroglycerin administration, the nurse knows the primary action of this medication works to relieve pain by

   A. decreasing plaque formation on vessel walls.

   B. increasing preload.

   C. reducing venous return by vasodilating the coronary arteries.

   D. increasing heart rate and strength of heart muscle contraction.

27. The nurse is evaluating a patient's home medication list and discovers the patient has been taking their warfarin dose twice daily instead of once daily. Which of the following orders would the nurse expect?

   A. PT/INR lab draw

   B. aPTT lab draw every 4 hours

   C. 2 units of packed FFP

   D. administer vitamin K

28. The nurse is evaluating a patient with pericarditis. Which of the following heart sounds would the nurse MOST likely hear?

   A. friction rub

   B. crackles

   C. wheezing

   D. S3 gallop

29. The nurse is evaluating a patient's lipid panel results and notes elevated LDL and triglyceride levels. Which of the following dietary recommendations should the nurse make to this patient?

   A. avoid saturated fats

   B. increase water intake

   C. reduce sodium intake

   D. increase fiber consumption

30. The cardiac vascular nurse is giving discharge instructions to a patient diagnosed with pericarditis. What is the BEST technique the nurse can use to demonstrate active listening?

   A. sit facing the patient while making eye contact

   B. speak clearly, loudly, and slowly

   C. ask the patient open-ended questions to ensure understanding

   D. move around the room while talking to the patient so they do not feel anxious

31. A student nurse tells the cardiac vascular nurse that he found a printout of a patient's lab report left on the table in the cafeteria. Which information listed on the paper is NOT considered personally identifiable information?

   A. patient Social Security number

   B. patient first and last name

   C. patient date of birth

   D. patient medical record number

32. A patient with stage 4 congestive heart failure agrees to palliative care. A family member is concerned that the patient will no longer receive appropriate care. What is the BEST way for the nurse to explain what palliative care is?

   A. Palliative care is for patients who have no other treatment options.

   B. Palliative care is focused on relieving the symptoms to help improve quality of life.

   C. Palliative care only begins once it is certain that the person will not survive for much longer.

   D. Palliative care only lasts for approximately 3 months.

33. A patient with abdominal pain and possible AAA dissection wants to leave the hospital. What should the nurse do next?

   A. Inform the patient he will be involuntarily committed to the hospital if he tries to leave.

   B. Inform the physician of the patient's wish to leave.

   C. Warn the patient he will die if he leaves the department.

   D. Give the patient directions to the exit.

34. The cardiac vascular nurse is discharging a 75-year-old patient. Which of the following support systems would be the MOST appropriate to help transport the patient to his car via wheelchair?

    A. the patient's wife

    B. a ride-sharing service

    C. a hospital volunteer

    D. the patient's daughter, who is an off-duty nurse

35. A nurse from the surgical unit is floated to the cardiac care unit. What is the BEST patient assignment to give the float nurse?

    A. The float nurse should receive the easiest assignment on the unit.

    B. The float nurse should be assigned postsurgical patients.

    C. The float nurse should receive the same assignment as any nurse on the unit.

    D. The float nurse should refuse any assignment, as a surgical nurse cannot care for cardiac patients.

36. The nurse is caring for a patient with DVT. Which of the following should be included in the plan of care?

    A. bed rest with the affected extremity elevated

    B. bed rest with the bed in reverse Trendelenburg

    C. walking slowly in the hall with assistance to prevent pneumonia

    D. sitting up in the chair for all meals and during visitation time

37. The nurse is evaluating patients for risk of heparin-induced thrombocytopenia (HIT). Which patient is at greatest risk for HIT, based on the nurse's assessment?

    A. a male patient who just completed a 1-week course of heparin

    B. a male patient taking enoxaparin for management of unstable angina

    C. a female patient receiving heparin for postsurgical thromboprophylaxis

    D. a female patient taking enoxaparin to prevent clots following a mild MI

38. Which of the following is most likely to be found in a patient with left-sided heart failure?

    A. JVD

    B. crackles

    C. hepatomegaly

    D. ascites

39. The cardiac vascular nurse is assessing a patient complaining of chest pain. A 12-lead ECG shows ST elevation in diffuse leads. The patient states the chest pain feels better when they are sitting up and leaning forward, and the nurse hears a friction rub on auscultation of the heart. The MOST likely diagnosis for this patient is

   A. V-fib.

   B. coronary thrombosis.

   C. pericarditis.

   D. congestive heart failure.

40. Which of the following is a modifiable risk factor that would place a patient at greater risk for cardiovascular disease?

   A. male gender

   B. age greater than 65 years old

   C. smoking one pack a day

   D. regular exercise

41. When evaluating a patient with mitral stenosis, the cardiac vascular nurse knows the patient is at higher risk for which cardiac dysrhythmia?

   A. A-fib

   B. V-fib

   C. SVT

   D. bradycardia

42. The nurse is evaluating the ECG rhythm of a patient with a first-degree heart block. Which of the following would be consistent with this diagnosis?

   A. widened QRS complex

   B. heart rate > 150 bpm

   C. inverted P waves

   D. PR interval > 0.20

43. A patient is being evaluated for a DVT. Which of the following risk factors would place the patient at greater risk for developing clot formation?

   A. a plane trip from Florida to California

   B. recent travel on a cruise ship

   C. recently began training for a running marathon

   D. works in a high-stress job

44. A patient diagnosed with an AAA states, "I just had a physical last month with blood work and imaging tests and nothing was wrong with me! You guys don't know what you're talking about!" What is the BEST response by the cardiac vascular nurse?

   A. "I understand you feel upset. What concerns you about your diagnosis the most?"

   B. "Your other physician was wrong. I can assure you that our results are correct."

   C. "You shouldn't worry because the aneurysm isn't large enough to require surgery."

   D. "Calm down. Let's discuss this rationally."

45. The cardiac vascular nurse and physician are at bedside obtaining consent for a procedure. The nurse is asked to sign as a witness to the consent. The nurse knows this means she is responsible for which of the following?

   A. ensuring the patient understands the risks and benefits of the procedure

   B. making certain the patient understands all the medications they will receive before, during, and after the procedure

   C. observing that the correct patient signed the consent form

   D. explaining how the procedure is performed

46. A patient asks about a holistic treatment plan for her CAD that is based on spirituality rather than taking pharmaceuticals. What might the cardiac vascular nurse refer the patient to?

   A. a religious-based hospital organization

   B. the chaplain

   C. a faith community nurse

   D. a physician who follows the same religion as the patient

47. A patient with hyperlipidemia can be taught to reduce cholesterol levels by all of the following EXCEPT

   A. maintaining an exercise program.

   B. eating a diet low in HDL and LDL cholesterol.

   C. quitting cigarette smoking.

   D. taking statin medications.

48. Which of following activities could the cardiac vascular nurse participate in to promote population health?

   A. organizing team-building activities for Nurse Appreciation Week

   B. running in a corporate 5k race

   C. volunteering at a free community blood pressure screening event

   D. participating in a research study

49. A patient presents to the ED with chest pain, dyspnea, and diaphoresis. The nurse finds a narrow complex tachycardia with a heart rate of 210 bpm, blood pressure of 122/72 mm Hg, and a respiratory rate of 18. The nurse should first prepare to

   A. administer adenosine 6 mg IV.

   B. perform synchronized cardioversion at 100 J.

   C. perform defibrillation at 300 J.

   D. perform vagal maneuvers.

50. Which of the following substances is contraindicated for an 80-year-old patient with acute heart failure?

   A. dopamine

   B. adrenaline

   C. digoxin

   D. dobutamine

51. Two weeks post–left-sided MI, a patient presents to the ED with dyspnea and cough with hemoptysis. The nurse should suspect the patient has developed which of the following?

   A. pneumonia

   B. over-coagulation

   C. pulmonary edema

   D. ruptured ventricle

52. A patient has an organized rhythm with a rate of 45 bpm and tall peaked T waves. The nurse should suspect

   A. hypokalemia.

   B. hyperkalemia.

   C. hyponatremia.

   D. hypernatremia.

53. A patient who was initially admitted for cardiac observation is told he needs more tests done and will need to stay a few days longer. The patient is competent, but he refuses to stay and states the hospital is just trying to make money off him by doing extra tests. What is the BEST action for the nurse to take?

   A. have the business office discuss a payment plan with the patient

   B. tell the patient he cannot leave because the tests are mandatory

   C. call the physician to have the patient involuntarily committed

   D. provide the patient with as much information as possible so he can make an informed decision regarding his care

54. Which of the following statements made by the cardiac vascular nurse is an example of motivational interviewing during smoking cessation counseling?

   A. "Smoking has been linked to cardiovascular disease and depression, so it is important that you stop immediately to prevent further damage to your heart."

   B. "Did you know that over 450,000 people die from smoking every year in the United States?"

   C. "What encourages you to stop smoking?"

   D. "I will contact the physician to write you a prescription-strength medication that will help you to quit smoking."

55. The cardiac vascular nurse is caring for a patient from a different culture than her own. Which of the following statements is appropriate for her to make regarding providing culturally competent care?

   A. "Do you have any special cultural needs we can provide for you during your stay?"

   B. "We may not be able to accommodate all your needs because we care for many different patients with different cultural needs."

   C. "Would you like me to call the chaplain to pray with you?"

   D. "We can only allow one visitor at a time, so your extended family will have to switch out with one another to visit with you."

56. Which of the following individualized learning activities would be MOST appropriate for a 25-year-old male patient admitted to the cardiac unit?

   A. attending a group classroom meeting

   B. role-playing

   C. an interactive, online educational game

   D. reading written information

57. The cardiac vascular nurse does not feel a pedal pulse in a patient's right foot. What is the next appropriate intervention?

   A. take the patient for a STAT CT to rule out a pulmonary embolus

   B. order a lower-extremity ultrasound to obtain blood flow measurements

   C. call the physician to report the patient does not have a pedal pulse

   D. use a Doppler to confirm if pulses are present

58. The American Heart Association recommends patients diagnosed with hypertension reduce their sodium intake. What is the current recommended ideal limit of daily sodium intake?

   A. 1,000 mg

   B. 1,500 mg

   C. 2,500 mg

   D. 3,000 mg

59. A competent 74-year-old patient has given power of attorney (POA) to his son. Upon admission to the cardiac unit, the patient is told he will need an implanted defibrillator due to his persistent third-degree heart block. The son agrees, but the patient refuses the surgery and wants to rescind the paperwork that designates his son as the POA. What is the MOST appropriate action for the nurse to take?

    A. to tell the patient he can revoke his son as POA and the hospital will follow his wishes regarding care

    B. to tell the patient that because his son is the POA, the son's decisions are final

    C. to tell the patient that the POA is legally binding and no changes can be made

    D. to tell the patient he needs to work out a compromise with his son and decide on a treatment plan

60. A patient with PVD is having a Doppler ultrasound of the lower extremities to rule out occlusion. Which explanation by the CV nurse BEST describes the purpose of this diagnostic test?

    A. "Having a Doppler ultrasound will help identify if you have cardiovascular disease."

    B. "You are having a Doppler ultrasound because it is faster and cheaper than other diagnostic tests to diagnose PVD."

    C. "The Doppler ultrasound helps rule out an aneurysm."

    D. "A Doppler ultrasound will measure blood flow and visualize any blocked arteries."

61. Which of the following is NOT considered a predisposing factor to clot formation?

    A. hypercoagulability

    B. venous stasis

    C. endothelial damage

    D. presence of heart murmur

62. The nurse is evaluating a patient's ECG rhythm after administering a dose of adenosine. Which of the following is an expected finding indicating treatment was effective?

    A. a flat line, followed by a normal sinus rhythm

    B. bradycardia

    C. a narrow-complex rhythm with a rate of 185 bpm

    D. an irregular, chaotic rhythm

63. A pediatric patient is being resuscitated in a trauma bay, and his father wants to be in the room. What should the nurse do?

    A. Tell the father he may not be in the trauma room during resuscitation.

    B. Allow the father in the trauma room with a knowledgeable staff member for support.

    C. Ask the father to stand just outside the trauma room.

    D. Call the legal department for advice.

64. A patient diagnosed with A-fib is taking warfarin for stroke prevention. Which of the following meal orders from the patient would cause the nurse to intervene and provide additional education?

    A. grilled cheese sandwich and baked chips

    B. turkey sandwich with reduced-fat cheese and carrots with ranch dip

    C. spinach and kale salad with tuna and light Italian dressing

    D. multigrain crackers and hummus with a baked sweet potato

65. The cardiac vascular nurse is caring for a patient with acute heart failure. Which of the following is the BEST way to evaluate fluid and electrolyte balance in this patient?

    A. record the patient's weight every morning

    B. draw labs every 4 hours to monitor for changes

    C. insert a Foley catheter

    D. reduce dietary sodium intake

66. A patient being discharged from the hospital on digoxin asks the nurse if she can continue using an herbal remedy of St. John's Wort. The nurse knows the interaction between these 2 medications is

    A. not significant, and the patient can continue taking both.

    B. not significant, but the patient should stop all medications prescribed by any other physician.

    C. significant, due to St. John's Wort's clotting factors.

    D. significant, because St. John's Wort can cause toxic effects when combined with digoxin.

67. Which of the following is considered objective data that would require reporting to the physician for a patient change in status?

    A. patient complaint of dizziness

    B. increased blood pressure of 200/98 mm Hg

    C. troponin of 0.02 ng/ml

    D. family member tells the nurse the patient seems more depressed

68. A patient being discharged with a LifeVest is shown by the nurse how to wear the vest and the monitor. The nurse asks the patient to demonstrate putting the LifeVest on and to explain what he is doing. What type of education is the nurse providing?

    A. procedural

    B. adherence

    C. memorization

    D. teach-back

69. A patient admitted with SSS needs to have an implanted pacemaker. Which of the following is required for the patient to sign informed consent?

   A. The patient is alert, oriented, and deemed competent to make their own medical decisions.

   B. The patient's insurance has been verified, and a complete history and physical are completed.

   C. The patient has been informed of only the benefits of the procedure.

   D. The patient expresses that he does not want the procedure done, so a family member signs the consent form for him.

70. Which laboratory finding indicates that a 62-year-old male patient is at risk for ventricular dysrhythmia?

   A. magnesium 0.8 mEq/L

   B. potassium 4.2 mmol/L

   C. creatinine 1.3 mg/dL

   D. total calcium 2.8 mmol/L

71. The triage nurse is assessing a patient with complaints of dyspnea. The nurse should suspect heart failure when the patient states:

   A. "I have been taking a beta blocker for many years."

   B. "I was diagnosed with a pulmonary embolism last year."

   C. "I get chest pain when I walk to the mailbox."

   D. "When I walk upstairs to my bedroom I have to stop and rest halfway up."

72. A patient's cardiac monitor shows the rhythm below. He is awake and alert but is pale and confused. His blood pressure reads 64/40 mm Hg. What is the priority nursing intervention for this patient?

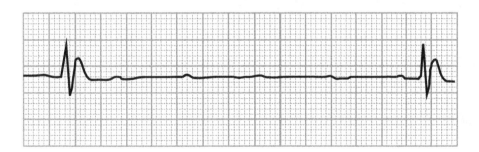

   A. defibrillate at 200 J

   B. prepare for TCP

   C. administer epinephrine 1 mg

   D. begin CPR

73. A patient is brought to the ED in SVT with a rate of 220. EMS has administered 6 mg of adenosine, but the patient remains in SVT. What is the next intervention the nurse should anticipate?

    A. administer 12 mg adenosine IV

    B. administer 1 mg epinephrine IV

    C. administer 300 mg amiodarone IV

    D. administer 0.5 atropine IV

74. Which of the following is NOT an appropriate way for the nurse to protect a patient's PHI?

    A. logging out of the computer each time the nurse is finished using it

    B. placing any documents with PHI that are no longer needed in the shred bin

    C. asking the HIPAA compliance officer of the hospital if the nurse has concerns about patient privacy

    D. giving a newly hired RN the nurse's password so they can assist with a medication pass and changing the password at the end of the shift

75. Which observation in a patient with AAA indicates the need for immediate treatment?

    A. complaints of yellow-tinted vision

    B. hemoptysis

    C. urinary output of 75 mL/hr per urinary catheter

    D. complaints of sudden and severe back pain and dyspnea

76. A patient on the cardiac care unit goes into sudden cardiac arrest. All of these actions are within the new graduate CV nurse's scope of practice EXCEPT

    A. administering epinephrine.

    B. preparing the patient for defibrillation.

    C. intubating the patient.

    D. inserting an IV.

77. A patient's troponin level comes back elevated. The patient is informed that he is having an acute MI and will need a cardiac catheterization. The patient states, "I exercise every day and I eat well, there is no possible way I'm having a heart attack." This statement is an example of what type of defense mechanism?

    A. passive coping

    B. avoiding

    C. active coping

    D. denial

78. The cardiac vascular nurse is assessing a patient before administering a scheduled dose of digoxin. What should the nurse assess first?

   A. apical pulse

   B. chest X-ray results

   C. blood glucose level

   D. blood pressure

79. The nurse is admitting a young female patient to the cardiac care unit. Which of the following is an open-ended interview question the nurse could ask?

   A. "Do you have any pain right now?"

   B. "Are you feeling any better after your last dose of pain medication?"

   C. "Is there any chance you could be pregnant?"

   D. "What is your main goal during your hospital stay?"

80. The cardiac vascular nurse receives an order to administer 4 mg of morphine to a patient having an acute MI. Which of the following is true about this medication?

   A. Morphine has a short half-life.

   B. Morphine decreases the oxygen demand of the heart.

   C. Morphine is contraindicated in an acute MI.

   D. Morphine reduces ST elevation.

81. When assessing a patient, which of the following would be considered part of the initial survey?

   A. vital signs

   B. skin color

   C. lab results

   D. chief complaint

82. The cardiac vascular nurse is caring for a patient who begins to experience sharp, severe chest pain that is radiating to the left arm. The nurse notifies the physician, performs an ECG, and administers a nitroglycerin tablet sublingually. What is the MOST appropriate way to document the situation?

   A. "Patient c/o chest pain, acute MI suspected. Physician notified. See EMAR for medications given."

   B. "Patient began having chest pain. Tech performed ECG. Medication administered STAT. Patient currently has no complaints."

   C. "Patient c/o sharp, severe chest pain radiating to left arm. Physician notified and received order to obtain ECG and administer 0.4 mg nitroglycerin tablet sublingually. Will continue to monitor patient for changes and medication side effects."

   D. No documentation is needed since the physician was notified.

83. When assessing a patient's risk stratification for a scheduled cardiac surgery, which of the following would place them at the highest risk?

   A. creatinine level of 1.3 mg/dL

   B. allergy to latex

   C. history of asthma

   D. MI within the last 6 months

84. A patient is scheduled for a contrast CT chest angiography. Which of the following is a priority to assess before the exam?

   A. allergies

   B. past medical history

   C. history of claustrophobia

   D. chief complaint

85. The nurse is assessing a patient suspected of having cardiac tamponade. Which assessment technique would help confirm this diagnosis?

   A. assessing for pedal edema

   B. performing a vagal maneuver

   C. percussion of the cardiac border

   D. auscultating heart sounds

86. The nurse knows that cardiovascular changes that occur with increasing age include which of the following?

   A. decreased blood pressure

   B. increased drug metabolism

   C. decreased CO

   D. increased CO

87. The cardiac vascular nurse is caring for a 2-year-old pediatric patient who experiences a sudden change in rhythm. The nurse notes the heart rate has dropped from 130 bpm to 50 bpm. What is the priority intervention the nurse should take?

   A. begin chest compressions

   B. prepare to transcutaneous pace

   C. provide bag-valve mask ventilations with 100% oxygen

   D. administer atropine 0.02 mg/kg

88. The cardiac vascular nurse is evaluating an infant who has been experiencing cyanotic episodes. Which of the following congenital heart defects is this presentation consistent with?

   A. patent ductus arteriosus

   B. tetralogy of Fallot

   C. atrial septal defect

   D. ventricular septal defect

89. A patient being treated for a DVT is scheduled for an IVC filter placement. The nurse knows the patient understands the purpose of the IVC filter when they state:

   A. "I will need to have the IVC filter surgically replaced approximately every 6 months."

   B. "Having an IVC filter will help dissolve the clot in my leg."

   C. "I won't be able to eat high-protein meals while the IVC filter is in place."

   D. "The IVC filter will prevent blood clots from dislodging through the bloodstream to the lungs."

90. A patient is being discharged after an ICD placement. The nurse provides patient education regarding wound care, including

   A. written instructions for how to perform wet to dry dressing changes.

   B. ensuring the patient is aware of signs and symptoms of infection of the incision site.

   C. stressing the importance of engaging in upper body exercise to improve circulation.

   D. emphasizing the importance of handwashing after completing a dressing change.

91. A patient goes into SVT and has a sustained heart rate of 225. After attempting vagal maneuvers and administering 2 doses of adenosine, the cardiologist tells the nurse to prepare for synchronized cardioversion. What should the nurse tell the patient about the procedure?

   A. "You will be awake during the procedure, and you should not feel any pain at all."

   B. "This procedure is optional. Your heart rate will likely return to normal soon without it."

   C. "You will be given medication before the procedure to sedate you so you don't feel pain."

   D. "This procedure will have to be repeated several times over the course of a few visits to be effective."

92. The cardiac vascular nurse is caring for a patient who suddenly develops a second-degree, type 2 heart block. The patient states they feel okay, but their heart rate is 45 bpm. There is no physician on the unit. What should the nurse do first to expedite care and ensure interdisciplinary collaboration?

   A. monitor the patient for any further changes in rhythm or symptoms since they are asymptomatic

   B. call a code blue

   C. use the telehealth cart to communicate with the physician remotely

   D. educate the patient on the symptoms of worsening heart blocks

93. A patient having a left ventricular assist device (LVAD) placed should receive which instruction before the procedure?

   A. "You will receive anticoagulation therapy during your hospital stay and at home to prevent clots, and your lab values will be closely monitored."

   B. "Most patients can typically be discharged home the same day as the procedure."

   C. "You will not have to take your medications after the device is placed."

   D. "You may still go into cardiac arrest with an LVAD, but standard resuscitation techniques such as chest compressions and defibrillation will improve your chance of survival."

94. The cardiac vascular nurse is working on a quality improvement project for the unit that aligns with a Healthy People 2020 objective. What is an example of a Healthy People 2020 objective the nurse can use to implement health promotion strategies for cardiac patients?

   A. decrease the number of adults with no cardiovascular history who take daily aspirin

   B. decrease the proportion of adults with prehypertension who meet the recommended guidelines for BMI

   C. increase the proportion of adults with hypertension who are taking the prescribed medications to lower blood pressure

   D. increase the proportion of adults aged 40 and older who are aware of the symptoms of and how to respond to a heart attack

95. A patient with heart failure is being discharged after a lengthy hospital stay. Which of the following discharge instructions should the cardiac vascular nurse provide?

   A. "You should weigh yourself daily and report a weight gain of 2 lbs. or more in 24 hours, or more than 5 lbs. per week."

   B. "You should make sure you do not eat any sodium because it causes fluid retention."

   C. "If you begin to experience difficulty breathing, you should use your nebulizer to give yourself a breathing treatment."

   D. "If you notice your feet swelling, you should put on compression socks."

96. A patient with diabetes admitted for an MI has an HgbA1C result of 9.0. Which of the following is important for the nurse to consider when developing a care plan for this patient?

   A. The patient has a normal HgbA1C value and should be encouraged to continue their current lifestyle.

   B. The patient has a low HgbA1C value and will need to take folic acid and vitamin C daily.

   C. The patient has an elevated HgbA1C value and should be given information about lifestyle modifications.

   D. The patient should have a fasting blood glucose level to confirm the HgbA1C result.

97. Which activity is part of the planning phase of the nursing process?

   A. auscultating heart sounds

   B. evaluating lab results

   C. checking a patient's blood pressure

   D. setting a goal to reduce pain

98. Which of the following anticoagulants would the nurse expect to administer to a patient having an MI?

   A. aspirin

   B. heparin

   C. nitrates

   D. clopidogrel

99. The nurse is evaluating a patient's ECG rhythm strip and notices a prolonged QT interval. Which of the following laboratory findings would the nurse expect to correlate to this?

   A. hypomagnesemia

   B. hypocalcemia

   C. hyperkalemia

   D. hyponatremia

100. The nurse is evaluating a patient's past medical history. Which of the following would the nurse consider a risk factor for developing an aneurysm?

   A. Addison's disease

   B. diabetes

   C. skin cancer

   D. Marfan syndrome

101. The cardiac vascular nurse is assessing a 55-year-old female with a chief complaint of chest pressure. Her blood pressure is 105/70 mm Hg, heart rate is 80 bpm, and pulse oximetry reads 98%. Her breathing is even and unlabored at a rate of 16 breaths per minute. What is the priority intervention for this patient?

   A. obtain a 12-lead ECG

   B. complete a full health history examination

   C. review hospital policies and procedures for admission

   D. obtain expert consultation

102. The nurse is evaluating the vital signs of a patient with an AAA. Which of the following vital signs would be MOST concerning?

    A.   oxygen saturation of 94%

    B.   temperature of 38°C (100.4°F)

    C.   blood pressure of 190/80 mm Hg

    D.   heart rate of 100 bpm

103. The cardiac vascular nurse is performing an initial admission health history for a cardiac patient. The patient tells her they have felt down lately, had less energy, and had difficulty falling asleep. The nurse should perform which type of screening?

    A.   depression

    B.   diabetes

    C.   dementia

    D.   drug abuse

104. The nurse is reviewing lab results of a patient admitted to the cardiac unit. Which of the following laboratory values is MOST concerning?

    A.   Hgb 11.9

    B.   WBC 5.2

    C.   INR 2.0

    D.   troponin 0.10

105. The nurse notes a patient who was previously in a sinus rhythm and is now in a second degree, type II heart block. How should the nurse initially respond to this change?

    A.   prepare to administer atropine

    B.   obtain orders for sedation to prepare for synchronized cardioversion

    C.   place pacing pads on the patient

    D.   continue to monitor the patient

106. The cardiac vascular nurse is helping a patient develop a home exercise plan. Which of the following statements by the patient shows they understand appropriate short-term goals?

    A.   "I will cut out all processed foods from my diet."

    B.   "I will start wearing a nicotine patch to help me quit smoking."

    C.   "Every time I go grocery shopping, I will check my blood pressure at the kiosk in the pharmacy."

    D.   "I will use an exercise log to record 15-minute daily walks at least 4 times a week."

107. The cardiac vascular nurse provides sodium reduction education to a patient with hypertension. The nurse knows his teaching was effective if the patient says she will eat which of the following meals?

   A.   canned vegetable soup with crackers

   B.   a sandwich made of deli meat and cheese and whole-wheat bread

   C.   baked chicken with sweet potatoes and a side salad

   D.   leftover pepperoni pizza with fresh fruit

108. The cardiac vascular nurse is evaluating a patient's adherence to treatment for hypertension. Which of the following indicates that he has followed his treatment plan?

   A.   He tells the nurse he feels much better since his last visit.

   B.   He has not refilled his medications.

   C.   He complains of intermittent chest pain.

   D.   He has a normal blood pressure.

109. The cardiac vascular nurse gets a phone call from a patient's husband asking how his wife is doing. What should the nurse do before giving the caller any information?

   A.   ask him to verify the patient's full name, birthdate, and room number

   B.   ask him for the security code or HIPAA password

   C.   give him vague information about the patient's status and tell him to come in person for updates on care

   D.   tell him that no information can be released over the phone for privacy reasons

110. A patient is advised to attend cardiac rehabilitation. The nurse explains that one reason patients can benefit from this is because

   A.   it is covered by all insurance plans.

   B.   it provides a support system for the patient during their recovery.

   C.   it is required so the cardiologist can continue providing follow-up care.

   D.   it ensures the patient does not have any further heart attacks.

111. The cardiac vascular nurse's husband has labs drawn at the hospital where she works. The nurse wants to check on the results and knows the BEST practice is to

   A.   access the chart to read the report since she is an employee of this hospital.

   B.   ask the physician to provide her with the results.

   C.   have her husband sign a release form to get the results.

   D.   ask her friend who is working to access the chart to read the results.

112. The CV nurse is caring for a patient diagnosed with endocarditis. Which of the following laboratory values would the nurse expect to be elevated?

    A. sedimentation rate

    B. lactic acid

    C. troponin

    D. BNP

113. Which of the following cardiovascular changes would be considered normal for a pregnant patient?

    A. tachycardia

    B. decreased cardiac output

    C. reduced blood volume

    D. hypertension

114. The cardiac vascular nurse is having a busy shift and is behind on tasks. Which task is the MOST appropriate for the nurse to assign to the patient care technician?

    A. assisting a patient to the bathroom

    B. taking a patient's vital signs

    C. hanging a normal saline IV bag

    D. inserting a Foley catheter to a patient with strict intake and output orders

115. The CV nurse is caring for a patient diagnosed with heart failure. Which of the following would be the priority nursing diagnosis related to heart failure?

    A. ineffective breathing pattern

    B. activity intolerance

    C. impaired urinary elimination

    D. risk for ineffective renal perfusion

116. A patient has been administered a fibrinolytic for an acute STEMI. What is an expected finding by the cardiac vascular nurse that would indicate treatment has been effective?

    A. The patient's troponin levels increase.

    B. There is no longer ST elevation present on the ECG.

    C. A new BBB is present.

    D. The patient's pain level has decreased.

117. Which of the following is an expected outcome for a patient on day 3 of admission for an MI?

   A. decreased pain

   B. increased mobility

   C. improved breathing pattern

   D. reduced urinary output

118. A patient complaining of crushing chest pain is diagnosed as a STEMI. The nurse knows that which condition is a contraindication to administering tPA?

   A. diabetes

   B. previous MI

   C. history of intracranial bleeding

   D. allergy to aspirin

119. The cardiac vascular nurse is caring for a patient following synchronized cardioversion. Which of the following is a priority to evaluate?

   A. post-cardioversion ECG rhythm

   B. ensure airway patency

   C. IV placement

   D. pulse strength

120. The nurse is caring for a low-vision, 85-year-old patient admitted to the cardiac care unit. How should she modify the room to create a safer environment?

   A. have a sitter stay with the patient at bedside

   B. place all furniture away from the patient's bed

   C. place the patient's glasses next to the call light on the bedside table within reach

   D. disconnect the television to reduce excess stimulation

121. A patient is discharged from the cardiac unit after being started on an ACE inhibitor to be continued at home. Which of the following common side effects should the nurse tell the patient they might experience while taking an ACE inhibitor?

   A. polyuria

   B. cough

   C. tachycardia

   D. nausea

122. The nurse is evaluating vital signs of a patient admitted with heart failure. She notes the oxygenation saturation is 88%, which is a change from the last documented reading of 98%. What is the nurse's priority intervention?

   A. ask the patient to bear down

   B. perform bag-valve mask ventilations

   C. apply oxygen

   D. prepare the patient for intubation

123. The cardiac vascular nurse inadvertently administers an incorrect dosage of a medication. She immediately notifies the physician and the patient and monitors for any side effects. The patient was not harmed, but the nurse worries she will be sued for negligence. Why is this unlikely?

   A. The nurse immediately notified the physician, which reduces the risk of litigation.

   B. The patient was not harmed.

   C. The patient was notified promptly.

   D. The nurse properly documented the incident and charted frequent assessments after the event.

124. A patient with cardiogenic shock is expected to have which of the following?

   A. hypertension; dyspnea

   B. decreased urine output; warm, pink skin

   C. increased urine output; cool, clammy skin

   D. hypotension; weak pulse; cool, clammy skin

125. The cardiac vascular nurse just started at a new facility and questions some of the practices of the organization. Which of these practices would be considered a HIPAA violation?

   A. giving information about the patient's condition over the phone to an approved family member

   B. leaving a printout of the patient's history and physical in plain view at the nurse's station

   C. faxing the patient's medical record to a new physician caring for the patient

   D. informing the billing department of the reason for the patient's visit

126. A patient is admitted to the ED after complaining of acute chest pain radiating down the left arm. She is diaphoretic and anxious and has dyspnea. In addition to troponin, which laboratory study would the nurse anticipate?

   A. potassium

   B. lactic acid

   C. INR

   D. CK-MB

127. A patient being admitted for ACS tells the nurse that her father also had ACS and took multiple cardiac medications, but he died at age 40 from a heart attack. What is the MOST appropriate place to chart this information?

   A. medication history

   B. social history

   C. past medical history

   D. family history

128. The cardiac vascular nurse is preparing to discharge a patient who has been started on warfarin during hospital admission and will be continuing this medication at home. Which part of the patient's social history would the nurse need to discuss with the patient prior to discharge?

   A. marital status

   B. upcoming plans to travel overseas

   C. daily alcohol consumption

   D. occupation of machinist

129. The nurse notes red, flat, and painless lesions on a patient's palms. Which of the following does she suspect?

   A. PAD

   B. heart failure

   C. endocarditis

   D. Wellens syndrome

130. Which of the following is the BEST choice of non-pharmacological venous thromboembolism (VTE) prophylaxis for a hospitalized cardiac patient?

   A. heparin injections

   B. intermittent pneumatic compression devices

   C. massage

   D. bed rest

131. The nurse is assisting a cardiac patient with dietary planning. Which of the following meals should be avoided?

   A. turkey meatballs with pasta sauce

   B. grilled chicken, baked potato, and green beans

   C. canned soup with a grilled ham and cheese sandwich

   D. salmon, brown rice, and salad

132. The nurse is prioritizing care after receiving the morning shift report. Which of the following patients requires immediate intervention and should be seen first?

    A. a patient admitted the night before for an NSTEMI who is requesting pain medication

    B. a new admission who is alert and oriented with a history of diabetes and who needs a blood sugar check before breakfast

    C. a patient with a new troponin lab result of 0.05 ng/ml, decreased from the previous troponin level of 0.10 ng/ml

    D. a patient admitted for hypertension who has a new complaint of severe back pain

133. A patient who experiences a sudden cardiac arrest in the cardiac care unit cannot be resuscitated. Two of the patient's family members are at the bedside and very emotional. What should the nurse do to help provide a therapeutic environment for the patient's family?

    A. ask the family if they would like a chaplain to visit

    B. discuss organ donation with the family

    C. escort the family to the waiting room so the patient can be prepared for transport to the morgue

    D. call additional family members to notify them of the patient's death so they can come stay with family already at the hospital

134. The nurse is caring for a patient on a heparin drip. The aPTT lab results come back as a critically high value. After stopping the heparin drip, what medication does the nurse anticipate administering?

    A. digoxin immune fab

    B. protamine sulfate

    C. vitamin K

    D. acetylcysteine

135. The nurse is applying an Unna boot to a patient with venous stasis in the lower extremities. Which of the following should the nurse ensure during this procedure?

    A. that the leg is moist to activate the gauze dressing

    B. that the dressing stops mid-calf to allow for vascular checks

    C. that the dressing is not used in a bed-bound patient

    D. that the dressing should be wrapped tightly to provide compression

136. The cardiac vascular nurse is caring for a patient after a heart catheterization in which the radial artery was used. The nurse knows which of the following is the BEST reason to use a radial compression device?

    A. to assist the puncture wound in healing faster

    B. to obtain a more accurate blood pressure reading

    C. to reduce the risk of blood clots after a transradial procedure

    D. to achieve hemostasis and prevent arterial damage

137. The nurse is caring for a STEMI patient who is receiving tPA. Which of the following is a priority for the nurse?

   A. monitoring the patient for bleeding

   B. administering pain medications through the intramuscular route

   C. assessing the patient for edema

   D. auscultating heart sounds

138. The nurse is evaluating the medication list of an infant diagnosed with tetralogy of Fallot. Which of the following medications would he expect to be ordered?

   A. adenosine

   B. dopamine

   C. digoxin

   D. potassium

139. Which of the following diet plans is the MOST appropriate for the nurse to recommend to a patient with hypertension?

   A. intermittent fasting

   B. DASH

   C. low carbohydrate

   D. gluten-free

140. The cardiac vascular nurse administers bumetanide to a patient admitted for heart failure. The nurse would expect which of the following when evaluating whether the medication was effective?

   A. decreased edema

   B. increased work of breathing

   C. wheezing lung sounds

   D. improved pain

141. A patient complaining of chest pain is administered a 0.4-mg nitroglycerin sublingual tablet. Upon reevaluation, the patient complains of a headache. Which of the following is the MOST appropriate action for the nurse to take?

   A. immediately notify the physician and discontinue the order for nitroglycerin

   B. administer acetaminophen for the headache

   C. switch the patient to an IV route of nitroglycerin

   D. prepare the patient for CT to rule out a brain hemorrhage

142. The cardiac vascular nurse is preparing to teach a patient about endocarditis. The first step is to assess the patient's

   A. current knowledge.

   B. IV drug use habits.

   C. social history.

   D. lab results.

143. The cardiac vascular nurse is discharging a patient who has been in the hospital for the last 5 days. The patient tells the nurse she will be flying out of the country. What is the MOST important discharge information the nurse can provide?

   A. suggesting she keep an exercise journal of her physical activity

   B. providing her with a list of heart-healthy foods for her trip

   C. giving her a physician's note in case she is stopped by airport security

   D. reminding her to stretch her legs and walk around occasionally while on the flight

144. A nursing student working with the cardiac vascular nurse is assisting with an ECG. The nurse determines that the patient has an inferior wall MI. The student asks the nurse how she knows which wall was affected. Which response by the nurse answers the student's question?

   A. "The patient's troponin level came back at 2.5."

   B. "Elevation is present in leads II, III, and aVF."

   C. "The patient had symptoms that correlated with an inferior wall MI."

   D. "The patient has a family history of an inferior wall MI."

145. The cardiac vascular nurse is working on the pediatric unit with a student nurse caring for a stable 1-year-old who is in SVT. The nurse knows the student nurse is aware of the proper treatment of this abnormal heart rhythm when he goes to the break room and returns with which of the following?

   A. a straw

   B. juice

   C. several bags of ice

   D. crackers

146. A local politician has a heart attack and is admitted to the cardiac care unit. A member of a local news station calls the nursing unit to ask for an update on the patient's status. Providing this information would be considered

   A. negligence.

   B. defamation.

   C. a HIPAA violation.

   D. non-maleficence.

147. The cardiac vascular nurse is discussing a patient's plan of care. What type of body positioning would indicate the nurse is using active listening?

A. The nurse is standing at the foot of the bed, with arms crossed, making good eye contact.

B. The nurse is sitting, facing the patient, and making good eye contact.

C. The nurse is leaning in close to the patient, nodding, and documenting in the computer.

D. The nurse is walking around the patient's room, occasionally nodding, while talking to the patient.

148. Which of the following labs would the nurse use to evaluate a patient suspected of a pulmonary embolism?

A. troponin

B. D-dimer

C. platelets

D. aPTT

148. A patient being treated for hemorrhagic stroke is determined to be brain dead, but his life can be sustained for organ procurement. The patient is identified as an organ donor. Which of the following is the next step for the nurse?

A. notify local organ procurement organization

B. remove all life-supporting interventions

C. perform postmortem care on the patient

D. complete the death certificate

150. When patients are transferred to higher levels of care, certain elements must be in place to be compliant with COBRA/EMTALA laws. Which of the following is necessary to transfer the patient?

A. There must be an accepting physician at a receiving hospital.

B. The patient must have insurance.

C. The transfer must be the fastest method of transport possible.

D. The receiving hospital must be the closest hospital.

ANSWER KEY

1. **A)**

A myocardial contusion is the most likely diagnosis, as it usually occurs after a direct injury to the chest and presents with tachycardia, hypotension, and shortness of breath.

2. **B)**

The patient should be instructed to tell airport security that he has an ICD prior to going through a metal detector. Carrying a note from the physician may also be helpful during travel. Most patients can fly within a few weeks after this procedure.

3. **B)**

Recent phosphodiesterase use is a contraindication to administering nitrates, as it can result in severe hypotension. An inferior wall infarction would also be a contraindication. Nitrates are not contraindicated in patients with ST elevation or beta blocker use.

4. **D)**

Dopamine (Intropin) is a positive inotrope, which will increase cardiac contractility and cardiac output, decrease the myocardial workload, and improve myocardial oxygen delivery.

5. **A)**

The NHLBI notes that stress can trigger an MI. Stress reduction techniques such as meditation and moderate exercise are recommended.

6. **C)**

The Healthy People 2020 goal HDS-5 focuses on reducing the proportion of individuals in the population with hypertension.

7. **B)**

Collaborative care that includes the patient in the decision-making process has been shown to increase compliance with the plan of care and reduce readmission rates. Providing too much information for patients can overwhelm them. Completing a discharge survey does not reduce readmission rates. Patients should not be kept in the hospital longer than necessary.

8. **C)**

Material written at an eighth-grade level is the best way to ensure the patient's comprehension. Photos should be used to supplement text if appropriate. Writing information in a large font will not ensure health literacy if the patient does not understand the content. Providing too much information may discourage patients or overwhelm them.

9. **D)**

Having A-fib increases a patient's risk of stroke. Blood pools in the heart's chambers, causing clots that might move to the brain and cause a stroke. Patients with A-fib are not at greater risk of developing arthralgia, influenza, or DIC.

10. **C)**

The nurse should ensure a qualified interpreter explains any changes in the treatment plan. Family members are not appropriate for translating medical care. A hospital employee cannot translate medical care unless they are designated as a qualified translator. The new medication should not wait until change of shift. A language line is the most appropriate intervention, as the nurse can speak directly to an interpreter and have the information translated immediately without delaying care.

11. **C)**

A history of hypertension will cause an increase in afterload. Diabetes will cause complications with microvascular disease, leading to poor cardiac function. Endocrine disorders will cause an increase in cardiac workload. Marfan syndrome causes the cardiac muscle to stretch and weaken.

12. **C)**

The cardiac vascular nurse can delegate appropriate tasks to LPNs, patient care techs, or medical assistants. The respiratory therapist is in an entirely different scope of practice, so it is not appropriate for the nurse to delegate tasks to this staff member.

13. **B)**

The most appropriate task to assign to a student nurse on their first day would be a simple one such as applying oxygen. Performing a procedure such as an arterial blood gas or calling the physician are not appropriate tasks for a student. A patient in heart failure would not be administered fluids.

14. **A)**

Magnesium sulfate is a CNS depressant and can cause marked bradycardia and respiratory depression. The nursing priority is to monitor the patient's vital signs for CNS depression after this drug is administered. Tachycardia and hyperventilation are not side effects of magnesium sulfate. A Swan-Ganz catheter and synchronized cardioversion are not indicated.

15. **C)**

ST elevation in the II, III, and aVF leads indicates an inferior MI. An anterior MI would have elevation in leads V1 – V4; a lateral MI would have elevation in I, aVL, V5, and V6; and a posterior MI would show ST depression in V1 and V2, and tall R waves.

16. **C)**

The patient should be reassured that they will be monitored for any changes in their post-procedure condition. The nurse should not give the patient false reassurance or provide results of the procedure. Anxiety medication may be indicated but is not the priority. Telling the patient that the physician will meet them soon does not address the patient's immediate concern.

17. **B)**

Elderly people tend to have decreased renal function. Digoxin is eliminated primarily in the kidneys, which increases the likelihood of digoxin toxicity.

18. **D)**

A patient's psychosocial and spiritual needs should be addressed to ensure a therapeutic environment is provided. Administering medications and assigning the same nurse to the patient each day are not part of creating a therapeutic environment.

19. **A)**

SMART goals should be specific, measurable, attainable, realistic, and timely. Option A defines a set amount of time, and this goal can be easily measured.

20. **B)**

Advance directives are used to help with difficult questions and the decision-making process for patients who are unable to make decisions for themselves. An alert and oriented patient can make decisions, so advance directives are not applicable. A stable patient being extubated after open heart surgery would not need advance directives unless they began to decline and were not able to communicate. Every patient who is discharged to a long-term facility does not necessarily need advance directives.

21. **B)**

The patient is in V-fib and is pulseless. After CPR is started, the next priority intervention is defibrillation. Epinephrine should not be administered until after defibrillation. Inserting an advanced airway may be indicated but is not the priority. A fluid bolus is not a priority for a patient in V-fib.

22. **C)**

A DNR order indicates that no heroic measures should be taken to prolong the patient's life. This includes chest compressions, defibrillation, and advanced airway placement. Administering oxygen is the most noninvasive option. The physician should be notified of the patient's status.

23. **B)**

A patient's goal should be specific and measurable (having a pain level of 5 or less), timely (by the end of the shift), and attainable (this is likely achievable by the end of the shift).

Being pain-free is an unrealistic goal. Taking all scheduled pain medication and taking less pain medication than the prior shift are not specific goals.

24. **A)**

Fluid boluses of 1 to 2 L normal saline should be used to treat hypotension. The patient is dehydrated at the cellular level and needs fluid resuscitation. Furosemide is used as a diuretic and would further dehydrate the patient, exacerbating the issue. Inotropes such as dopamine are used to promote cardiac contractility and will not hydrate the patient. D5W is not indicated because it is not an isotonic solution that will add to the systemic fluid volume.

25. **A)**

Use of nitrates is contraindicated in patients who have taken phosphodiesterase inhibitors (erectile dysfunction medications) because the combination can cause a dangerous drop in blood pressure.

26. **C)**

Nitroglycerin works through vasodilation that improves blood flow and helps reduce venous return. Nitroglycerin reduces preload and does not increase the heart rate or reduce plaque formation.

27. **A)**

The PT/INR level should be drawn first to determine how the warfarin has affected the patient's ability to clot. An aPTT lab monitors the effects of heparin. Administration of FFP or vitamin K may be necessary depending on the results of the PT/INR.

28. **A)**

Pericarditis has a typical friction rub, or "leathery" sound. Crackles would be heard in pulmonary edema or pneumonia. Wheezing would be heard with asthma. An S3 gallop may be heard with mitral regurgitation.

29. **A)**

A patient with increased LDL and triglyceride levels should avoid foods high in saturated fats. The other options would not directly affect cholesterol levels.

30. **A)**

The best technique for active listening is to sit facing the patient while making eye contact. Speaking clearly is important, but it is not necessary to speak loudly and slowly. Asking open-ended questions is not a component of active listening. Moving around the room is not a component of active listening.

31. **C)**

Personally identifiable information (PII), such as a patient's Social Security number, first and last name, and medical record numbers, should be kept confidential. A date of birth, with no other identifying information, is not considered PII.

32. **B)**

Palliative care is focused on relieving the symptoms to help improve quality of life and can be used at any time. A patient does not have to be terminal to receive palliative care, and it can be used in combination with other treatments. Palliative care can last more than 3 months, if needed.

33. **B)**

The physician will counsel the patient on the risks associated with leaving against medical advice (AMA). Whenever possible, the patient should be counseled by the physician, sign AMA paperwork, and then leave the department. A patient with appendicitis will not be involuntarily committed. It is not appropriate to tell a patient he will die if he leaves, although he should be informed of possible negative consequences. The patient should speak with the physician before he tries to leave.

34. **C)**

The hospital volunteer is an appropriate choice to wheel the patient to his car. The patient's wife or daughter should not be given this task. A ride-sharing service is not appropriate to assist in helping the patient to his car.

35. B)

The float nurse should be assigned patients like the patients they usually care for. In this situation, postsurgical patients would be most appropriate. Nurses from another unit may not be familiar with specific protocols for cardiac patients, but they can still care for them.

36. A)

Patients with DVT should be on bed rest to prevent movement of the DVT and pressure changes that occur with walking and other weight-bearing activities. The affected extremity should be elevated. Placing the bed in reverse Trendelenburg will increase pressure on the affected extremity. Walking is contraindicated for patients with DVT, and while preventing hospital-acquired pneumonia is important, patient safety takes priority over pneumonia prevention in this situation. The patient may still use an incentive spirometer and practice coughing and deep breathing to clear the lungs without ambulating. Sitting up in a chair is also contraindicated until the DVT has resolved and the health care provider has prescribed activity for the patient.

37. C)

Increased risk factors for heparin-induced thrombocytopenia (HIT) include being female and heparin use for postsurgical thromboprophylaxis. HIT is more common in patients who have been on unfractionated heparin or who have used heparin for longer than 1 week. Enoxaparin is a low-molecular-weight heparin, which carries a lower risk of causing HIT. It is often prescribed for patients with unstable angina to help increase blood flow through the heart.

38. B)

Left-sided heart failure manifestations include pulmonary symptoms such as crackles and dyspnea. Right-sided heart failure causes systemic congestion, leading to hepatomegaly, dependent edema, jugular vein distention, and ascites.

39. C)

Pericarditis has a characteristic friction rub sound on auscultation due to inflammation, and pain is typically relieved when leaning forward.

40. C)

Smoking is one of the main risk factors for cardiovascular disease. The cardiac vascular nurse should provide the patient with smoking cessation resources and encourage them to quit smoking. Gender and age are non-modifiable risk factors. Regular exercise improves heart health.

41. A)

Mitral stenosis causes increased pressure and increased blood volume in the left atrium, which causes enlargement. The enlarged atrium can lead to A-fib because the heart cannot pump as effectively.

42. D)

A defining characteristic of a first-degree block is a prolonged PR interval > 0.20.

43. A)

Travel that requires long periods of immobility such as plane or car rides is associated with increased risk of blood clot formation due to physical inactivity.

44. A)

The nurse should acknowledge the patient's feelings and then attempt to discuss the results and diagnosis. The nurse should avoid blaming the other physician or facility or downplaying the diagnosis by telling the patient not to worry. The nurse should avoid telling the patient what to do and focus on why he is upset.

45. C)

When the nurse signs as a witness on a consent form, the nurse is only stating that they observed the patient sign that form. It is the role of the physician to explain the procedure and ensure the patient understands the risks and benefits. The patient can be educated on medications they will receive, but this is not a prerequisite to completing a consent form.

46. C)

The faith community nurse, or parish nurse, is the best option to provide health care using a holistic approach by focusing on spirituality and faith-based care.

47. B)

HDL cholesterol is considered "good cholesterol," and higher levels can lower cardiovascular diseases. Cholesterol can be lowered by maintaining an exercise program, smoking cessation, and medications.

48. C)

To promote population health, the cardiac vascular nurse could participate in a free community blood pressure screening event because hypertension is the number one risk factor for cardiovascular disease. Organizing team-building activities, running in a 5k, and participating in a research study do not help improve population health.

49. D)

The patient is stable in SVT, so the most noninvasive treatment (vagal maneuvers) should be performed first. Adenosine is the first drug of choice if vagal maneuvers are unsuccessful. Defibrillation is not used in conscious patients with organized heart rhythms. Synchronized cardioversion is not indicated for a stable patient in SVT.

50. C)

Adrenaline, dopamine, digoxin, and dobutamine are all positive inotropes and can be helpful in the management of heart failure. However, digoxin is not recommended in the treatment of acute heart failure in an 80-year-old patient because elderly patients are more susceptible to digoxin toxicity.

51. C)

The patient is experiencing symptoms of pulmonary edema, a complication of left-sided heart failure. Coagulation is not a secondary effect of MI. Pneumonia is not generally related to post–MI concerns. A ruptured ventricle would present symptoms closer to the time of injury.

52. B)

Hyperkalemia will cause bradycardia and tall peaked T waves. Patients with hypokalemia will have ventricular dysrhythmias such as PVCs, V-tach or V-fib, or the presence of U waves. Hyponatremia can cause neurologic effects such as a decreased level of consciousness or seizure activity.

53. D)

The nurse should provide the patient with as much information as possible regarding his diagnosis and treatment plan so that he can make an informed decision regarding his care. A competent patient cannot be forced to stay and has the right to refuse tests or leave the hospital. Having the business office discuss a payment plan may be helpful, but it is not the best action for the nurse to take in this situation.

54. C)

Discussing beneficial reasons for the patient to quit smoking is an example of motivational interviewing. Giving statistics and consequences for smoking may be helpful for some patients, but this is not an example of motivational interviewing. Telling the patient to use a prescription-strength medication might be an option for a patient wanting to stop smoking but is not an example of motivational interviewing.

55. A)

Asking about special cultural needs is the appropriate action when caring for a patient from a different culture. The nurse should make every attempt to accommodate the patient's needs. The nurse should not assume the patient would like a chaplain to pray with unless requested. The nurse may be able to make an exception to the visitor policy if it is for a cultural purpose, but this statement does not help provide culturally competent care.

56. C)

Patients in the millennial age group generally prefer learning strategies focused on technology. Role-playing is more appropriate for younger age groups. Older generations may prefer classroom or self-paced learning by reading.

57. D)

The priority intervention is to use a Doppler to confirm if pulses are present. If pulses are not present using the Doppler, a call to the physician would be appropriate. An ultrasound or CT may be appropriate but is not the priority.

58. B)

The American Heart Association currently recommends a 1,500 mg limit of sodium intake for cardiac patients to improve hypertension and heart health.

59. A)

A patient who is competent can still make decisions regarding their care, which overrides a POA documentation. The patient is within his rights to revoke his son as POA and the patient can alter it as long as he is mentally capable to do so.

60. D)

The main purpose of a Doppler ultrasound is to measure the patient's blood flow and help identify any blocked arteries. It does not identify cardiovascular disease. Time and cost are not the main reasons to have a Doppler. A lower-extremity Doppler will not rule out an aneurysm.

61. D)

Hypercoagulability, venous stasis, and endothelial damage (also known as Virchow's triad) are the main factors that predispose an individual to clot formation. A heart murmur is not part of Virchow's triad and is not considered a major contributing factor to clot formation.

62. A)

Administration of adenosine can cause a brief period of asystole on the monitor, followed by conversion to a normal sinus rhythm.

63. B)

A family member at the bedside for resuscitation has been demonstrated in the evidence as a preference for patients and families and should be offered when possible and appropriate. Family members should be present only if they are not disruptive to patient care.

64. C)

Eating a diet too rich in vitamin K can decrease the effects of warfarin. The patient should be taught to avoid excessive intake of leafy greens such as spinach and kale, which are high in vitamin K. Tuna packed in oil is also high in vitamin K. The other options are not high in vitamin K.

65. A)

Monitoring the patient's weight every morning is the best way to evaluate fluid and electrolyte balance. A weight gain of more than 2 pounds a day or 5 pounds in a week should be reported. Weight gain is considered the first sign of worsening heart failure. Foley catheters should be avoided when possible to prevent urinary tract complications. Reducing sodium intake is necessary for heart failure patients but does not help evaluate fluid/electrolyte balance.

66. D)

The combined use of St. John's Wort and digoxin can result in toxic effects. St. John's Wort can cause excessive bleeding when combined with anticoagulants, not excessive clotting.

67. B)

The elevated blood pressure is a critical finding and is considered objective data because it can be measured. The troponin level is an example of objective data, but it is a normal finding that does not need to be reported. The patient complaint of dizziness or a family member reporting that the patient seems more depressed should be followed up on, but these are considered subjective data.

68. D)

In the teach-back method, the nurse has the patient demonstrate or repeat back what they have learned. Procedural education is given before a procedure so the patient knows what to expect before, during, and after. Adherence is how compliant the patient is with their plan of care. Memorization is committing something to memory.

69. A)

A patient must be alert, oriented, and deemed competent to make their own medical decisions in order to sign informed consent. The patient does not need to have their insurance verified or a complete history and physical completed before the procedure. The patient should be informed of the benefits and risks of the procedure before signing the consent form. If a patient refuses the procedure, another family member cannot sign for them.

70. A)

Abnormalities in magnesium levels may put the patient at risk for ventricular dysrhythmia. A hypomagnesemia level of 0.8 mEq/L would be of concern (normal range is 1.5 – 2.5 mEq/L). The other values are within normal ranges.

71. D)

Patients with heart failure have difficulty with exertional activity such as walking up stairs. Beta blockers are used for hypertension, but they do not indicate or contribute to heart failure. Pulmonary emboli may affect the heart, but not in a chronic way like heart failure. Chest pain is not commonly associated with heart failure.

72. B)

The patient is unstable in a third-degree or complete heart block, so TCP is indicated.

73. A)

The drug of choice for SVT is adenosine. The first dose of 6 mg has already been given, so the next appropriate dose would be 12 mg. The other options are not the next appropriate intervention for a patient in SVT.

74. D)

The nurse should properly log out of the computer when he is finished so that no one else can access the information. Any paper documents that are no longer needed

should be shredded. The nurse can ask the HIPAA compliance officer questions or state concerns regarding HIPAA policies. The nurse should never share passwords under any circumstances.

75. D)

Sudden back pain and dyspnea indicate rupture of the aneurysm, which is an emergency. The nurse should notify the health care provider, monitor neurological and vital signs, and remain with the patient. Yellow-tinted vision is a finding of digitalis toxicity. Hemoptysis a sign of pulmonary edema. Urinary output of 75 mL/hr is normal.

76. C)

The new graduate CV nurse should be prepared to insert an IV, administer epinephrine, and prepare the patient for defibrillation. Intubating the patient is typically not done by the bedside nurse and should not be done by a new graduate nurse.

77. D)

Denial is refusing to accept or believe something. Passive coping is feeling helpless to deal with the stress or change required to cope with a situation. Active coping is characterized by problem solving and seeking support to deal with an issue. Avoiding involves changing one's behavior to keep from thinking about the problem.

78. A)

The nurse should assess the apical pulse for a full minute before administering digoxin. If the pulse is less than 60 bpm, the nurse should hold the dose and notify the physician. The chest X-ray results and glucose levels are not related to administering digoxin. Digoxin can affect the blood pressure, but it primarily affects the heart rate.

79. D)

Asking the patient about their goals is an example of an open-ended question that may help the nurse gather more information from the patient. The other questions can all be answered with a yes or no.

80. B)

Morphine is the pain medication of choice for an acute MI because it decreases the oxygen demand of the heart. The half-life of morphine is 2 – 4 hours. Morphine does not reduce ST elevation.

81. B)

The initial survey includes a rapid assessment to identify emergent conditions and includes LOC, breathing pattern, and skin color.

82. C)

Documentation for any change in patient status is always necessary and should be as descriptive as possible. Documentation should not include a suspected diagnosis.

83. D)

A recent MI would place the patient in a higher risk category for cardiac surgery. A creatinine level of 1.3 mg/dL is normal. An allergy to latex and history of asthma would not place the patient at a higher risk for cardiac surgery.

84. A)

Patients allergic to the iodine dye used in contrast CT studies may need a different exam or may need to be pre-medicated before the CT.

85. D)

Classic signs of cardiac tamponade include muffled heart tones, JVD, and hypotension (symptoms known as Beck's triad). Auscultating heart sounds would be helpful to identify the presence of muffled heart tones.

86. C)

Decreased CO usually occurs with increasing age due to cardiac muscles hardening, which results in decreased filling and emptying of the heart. Drug metabolism is typically reduced, and blood pressure usually increases with age.

87. C)

The most likely cause of bradycardia in pediatrics is hypoxia, so reoxygenation should be the priority intervention for any pediatric patient in bradycardia.

88. B)

Tetralogy of Fallot is a congenital heart defect in which blood flow to the lungs is reduced. Oxygen-poor blood flows to the right atrium and ventricles and is then pumped through the aorta to the rest of the body. This shunting of oxygen-poor blood causes cyanosis. Infants experiencing cyanotic events are said to be having "tet spells."

89. D)

IVC filters are used to prevent clots from causing a pulmonary embolism. They can be removed when necessary but are not routinely replaced every 6 months. Patients can eat a normal diet with IVC filters in place.

90. B)

The patient with a new ICD should monitor the incision for signs and symptoms of infection and report them to the physician. The appropriate wound care for the incision is a dry dressing change. Patients should be taught about activity restrictions post-surgery, including limiting heavy lifting with the affected arm. The importance of handwashing should be emphasized both before and after dressing changes.

91. C)

Prior to synchronized cardioversion, patients should be sedated so they do not feel the pain associated with the electrical shock. Patients should only be awake if they are unstable and there is no time for sedation. The procedure should not need to be repeated. The patient has a choice in refusing the procedure, but they may deteriorate without it.

92. C)

Telehealth can expedite care and allow the nurse to discuss patient changes with the physician remotely to develop a new plan of care. A code blue should only be called for a cardiac arrest. A patient in a second-degree, type 2 heart block should be immediately reported to the physician, and staff should take steps to prepare to transcutaneous pace.

93. A)

Patients need anticoagulation therapy to prevent clots after a surgical cardiac procedure such as an LVAD. Patients typically need to stay in ICU postoperatively and should plan on staying in the hospital for approximately 2 weeks. Several medications will be prescribed to keep the heart functioning properly. Chest compressions should not be performed on a patient with an LVAD unless it is an absolute last resort, as it may cause the LVAD to become dislodged.

94. C)

Increasing the proportion of adults with hypertension who are taking the prescribed medications to lower blood pressure is a Healthy People 2020 objective the nurse can use for this quality improvement project. The number of adults with no cardiovascular history who take daily aspirin should be increased. The number of adults with prehypertension who meet the recommended guidelines for BMI should be increased. The proportion of adults 20 and older who are aware of the symptoms of and how to respond to a heart attack is a Healthy People 2020 objective.

95. A)

Patients with heart failure should be instructed to weigh themselves daily to monitor fluid balance. Patients should be taught sodium reduction, not complete restriction. If a patient has difficulty breathing, they should be taught to go to the ED. If a patient notices pedal edema, they should report this finding to their provider, as it may indicate worsening heart failure.

96. C)

An HgbA1C of 9.0 is elevated and reflects poor blood sugar control over the prior 3 months. The nurse and the patient should develop a plan of care to improve diet, exercise, and medication compliance.

97. D)

Goal setting is part of the planning process. Auscultating heart sounds is part of the assessment, evaluating lab results is part of the evaluation process, and checking a patient's blood pressure is part of the intervention phase.

98. B)

Heparin is an anticoagulant commonly administered to a patient having an MI. Aspirin and clopidogrel are antiplatelet medications. Nitrates are vasodilators.

99. B)

Hypocalcemia can cause a prolonged QT interval. Hypomagnesemia would cause a prolonged PR interval and widenings of the QRS complex. Hyperkalemia can cause peaked T waves. Hyponatremia does not typically cause ECG changes.

100. D)

Marfan syndrome causes connective tissue to degenerate. As a result, blood vessel walls can weaken due to stretching and cause an aneurysm.

101. A)

The priority intervention for any patient with chest discomfort or pressure is to obtain a 12-lead ECG. Expert consultation would not be needed at this time. A health history and reviewing admission policies are important but are not the priority.

102. C)

Hypertension puts continuous pressure on the vessel walls, which causes them to weaken and form an aneurysm. Blood pressure control should be a priority for a patient with an AAA.

103. A)

The patient feeling down, having trouble sleeping, and reporting decreased energy levels warrants a depression screening. Depression is a known risk factor for cardiac disease. All cardiac patients are recommended to be screened for depression.

104. D)

A troponin of greater than 0.05 indicates cardiac damage and should be followed up on. This patient would need serial cardiac enzymes to ensure the troponin does not continue to increase.

105. C)

The nurse should anticipate that a patient in a second degree, type II heart block could progress to a third degree block and need transcutaneous pacing. Synchronized cardioversion is not indicated for this patient. The nurse should not continue to monitor the patient without intervention, as this type of heart block can progress to a complete heart block.

106. D)

Short-term goals should be measurable and specific. Using an exercise log to record 15-minute daily walks at least 4 times a week is a clear, specific, and measurable goal. Cutting out processed foods, wearing a nicotine patch, and intermittently checking blood pressure are not specific and measurable goals.

107. C)

Baked chicken with vegetables is a healthy, low-sodium option for a cardiac patient. Canned soups, deli meats and cheeses, and pizza are high-sodium foods that should be avoided or eaten sparingly.

108. D)

The patient who has been following his treatment plan for hypertension would be expected to have a normal blood pressure. A patient stating that they feel better is subjective, whereas measuring their blood pressure is an objective way of determining compliance. Not refilling medication is a sign of noncompliance. A patient complaint of intermittent chest pain does not necessarily indicate compliance, and the patient will need follow-up.

109. B)

Before giving out any patient information, the nurse should make sure the patient has given permission to discuss their care with the person asking for it. This can be done using a security code or HIPAA password that is given only to people the patient approves. Verifying the name, birthdate, and room number are not valid reasons to give out patient information. Even vague information should not be given out, in order to protect the patient's privacy. Information can be given over the phone if the patient has given permission and the caller's identity is confirmed.

110. B)

Cardiac rehabilitation helps provide a support system for patients during their recovery. It may not be covered fully by all insurance plans and is not required for cardiologists to treat patients with follow-up care. While cardiac rehabilitation reduces the chance of having subsequent heart attacks, it does not completely prevent them.

111. C)

To access the results, the nurse should have her husband sign a release form. The nurse may not access information for any patient not under her care. The physician should not provide results regarding her husband's care. Asking a friend who is working to access the chart is considered a breach of confidentiality.

112. A)

Increased WBCs and an increased sedimentation rate are expected findings in a patient diagnosed with endocarditis due to inflammation. Elevated lactic acid, troponin, and BNP are not expected findings for endocarditis.

113. A)

Increased heart rate, increased blood volume, and increased CO are expected changes for a pregnant patient. Blood pressure should not be affected and can be dangerous if elevated.

114. A)

Assisting a patient to the bathroom is the most appropriate task for an unlicensed assistive personnel (UAP) such as a patient care technician. The patient care technician can also assist with vital signs, but assisting the patient to the bathroom is more appropriate. It is not appropriate for patient care technicians to hang IV fluids or insert a catheter.

115. A)

The priority nursing diagnosis would be focused on addressing breathing issues. Activity intolerance, urinary issues, or renal perfusion may be considered in patients with heart failure, but ineffective breathing due to excess fluid would be the priority focus.

116. B)

Administration of a fibrinolytic should result in resolution of ST elevation. Effectiveness of the fibrinolytic would not be based on troponin levels, a new bundle branch block, or a decrease in pain level.

117. A)

An expected outcome for a patient on day 3 of admission is to achieve a controlled pain level.

118. C)

A history of intracranial bleeding is a contraindication to administering tPA due to the risk of bleeding.

119. B)

Airway patency is the priority for any patient following synchronized cardioversion, as the patient has likely been sedated and will need airway monitoring. The other options are important, but airway patency takes priority.

120. C)

The nurse should address any specific needs the patient may have. Placing necessary items within reach can help the patient feel safer and more comfortable.

121. B)

A common side effect of an ACE inhibitor is a dry cough, and patients should be informed of this before starting the medication.

122. C)

The nurse should first apply oxygen by the least invasive means possible. Asking the patient to bear down could cause bradycardia and worsen oxygenation.

123. B)

The patient was not harmed, so it is unlikely they would be successful in suing the nurse for negligence. Notifying the physician and patient, monitoring for side effects, and proper documentation are all important, but the extent of the patient injury is the determining factor.

124. D)

Classic signs of cardiogenic shock include a rapid pulse that weakens; cool, clammy skin; and decreased urine output. Hypotension is another classic sign.

125. B)

Leaving a printout of the patient's personal information in plain view at the nurse's station where it could be read by any staff member or visitor is a HIPAA violation. Information about a patient's status can be given over the phone if the patient has given approval. Faxing patient information to another physician caring for the patient is necessary for continuity of care. Giving pertinent information to the billing department is permitted.

126. D)

Creatine kinase muscle/blood (CK-MB) is a cardiac enzyme specific to heart muscle and should be drawn along with troponin for any patient with complaints of chest pain. A potassium level may be indicated but is not the priority. An INR level is not necessary.

127. D)

The most appropriate place to chart information about a family member's health history is in the family history section. Medication history includes which medications the patient is on, and past medical history includes the patient's medical history diagnoses. Social history includes details about the patient's personal life that may be pertinent (e.g., occupation or recreational activities).

128. C)

Increased alcohol consumption can increase the effect of warfarin and cause excessive bleeding. The patient should be instructed to abstain from alcohol consumption while taking this medication.

129. C)

One physical sign of endocarditis is red, flat, and painless lesions known as Janeway lesions. These are often seen in patients with endocarditis along with fever, chest pain, petechiae, and flu-like symptoms.

130. B)

Intermittent pneumatic compression devices use cuffs that wrap around the legs and intermittently fill with air to squeeze the legs to increase blood flow. Heparin is a pharmacological type of VTE prophylaxis. Massage and bed rest are not considered best practice for VTE prophylaxis.

131. C)

Canned soup and sandwiches with processed meats and cheeses are typically high in sodium and should be avoided on a cardiac diet.

132. D)

The patient with hypertension and severe back pain (especially if described as "tearing") could have an AAA rupture, which is emergent. A patient needing a blood sugar check can be delegated to a UAP. A decreased troponin result is an improvement and does not require immediate intervention. A patient requesting pain medicine can be covered by another RN or seen after the patient with tearing pain is assessed.

133. A)

Arranging for a chaplain can help meet the psychosocial and spiritual needs of the family after a loss. The nurse should not discuss organ donation with the family members at this time. The family should be allowed to stay with the patient and not rushed to leave after a patient's death.

134. B)

The antidote for heparin is protamine sulfate. Vitamin K is the antidote for warfarin. Digoxin immune fab is the antidote for

digoxin. Acetylcysteine is the antidote for acetaminophen.

135. C)

The Unna boot moves fluid with activity to improve venous flow and so is not recommended for bed-bound patients. The leg should be dry before the boot is applied. The dressing should not stop mid-calf or be wrapped too tightly, as there should be room for natural swelling to occur.

136. D)

A radial compression device is often used after a transradial procedure to achieve hemostasis and prevent arterial damage.

137. A)

Any patient receiving a thrombolytic should be monitored for signs of bleeding. Intramuscular injections should be avoided since the patient is at risk for bleeding. Assessing the patient for edema and auscultating heart sounds are not priorities for a patient receiving tPA.

138. C)

An infant with tetralogy of Fallot would be ordered digoxin to slow down and control the heart rate.

139. B)

The Dietary Approaches to Stop Hypertension (DASH) diet is composed of fruits, vegetables, and low-fat dairy products. It features low cholesterol, low fat, and low sodium and is recommended for hypertension patients.

140. A)

Bumetanide is a diuretic, so decreased edema is an expected result if the medication is effective. Work of breathing should improve due to reduced fluid in the heart and lungs. Wheezing is a lower-airway obstruction and is not expected when administering bumetanide. Improved pain is not an expected side effect.

141. B)

A headache is a common side effect of nitroglycerin, which causes vasodilation.

Acetaminophen can be administered to help with a headache.

142. A)

The nurse should first assess what the patient already knows about endocarditis. The patient's social history, IV drug habits, and lab results are important but are not the priority when performing patient education.

143. D)

A patient who has been hospitalized for several days and then takes a long flight is at risk for a DVT. She should be encouraged to stretch her legs and walk around the airplane occasionally to increase blood flow and prevent clots. Although heart-healthy foods and exercise logs are important, preventing a DVT takes priority.

144. B)

Elevation in leads II, III, and aVF on an ECG indicates an inferior wall MI. Troponin levels will not indicate which wall is affected. Symptoms and family history do not correlate to the specific wall affected.

145. C)

A stable 1-year-old in SVT is treated with ice to the face to stimulate the vagal nerve. A straw can be used to stimulate the vagal nerve in older children who can follow directions. Returning with juice and crackers would not indicate that the student has knowledge of treating SVT.

146. C)

Disclosing personal patient information to parties who do not have a need to know and to whom the patient has not given permission is considered a HIPAA violation. Negligence is failure to act as another nurse reasonably would in the same situation. Defamation is providing information that damages someone's reputation. Non-maleficence is doing no harm.

147. B)

The best body positioning for the nurse to use is sitting, facing the patient, and making good eye contact, as these all demonstrate active listening. Standing at the foot of the bed, walking around the room, and documenting in the computer do not demonstrate proper active listening skills.

148. B)

The D-dimer can help diagnose the presence of a clot. A patient with an elevated D-dimer level should be further assessed with a CT of the chest to rule out a pulmonary embolism.

149. A)

When an organ donor patient dies, the nurse should first contact the organ procurement organization because of time sensitivity. Life-supporting interventions such as ventilators and medications should be continued until the organ procurement agency arrives. Postmortem care and completing the death certificate can be performed after organ procurement has taken place.

150. A)

In order to be compliant with COBRA/EMTALA, there must be an accepting physician at an accepting hospital, the patient must consent when he or she has decisional capacity, and the transport method must be congruent with the patient's condition. The hospital must have the services the patient's condition requires.

To access your second cardiac vascular nursing exam, follow the link below:

http://ascenciatestprep.com/cvrn-online-resources

APPENDIX: SIGNS and SYMPTOMS GLOSSARY

angioedema: edema of subcutaneous tissues

aphasia: impairment in ability to speak, write, and understand others

apnea: temporary cessation of breathing

arthralgias: joint pain

ascites: abdominal swelling caused by fluid in the peritoneal cavity

bradycardia: slow heart rate

bradypnea: slow respiration rate

carotid bruits: murmur heard over the carotid artery

cardiomegaly: enlarged heart

cyanosis: blueish skin

diaphoresis: excessive sweating

dysarthria: slurred speech caused by muscle weakness

dyspnea: difficulty breathing

ecchymosis: bruising

edema: swelling caused by excess fluid

effusion: accumulation of fluid

epistaxis: bleeding from the nose

erythema: redness of the skin

erythema multiforme: skin rash characterized by target-shaped lesions

hematuria: blood in urine

hemoptysis: blood in expectorate from respiratory tract

hepatomegaly: enlargement of liver

Homans' sign: discomfort behind the knee or increased resistance in response to dorsiflexion of the foot

hypertension: high blood pressure

hypotension: low blood pressure

hypoxemia: low levels of oxygen in the blood

hypoxia: lack of oxygen supplied to tissues

ileus: lack of movement in the intestines

ischemia: restricted blood flow to tissue

jaundice: yellowing of the skin or sclera

Kussmaul respirations: deep, labored breathing

Levine's sign: a clenched fist held over the chest in response to ischemic chest pain

nocturia: excessive urination at night

oliguria: low urine output

orthopnea: dyspnea that occurs while lying flat

orthostatic (postural) hypotension: decrease in blood pressure after standing

pallor: pale appearance

palpitations: sensation of the heart racing, fluttering, or pounding

paresthesia: abnormal dermal sensation such as burning or "pins and needles"

petechiae: tiny red or brown spots on the skin caused by subcutaneous bleeding

poikilothermia: inability to regulate body temperature

polydipsia: excessive thirst

polyphagia: excessive hunger

polyuria: abnormally high urine output

pulsus alternans: alternating strong and weak pulse

stenosis: narrowing of a passage

stridor: high-pitched wheezing sound caused by a disruption in airflow

syncope: temporary loss of consciousness

tachycardia: fast heart rate

tachypnea: fast respiratory rate

varicose veins: swollen veins

APPENDIX: ABBREVIATIONS

A

AAA: abdominal aortic aneurysm (triple A)

AACVPR: American Association of Cardiovascular and Pulmonary Rehabilitation

ABCM: American Board of Cardiovascular Medicine

ABCs: airway, breathing, circulation

ABG: arterial blood gas

ABI: ankle-brachial index

ACC: American College of Cardiology

ACE-Is or **ACE inhibitors:** angiotensin-converting enzyme inhibitors

ACLS: advanced cardiovascular life support

ACPE: acute cardiogenic pulmonary edema

ACS: acute coronary syndrome

ADHD: attention deficit hyperactivity disorder

ADLs: activities of daily living

ADP: adenosine diphosphate

ADPIE model: assessment, diagnosis, planning, intervention, evaluation

A-fib: atrial fibrillation

AHA: American Heart Association

ALP: alkaline phosphatase

ALT: alanine aminotransferase

AMA: against medical advice

ANA: American Nurses Association

ANCC: American Nurses Credentialing Center

AND: allow natural death

aPTT: activated partial thromboplastin time

AR: aortic regurgitation

ARB: angiotensin II receptor blocker

AS: aortic stenosis

ASAP: as soon as possible

ASCVD: atherosclerotic cardiovascular disease

ASD: atrial septal defect

AST: aspartate aminotransferase

AV: atrioventricular

aVF: augmented vector foot (ECG lead)

aVL: augmented vector left (ECG lead)

aVR: augmented vector right (ECG lead)

B

BBB: bundle branch block

BHV: bioprosthetic heart valves

BiPAP: bilevel positive airway pressure

BMI: body mass index

BNP: B-type natriuretic peptide

BP: blood pressure

BPEG: British Pacing and Electrophysiology Group (pacemaker codes)

BPH: benign prostatic hyperplasia

bpm: beats per minute

BPM: breaths per minute

BUN: blood urea nitrogen

C

CABG: coronary artery bypass graft

CAD: coronary artery disease

cAMP: cyclic adenosine monophosphate

CAOD: carotid artery occlusive disease

CBC: complete blood count

CEA: carotid endarterectomy

CI: cardiac index

CK: creatine kinase

CK-MB: creatine kinase–muscle/brain

CLL: chronic lymphocytic leukemia

CML: chronic myelogenous leukemia

CMP: comprehensive metabolic panel

CNS: central nervous system

CO: cardiac output

COBRA: Consolidated Omnibus Budget Reconciliation Act

COPD: chronic obstructive pulmonary disease

CPR: cardiopulmonary resuscitation

CRT: capillary refill time

CT scan: computed tomography scan

CV nurse: cardiac vascular nurse

CVA: cerebrovascular accident

CVD: cardiovascular disease

CVI: chronic venous insufficiency

CVP: central venous pressure

CVRN: cardiac vascular registered nurse

D

D5W: dextrose 5% in water

DASH: dietary approaches to stop hypertension

DBP: diastolic blood pressure

DCCM: dilated congestive cardiomyopathy

DNI: do not intubate

DNR: do not resuscitate

DOB: date of birth

DVT: deep vein thrombosis

E

ECG: electrocardiogram

ED: emergency department

EMTALA: Emergency Medical Treatment and Active Labor Act

EPS: electrophysiology studies

EVAR: endovascular aneurysm repair

F

FDP: fibrin degradation products

FFP: fresh frozen plasma

FSP: fibrin split products

G

GCS: Glasgow Coma Scale

GGT: gamma-glutamyltransferase

GI: gastrointestinal

H

Hct: hematocrit

HCM: hypertrophic cardiomyopathy

HDL: high-density lipoprotein

HDL-C: high-density lipoprotein cholesterol

HF: heart failure

HFpEF: heart failure with preserved ejection fraction

HFrEF: heart failure with reduced ejection fraction

HgB: hemoglobin

HIPAA: Health Insurance Portability and Accountability Act

HIT: heparin-induced thrombocytopenia

HR: heart rate

I

IABP: intra-aortic balloon pump

IADLs: instrumental activities of daily living

ICD: implantable cardioverter defibrillator

ICM: insertable cardiac monitor

ICP: intracranial pressure

ID: identification

INR: international normalized ratio

IV: intravenous

IVC: inferior vena cava

J

JNC: Joint National Committee on Prevention, Detection, Evaluation, and Treatment of High Blood Pressure

JVD: jugular vein distention

L

LAD: left anterior descending (artery)

LBBB: left bundle branch block

LD (or LDH): L-lactate dehydrogenase

LDL: low-density lipoprotein

LDL-C: low-density lipoprotein cholesterol

LLQ: left lower quadrant

LMWH: low molecular weight heparin

LOC: level of consciousness

LPN: licensed practical nurse

LUQ: left upper quadrant

LV: left ventricle

LVAD: left ventricle assist device

LVEDP: left ventricular-end diastolic pressure

LVN: licensed vocational nurse

M

MAP: mean arterial pressure

MCH: mean corpuscular hemoglobin

MCHC: mean corpuscular hemoglobin concentration

MCT: mobile cardiac telemetry

MCV: mean corpuscular volume

mEq: milliequivalent

MHV: mechanical heart valves

MI: myocardial infarction

MONA: morphine, oxygen, nitroglycerin, aspirin

MR: mitral regurgitation

MRA: magnetic resonance angiography

MRI: magnetic resonance imaging

MS: mitral stenosis

N

NASPE: North American Society of Pacing and Electrophysiology (pacemaker codes)

NHLBI: National Heart, Lung, and Blood Institute

NIH: National Institutes of Health

NIHSS: National Institutes of Health Stroke Scale

NPH: neutral protamine Hagedorn (insulin)

NPO: *nil per os* (nothing by mouth)

NSAID: nonsteroidal anti-inflammatory drug

NSTEMI: non-ST-elevation myocardial infarction

NVS: Newest Vital Signs

P

PAD: peripheral artery disease

PAH: pulmonary arterial hypertension

PAOP: pulmonary artery occlusion pressure

PAP: pulmonary artery pressure

PCI: percutaneous coronary intervention

PCWP: pulmonary capillary wedge pressure

PDA: patent ductus arteriosus

PE: pulmonary embolism

PEA: pulseless electrical activity

PERRLA: pupils equal, round, and reactive to light and accommodation (motor function assessment)

PET: positron emission tomography

PFO: patent foramen ovale

PH: pulmonary hypertension

PHI: protected health information

PII: personally identifiable information

PO: *per os* (by mouth)

POA: power of attorney

PQRST: provoking, quality, region, severity, timing (to assess pain in a patient)

PRN: *pro re nata* (as needed)

PSVT: paroxysmal supraventricular tachycardia

PT: prothrombin time

PTA: percutaneous transluminal angioplasty

PTCA: percutaneous transluminal coronary angioplasty

PT/INR: prothrombin time and international normalized ratio

PTT: partial thromboplastin time

PVD: peripheral vascular disease

PVR: pulmonary vascular resistance

R

RA: right atrial

RAP: right atrial pressure

RBBB: right bundle branch block

RBC: red blood cell

RCA: right coronary artery

RCM: restrictive cardiomyopathy

REALM: Rapid Estimate of Adult Literacy in Medicine

RHD: rheumatic heart disease

RLQ: right lower quadrant

RR: respiration rate

RUQ: right upper quadrant

RV: right ventricle

RVEDP: right ventricular end-diastolic pressure

S

SA: sinoatrial

SBAR: situation, background, assessment, recommendations

SBP: systolic blood pressure

SCD: sequential compression devices

SIADH: syndrome of inappropriate antidiuretic hormone secretion

S-ICD: subcutaneous implantable cardioverter defibrillator

SMART: specific, measurable, attainable, realistic, time-restricted

SND: sinus node dysfunction

SSS: sick sinus syndrome

STEMI: ST-elevation myocardial infarction

SV: stroke volume

SVN: Society for Vascular Nursing

SVR: systemic vascular resistance

SVT: supraventricular tachycardia

T

TCP: transcutaneous pacing

TEE: transesophageal echocardiogram

TED: thromboembolic deterrent stockings

TF: tissue factor

TIA: transient ischemic attack

TOFHLA: Test of Functional Health Literacy in Adults

tPA: tissue plasminogen activator

TTE: transthoracic echocardiogram

TV-ICD: transvenous implantable cardioverter defibrillator

U

UAP: unlicensed assistive personnel

ULQ: upper left quadrant

URQ: upper right quadrant

UTI: urinary tract infection

V

V-fib: ventricular fibrillation

V-tach: ventricular tachycardia

VAD: ventricular assist device

VSD: ventricular septal defect

VTE: venous thromboembolism prophylaxis

vW: von Willebrand factor

W

WBC: white blood cell

WHO: World Health Organization

APPENDIX C: DIAGNOSTIC TESTS and CRITICAL VALUES

Test	Description	Normal Range
Basic Metabolic Panel		
Potassium (K+)	electrolyte that helps with muscle contraction and regulates water and acid-base balance	3.5 – 5.2 mEq/L
Sodium (Na+)	maintains fluid balance and plays a major role in muscle and nerve function	135 – 145 mEq/L
Calcium (Ca+)	plays an important role in skeletal function and structure, nerve function, muscle contraction, and cell communication	8.5 – 10.3 mg/dL
Chloride (Cl−)	electrolyte that plays a major role in muscle and nerve function	98 – 107 mEq/L
Blood urea nitrogen (BUN)	filtered by the kidneys; high levels can indicate insufficient kidney function	7 – 20 mg/dL
Creatinine	filtered by the kidneys; high levels can indicate insufficient kidney function	0.6 – 1.2 mg/dL
BUN to creatinine ratio	increased ratio indicates dehydration, AKI, or GI bleeding; decreased ratio indicates renal damage	10:1 – 20:1
Glucose	tests for hyper- and hypoglycemia	non-fasting: < 140 mg/dL fasting: 70 – 99 mg/dL
Bicarbonate (HCO_3 or CO_2)	measures amount of CO_2 in the blood; decreased levels indicate acidosis or kidney damage; increased levels indicate alkalosis or lung damage	23 – 29 mEq/L
Other Serum Tests		
Magnesium	electrolyte that regulates muscle, nerve, and cardiac function	1.8 – 2.5 mg/dL
Glomerular filtration rate (GFR)	volume of fluid filtered by the renal glomerular capillaries per unit of time; decreased GFR rate indicates decreased renal function	men: 100 – 130 mL/min/1.73m^2 women: 90 – 120 mL/min/1.73m^2 GFR < 60 mL/min/1.73m^2 is common in adults > 70 years

Test	Description	Normal Range
Other Serum Tests (continued)		
Total cholesterol (LDL and HDL)	a steroid produced by the liver that is needed to build and maintain animal cell membranes and that has protective properties for the heart; goals for low-density lipoprotein (LDL) and high-density lipoprotein (HDL) levels are based on the patient's risk factors for cardiovascular disease	< 200 mg/dL LDL: < 100 mg/dL HDL (men): 40 – 50 mg/dL HDL (women): 50 – 59 mg/dL
Triglycerides	stores fat	< 150 mg/dL
B-type natriuretic peptide (BNP)	protein produced by the heart; high levels can indicate heart failure	< 100 pg/ml
Highly selective CRP test for C-reactive protein	marker for inflammation used to determine a patient's risk for heart disease	low risk: < 1.0 mg/L average risk: 1.0 – 3.0 mg/L high risk: > 3.0 mg/L
Homocysteine	an amino acid used as a marker for heart disease and vitamin deficiency (B_6, B_{12}, and folate)	4 – 14 μmol/L
Prostate-specific antigen (PSA)	enzyme produced by prostate gland; high levels can indicate prostate cancer, prostatitis, or BPH	< 4 ng/mL
Erythrocyte sedimentation rate (ESR or sed rate)	measures rate at which RBCs sediment (fall); increased ESR may indicate inflammation, anemia, or infection; decreased ESR may indicate heart failure or liver or kidney disease; ESR increases with age	men: 12 – 14 mm/h women: 18 – 21 mm/h
Ammonia	produced by bacteria in the intestines during the breakdown of proteins; increased levels may indicate liver or kidney damage; decreased levels are associated with hypertension	15 – 45 mcg/dL
Serum lipase (LPS)	protein secreted by the pancreas that helps break down fats; increased levels can indicate damage to the pancreas	0 – 160 U/L
Amylase	enzyme produced by pancreas and salivary glands; increased levels may indicate damage to the pancreas	23 – 85 U/L
Complete Blood Count (CBC)		
White blood cells (WBCs)	number of WBCs in blood; an increased number of WBCs can be an indication of inflammation or infection	4,500 – 10,000 cells/mcL
Red blood cells (RBCs)	carry oxygen throughout the body and filter carbon dioxide	men: 5 – 6 million cells/mcL women: 4 – 5 million cells/mcL
Hemoglobin (HgB)	protein that holds oxygen in the blood	men: 13.8 – 17.2 g/dL women: 12.1 – 15.1 g/dL
Hematocrit (Hct)	percentage of the blood composed of red blood cells	men: 41% – 50% women: 36% – 44%

Complete Blood Count (CBC) (continued)

Red blood cell indices	mean corpuscular volume (MCV): average size of the red blood cells mean corpuscular hemoglobin (MCH): average amount of hemoglobin per RBC mean corpuscular hemoglobin concentration (MCHC): average concentration of hemoglobin in RBCs	MCV: 80 – 95 fL MCH: 27.5 – 33.2 pg MCHC: 334 – 355 g/L
Platelets	play a role in the body's clotting process	150,000 – 450,000 cells/mcL

Coagulation Studies

Prothrombin time (PT)	tests how long it takes blood to clot	10 – 13 seconds
International normalized ratio (INR)	determines the effectiveness of an anticoagulant in thinning blood	healthy adults: < 1.1 patients receiving anticoagulants: 2.0 – 3.0
Partial thromboplastin time (PTT)	assess the body's ability to form blood clots	60 – 70 sec
Activated partial thromboplastin time (aPTT)	measures the body's ability to form blood clots using an activator to speed up the clotting process	20 – 35 sec

Cardiac Biomarkers

Troponin I (cTnI) and troponin T (cTnT)	proteins released when the heart muscle is damaged; high levels can indicate a myocardial infarction but may also be due to other conditions that stress the heart (e.g., renal failure, heart failure, PE); levels peak 24 hours post MI and can remain elevated for up to 2 weeks	cTnI: cutoff values for MI vary widely between assays cTnT: possible MI: > 0.01 ng/mL
Creatine kinase (CK)	responsible for muscle cell function; an increased amount indicates cardiac or skeletal muscle damage	22 – 198 U/L
Creatine kinase–muscle/brain (CK-MB or CPK-MB)	cardiac marker for damaged heart muscle; often used to diagnose a second MI or ongoing cardiovascular conditions; a high ratio of CK-MB to CK indicates damage to heart muscle (as opposed to skeletal muscle)	5 – 25 IU/L possible MI: ratio of CK-MB to CK is 2.5 – 3

Urinalysis

Leukocytes	presence of WBCs in urine indicates infection	negative
Nitrate	presence of nitrates in urine indicates infection by gram-negative bacteria	negative
Urobilinogen	produced during bilirubin reduction; presence in urine indicates liver disease, bilinear obstruction, or hepatitis	0.2 – 1 mg
Protein	presence of protein in the urine may indicate nephritis or eclampsia	negative

Test	Description	Normal Range
Urinalysis (continued)		
pH	decreased (acidic) pH may indicate systemic acidosis or diabetes mellitus; increased (alkali) pH may indicate systemic alkalosis or UTI	4.5 – 8
Blood	blood in urine may indicate infection, renal calculi, neoplasm, or coagulation disorders	negative
Specific gravity	concentration of urine; decreased may indicate diabetes insipidus or pyelonephritis; increased may indicate dehydration or SIADH	1.010 – 1.025
Ketone	ketones are produced during fat metabolism; presence in urine may indicate diabetes, hyperglycemia, starvation, alcoholism, or eclampsia	negative
Bilirubin	produced during the breakdown of heme; presence in urine may indicate liver disease, biliary obstruction, or hepatitis	negative
Glucose	presence of glucose in urine indicates hyperglycemia	0 – 15 mg/dL
Urine hCG	determination of pregnancy	N/A
Urine culture and sensitivity	study of urine with growth on a culture medium to determine which pathogenic bacteria is present and which antibiotic the pathogen is sensitive to	N/A
Liver Function Tests		
Albumin	a protein made in the liver; low levels may indicate liver damage	3.5 – 5.0 g/dL
Alkaline phosphatase (ALP)	an enzyme found in the liver and bones; increased levels indicate liver damage	45 – 147 U/L
Alanine transaminase (ALT)	an enzyme in the liver that helps metabolize protein; increased levels indicate liver damage	7 – 55 U/L
Aspartate transaminase (AST)	an enzyme in the liver that helps metabolize alanine; increased levels indicate liver or muscle damage	8 – 48 U/L
Total protein	low levels of total protein may indicate liver damage	6.3 – 7.9 g/dL
Total bilirubin	produced during the breakdown of heme; increased levels indicate liver damage or anemia	0.1 – 1.2 mg/dL
Gamma-glutamyl-transferase (GGT)	an enzyme that plays a role in antioxidant metabolism; increased levels indicate liver damage	9 – 48 U/L
L-lactate dehydrogenase (LD or LDH)	an enzyme found in most cells in the body; high levels may indicate liver damage, cancer, or tissue breakdown	adult: 122 – 222 U/L

Arterial Blood Gas (ABG)

pH	measure of blood pH	7.35 – 7.45
Partial pressure of oxygen (PaO_2)	amount of oxygen gas in the blood	75 – 100 mm Hg
Partial pressure of carbon dioxide ($PaCO_2$)	amount of carbon dioxide gas in the blood	35 – 45 mm Hg
Bicarbonate (HCO_3)	amount of bicarbonate in the blood	22 – 26 mEq/L
Oxygen (O_2) saturation	measurement of the amount of oxygen-saturated hemoglobin relative to unsaturated hemoglobin	94 – 100%
Lactate	molecule produced during anaerobic cellular respiration; high levels indicate lack of available oxygen in cells	4.5 – 14.4 mg/dL